FUTURE HISTORY

GOD'S
INTELLIGENCE
BRIEFING
ON THE
END TIMES

BY
DR. PAUL FELTER

Future History
God's Intelligence Briefing on The End Times

Published by
Harpazo Publishing Company
Houston, Texas
Copyright © 2017, 2021, 2023 by Paul Felter, MBS, PhD

Printed in the United States of America

Cover Image "Binary Planet" Copyright:
https://www.123rf.com/profile_anterovium'>anterovium / 123RF
Stock Photo – Extended License on File

All Scripture quotes are from the public domain King James Version.

File Creation Date: April 30, 2021
Version Date: April 30, 2021

ISBN: 978-0-9829954-2-6

TABLE OF CONTENTS

AUTHOR PAGE

Author: Dr. Paul Felter

- Christian since June 1977
- Taught Bible study for decades
- Graduate of Florida Atlantic University BA
- Graduate of Newburgh Theological Seminary – Master of Biblical Studies and Doctorate in Christian Apologetics
- Visit https://BreadofLife.media
- Articles, books, eBooks and podcast
- Currently living in Houston, Texas where I teach and sub for my Pastor.

INTRODUCTION

If you ask a dozen Bible Prophecy "experts" what's next on God's prophetic timetable, you'll likely get thirteen or more scenarios they think might soon play out. Some are looking for a revived Roman Empire from Europe. Others the Gog Magog war against Israel with Iran, Turkey, and Russia at the helm. With the war in Syria, the prophesied destruction of Damascus is high on many prophetic watch lists. Many are even looking for the Antichrist's arrival to confirm a peace treaty in the Middle East kicking off the 7-year Tribulation.

Granted, all these things and much more will happen, but I found that God has His timetable in my many years of study and life experiences. He will fulfill His Prophetic Scriptures when and how He chooses. However, even though He is Almighty God, He will never violate His Word. All Prophetic Scripture must be fulfilled. They cannot be canceled, ignored, or changed. The Lord will fulfill His Prophetic Word down to the most minute detail because He is "faithful and true."

Many believers have difficulty with Bible Prophecy. There are so many bits and pieces scattered throughout the Bible, the task of piecing them together into a coherent picture can seem daunting. Like a thousand-piece jigsaw puzzle, you need a clear picture of the image to help align the individual pieces. Starting in Genesis chapter 3 going through Revelation chapter 22, many Scriptures predict events that are yet future. But piecing them together to understand God's plan for the Last Days; therein lies your great challenge and the source of much confusion.

So, has God given us a high-level picture of His Prophetic timetable into which all the detailed pieces must neatly fit? Of course, God is not the author of confusion, men and the devil are. One source of confusion persists with believers that don't study the Old Testament. Many believe the Old Testament is simply about creation and the history of the Jews, not relevant in the 21st century. Adopting this attitude enhances your ignorance. After all, if you convince yourself the Old Testament is not necessary for the post-modern believer. You have marginalized two-thirds of your Bible and alleviated yourself of much reading and study. Let's concentrate on the words of Jesus. He is our Lord and Savior. Indeed, His words are the most important. Faulty thinking like this creates much error in churches and pulpits across America.

Jesus said, *"These are the words which I spoke unto you, while I was yet with you, that all things must be fulfilled, which were written in the law of Moses, and the prophets, and the psalms, concerning me." - Luke 24:44 KJV.*

The "law of Moses, and in the prophets, and the psalms" that sounds like the Old Testament to me. Now someone might say that Jesus was referring to His ministry and crucifixion and not end times prophecy. At the time the Old Testament was written, that was Prophecy. You will see in this study that ALL Prophecy is centered around the Lord Jesus Christ. *"For the testimony of Jesus is the spirit of prophecy." - Revelation 19:10 KJV.*

Many proclaim end times prophecy was fulfilled in 70 A.D. with the conquering of Jerusalem and the destruction of the Jewish Temple. Others say that books like Revelation are just allegories depicting the ongoing battle of good and evil. A prominent view of Catholicism and mainstream Protestantism is that the Church has replaced Israel, and the Church will conquer the world for Jesus. Big words like Preterism,

Futurism, Premillennialism, Postmillennialism, Amillennialism, Pretribulationalism, Posttribulationalism, etc., are used by so-called "scholars" to muddy the prophetic waters. Set all that aside. Let's make this easy. How about we just let the Prophetic Scriptures speak for themselves. As we read a Scripture passage, we can simply ask ourselves, have the details of the passage already been fulfilled? If "yes," then the passage is historical. If "no," then the fulfillment is yet future. We will let the Word speak to us without the filter of a preconceived end times paradigm. You will find this to be a freeing experience.

In this study, we will focus on the overarching panorama of God's plan for the ages. Once we see the big picture, piecing in the details becomes much more manageable as all Prophetic Scriptures must harmonize and fit together. Beware of those that build an end-times scenario from a few selected Scriptures. They create a scenario based on their understanding and add a few Scriptures to give it credibility. That is not proper Bible study. In this study, we let the Scriptures say what the Spirit wants to say, letting God's Word present the prophetic scenario. So, let's take Jesus' advice and begin our study in the Old Testament. We'll save the Book of Revelation for later. There is a good reason why it's the last book of the Bible. Thanks for joining me in this study.

But before we begin, let's ask the Lord to help and guide us with this prayer:
"Father in heaven, we ask you to teach us and guide us in the study of your Prophetic Scriptures. Open the eyes of our understanding and wisdom to receive your Truth from your Holy Spirit. Let everything be said and done for your glory and honor, lifting the name of our Lord and Savior Jesus Christ, for we pray in His precious, holy name. Amen"

THE TRUE GOSPEL OF JESUS CHRIST

Before we jump into the Old Testament prophecies, I want to make sure everyone knows the true gospel of Jesus Christ. That is critical because only the true gospel can save your soul. There are many narratives today that claim to be the gospel of Jesus Christ. The Apostle Paul warns us of fake gospels.

*"I marvel that ye are **so soon removed** from him that called you into the grace of Christ **unto another gospel. Which is not another,** but there be some that trouble you and **would pervert the gospel of Christ**. But though we, or an angel from heaven, **preach any other gospel** unto you than that which we have preached unto you, **let him be accursed**. As we said before, so say I now again, **If any man preach any other gospel unto you than that ye have received, let him be accursed**."* - Galatians 1:6-9 KJV

The Apostle Paul has some strong words for those that preach "another" gospel or pervert the true gospel, let them "be accursed." That is a profoundly serious issue with God. Many today preach fake, watered-down versions of the gospel that do not save anyone. They sound nice, are politically correct, and don't offend anyone. Here are some examples.

- The prosperity gospel.
- The Word-Faith name it and claim it gospel.
- The gospel of love where God loves everyone.
- The emergent gospel where anything goes if you are sincere.
- The ecumenical gospel.

These are all fake gospels that save no one. So, what is the true gospel? We find the true gospel in 1 Corinthians chapter 15.

*"Moreover, brethren, **I declare unto you the gospel** which I preached unto you, which also ye have received, and wherein ye stand; **By which also ye are saved**, if ye keep in memory what I preached unto you, unless ye have believed in vain. For I delivered unto you first of all that which I also received, **how that Christ died for our sins according to the scriptures; And that he was buried, and that he rose again the third day according to the scriptures:**" - 1 Corinthians 15:1-4 KJV*

Here are the elements of the true gospel:
1. "Christ died for our sins according to the scriptures" – Jesus died on the cross for our sins. He shed His blood for the remission of our sins. We must repent of our sin and receive the cleansing power of His blood.
2. "he was buried" – Jesus died on the cross and was buried. It was not a fake death, as some presume.
3. "he rose again the third day according to the scriptures." The resurrection of Jesus Christ proves he is the Son of God, the Lamb of God that taketh away the world's sin.

The gospel core is that Jesus died on the cross for our sins, was buried, and rose on the third day. All this "according to the scriptures." The fact that God loves you, has a plan for your life, and wants to bless you are true, but not the gospel.

There are three aspects to salvation by the true gospel.
1. Knowledge – you must hear the true gospel. One cannot believe in something about which he knows nothing.
2. Belief – A person may know about a thing but not believe it.

3. Dependence – we can know something, believe it, and yet put no dependence on it. We must trust in it and rely upon it.

Simple knowledge and belief are not enough to save one's soul, as the below verse states.

"Thou believest that there is one God; thou doest well: the devils also believe, and tremble." - James 2:19 KJV

Satan and his demons believe in Jesus Christ, but they do not obey Him or trust in Him. They are not dependent upon Jesus for His divine promises of salvation and eternal life. To be saved, we must believe and trust in Jesus Christ by surrendering our life to Him and entirely depend on Him to fulfill His promises to us. We must be "in" Christ. Have you given your life to Jesus Christ? You believe in Jesus, but do you Trust Him completely with your life? If not, do it now; time is short. Give your life to Jesus Christ now!

"Trust in the LORD with all thine heart; and lean not unto thine own understanding." - Proverbs 3:5 KJV

HEAVY METAL

The Great Image

Let's begin our study with the book of Daniel. This book by the beloved Prophet is foundational to your proper understanding of End Times Prophecy. Daniel, inspired by the Holy Spirit, lays out the panorama of Gentile kingdoms that will control the land of Israel for centuries to come. As a young teenager, Daniel trained at Jerusalem for service to the king. Daniel was taken captive from Judah to Babylon around 606 B.C. after the invasion of the southern kingdom. Daniel spent the rest of his life in captivity in Babylon. He was a bright, talented young man destined to serve in the king's court. Just the type of young man Nebuchadnezzar, the king of Babylon, needed to help conduct business and government.

Some claim Daniel could not have authored the book bearing his name as the details are far too accurate. It had to be written by someone else at a much later date between 100-200 B.C. However, Jesus validates the Book of Daniel in Matthew Chapter 24 with His reference to the Abomination of Desolation, which I'll cover later. The prophet Daniel is the author writing in the sixth century B.C., but God gives the prophecies through His angel.

We begin with chapter two wherein Nebuchadnezzar, king of Babylon, had a night's dream but cannot remember the dream upon awakening even though the dream had upset him. The king calls the magicians, the astrologers, the sorcerers, and the Chaldeans to tell him the dream and the interpretation upon pain of death. Of course, they cannot give the king the dream and are outraged that the king would make such a request. They kept asking the king for the details of the dream, but the king could not remember, so he threatened them with their death and the death of their families as well if they could not give the dream and its interpretation.

Daniel was part of the king's court, so this threat of death fell upon him as well. But Daniel knew that God could provide the dream and the interpretation, so he asks the king for more time. That night God gives Daniel the vision and the interpretation. The following day Daniel requests an audience with the king to proclaim what God revealed to him. Here is Daniel's proclamation.

*"Thou, O king, saw, and behold a **great image**. This great image, whose brightness was excellent, stood before thee; and the form thereof was terrible. This image's head was of **fine gold**, his breast and his arms of **silver**, his belly and his thighs of **brass**, His legs of **iron**, his feet **part of iron and part of clay**. Thou saw till that a **stone** was cut out without hands, which **smote the image upon his feet** that were of iron and clay and brake them to pieces. Then was the **iron, the clay, the brass, the silver, and the gold, broken to pieces together**, and became like the chaff of the summer threshing floor; and the wind carried them away, that no place was found for them: and **the stone that smote the image became a great mountain, and filled the whole earth**. This is the dream; and we will tell the interpretation thereof before the king." - Daniel 2:31-36 KJV*

Next, Daniel gives the king the interpretation of the dream.

*"Thou, O king, art a king of kings: for the God of heaven hath given thee a kingdom, power, and strength, and glory. And wheresoever the children of men dwell, the beasts of the field and the fowls of the heaven hath he given into thine hand, and hath made thee ruler over them all. **Thou art this head of gold**." - Daniel 2:37-38 KJV*

14

So, the head of gold is Nebuchadnezzar and the Babylonian Kingdom.

*"And after thee shall arise **another kingdom** inferior to thee, and another **third kingdom of brass**, which shall bear rule over all the earth. And the **fourth kingdom** shall be strong as iron: forasmuch as iron breaks in pieces and subdues all things: and as iron that breaks all these, shall it break in pieces and bruise."* - Daniel 2:39-40 KJV

We see that the image represents kingdoms. Each metal represents a succeeding kingdom that follows Babylon.

Substance	Body Area	Definition
Gold	Head	Babylon
Silver	Chest and Arms	Media/Persia
Brass	Belly and Thighs	Greece
Iron	Legs	Rome
Iron and Clay	Feet and Toes	End Times kingdom
Stone	Crushes the Image	Christ's Kingdom

One might think that the first four kingdoms, Babylon, Media/Persia, Greece, and Rome are historical, but each has its end-time manifestation. Babylon is Iraq. Media/Persia is the Kurds and Iran. Greece is Lydia, western Turkey, and Rome, a reference to Europe as Rome was primarily a European Empire. The feet of "iron and clay" is the end-times kingdom that rules during the 7-year Tribulation. We will see this kingdom again in Daniel chapter 7.

The Stone Kingdom
But then a "stone" comes and hits the image on the feet. That's a bit strange. Should you not hit the image on the head if you want to

destroy it? The "stone" hits the image's feet because the feet with ten toes represent the governing power in the end times. Destroy the feet, and the rest of the image crumbles. The "stone" cut out without hands is not a creation of man. The stone comes from God and grows into a "great mountain" after crushing the image. A significant key to understanding Prophetic Scriptures is that mountains are kingdoms.

*"And in the days of these kings (10 toes) shall the **God of heaven set up a kingdom**, which shall never be destroyed: and the kingdom shall not be left to other people, but **it shall break in pieces and consume all these kingdoms**, and it shall **stand forever.**"* - Daniel 2:39-40, 44 KJV

The "great stone mountain" is the Millennial Kingdom of Jesus Christ. Upon His return at the end of the 7-year Tribulation, He destroys the kingdom of Antichrist and inaugurates His Millennial Kingdom upon the whole world. That has never happened in history, so it must be yet future.

Our takeaway here is that there is a powerful earthly kingdom (feet and toes of iron and clay) that exists prior to the Second Coming of Jesus Christ in the last days. Ten kings control this powerful kingdom which Jesus destroys upon His return. Then Jesus establishes His Kingdom on earth, which lasts for a thousand years, as you will see. As you get further into the Book of Daniel, you will know where this end-time earthly kingdom originates. Remember, our purpose here is to discern a high-level paradigm for the last days, not a detailed explanation of each verse.

So, here is a table of what we have so far:

Event/Activity	Timeframe
Gentile Nations rule the Middle East	The Present Time and the End Times
Second Coming of Jesus Christ	Gentile rule destroyed
The Millennial Kingdom	Thousand-year reign of Jesus Christ

You can see a pattern building here. But let's tackle a few issues before we move on to Daniel chapter 7. Although the first three kingdoms in Nebuchadnezzar's dream image are easy to discern since the text tells us the golden head is Babylon and the other two, Media/Persia and Greece, follow in succession. This fact is also clear from history. The legs of iron are Rome. Remember that the Old Testament prophets like Daniel knew nothing about a 2000-year church age, so that time element is missing in their prophecies. We see the Coming of Jesus Christ in the dream represented by the "stone cut out without hands." But there is no imagery for the first coming of Jesus, His crucifixion, and resurrection. The writers of Old Testament prophecy include the first and second advents of Jesus Christ in a single event. They make no time distinction between the first coming and the second coming even though we know there's a least a 2000-year gap.

Let's look at Isaiah chapter 61:
"The Spirit of the Lord GOD is upon me; because the LORD hath anointed me to preach good tidings unto the meek; he hath sent me to bind up the brokenhearted, to proclaim liberty to the captives, and the opening of the

prison to them that are bound; To proclaim the acceptable year of the LORD, **and the day of vengeance of our God**, to comfort all that mourn;" - Isaiah 61:1-2 KJV.

You at once recognize this text being what Jesus quoted (Luke 4:18-19) when he started his ministry in Nazareth. But Jesus stopped at the **"acceptable year of the LORD,"** He did not say **"and the day of vengeance of our God."** We have been paused on that comma for almost 2000 years. The first coming of Jesus was about atonement and salvation. The second coming of Jesus brings the vengeance and wrath of God. The prophetic gap in Isaiah becomes evident once you analyze the passage. Jesus made a distinction between His prophesied first coming and His later return as King of Kings.

Event/Activity	Timeframe
the acceptable year of the LORD	First Coming of Jesus Christ - Past
2000-year Gap	The Church Age - Present
the day of vengeance of our God	Second Coming of Jesus Christ - Future

We read in Isaiah chapter 63 about the return of Jesus Christ:

"*Wherefore art thou **red in thine apparel**, and thy garments like him that treadeth in the winefat? I have trodden the winepress alone; and of the people there was none with me: for I will **tread them in mine anger**, and trample them in my fury; and their **blood shall be sprinkled upon my garments**, and I will stain all my raiment. For the **day of vengeance** is in mine heart, and the **year of my redeemed** is come.*" - Isaiah 63:2-4 KJV.

When Jesus returns, He will fulfill the "day of vengeance" that He did not perform at His first coming. You can see in Isaiah Chapter 61 that between the "acceptable year of the LORD" and the "day of vengeance," there is a gap of almost 2000 years. But Isaiah could not see this gap, neither could any of the other prophets, including Daniel.

The gap was hidden from their eyes as we shall see. That is a critical point to understand and must be applied to the Old Testament Prophetic Scriptures where applicable based on the context. The Church age, the dispensation of grace, was not revealed in the Old Testament. It was a secret hid in God, as Paul states below.

*"And to make all men see what is the fellowship of the mystery, **which from the beginning of the world hath been hid in God**, who created all things by Jesus Christ:" - Eph 3:9 KJV*

Another obvious prophetic gap is found in a very familiar verse in Isaiah Chapter 9:

*"For unto us a **child is born**, unto us a **son is given**: and the **government** shall be upon his shoulder: and his name shall be called Wonderful, Counsellor, The mighty God, The everlasting Father, The Prince of Peace. Of the increase of his government and peace there shall be no end, upon the **throne of David**, and upon his kingdom, to order it, and to establish it with judgment and with justice from henceforth even forever. The zeal of the LORD of hosts will perform this." - Isaiah 9:6-7 KJV.*

Much of this Scripture is yet to unfold. The "child is born" phrase was the birth of Jesus at Bethlehem. The "a son is given" phrase was fulfilled at Golgotha, where Jesus gave His life as the atonement for sin. But Jesus is yet to sit on David's throne and have government responsibility upon His shoulder. When Jesus walked the earth, there was no throne of David. That happens after the Second Coming of

Jesus Christ at the end of the 7-year Tribulation. The first and second comings of Jesus Christ are in one contiguous statement in Isaiah 9 with no apparent gap. But we have the advantage of historical perspective and know the gap exists. We are currently in the Prophetic Gap between **"unto us a son is given"** and **"the government shall be upon his shoulder."**

We see similar language when the angel Gabriel announced to Mary that she would give birth to the Messiah.

*"And the angel said unto her, Fear not, Mary: for thou hast found favor with God. And, behold, thou shalt conceive in thy womb, and bring forth a son, and shalt call his name JESUS. He shall be great, and shall be called the Son of the Highest: and **the Lord God shall give unto him the throne of his father David.**"* - Luke 1:30-32 KJV.

This verse was fulfilled during Jesus first coming except the giving to Him the "throne of his father, David." That will happen after Jesus' Second Coming. Here again, the Prophetic Gap is evident to us but was not to Mary. Hindsight is 20/20. Since we live in the last days, we have the facts of history to clarify Prophetic Scriptures.

Even in the New Testament, we find the Apostle Peter exposing the Prophetic Gap.

*"Of which salvation the **prophets have enquired and searched diligently**, who prophesied of the grace that should come unto you: Searching what, or **what manner of time** the Spirit of Christ which was in them did signify, when it testified beforehand the **sufferings of Christ, and the glory that should follow.** "* - 1Peter 1:10-11 KJV.

Peter clearly states that the Prophets of old searched and enquired of God as to the timing of the salvation by grace we enjoy today. They did not see that between the "sufferings of Christ" and the "glory that should follow," there would be a dispensation of grace as the Apostle Paul calls it, more commonly, the Church age. The "sufferings of Christ" was the Cross, but the "glory that should follow" will be the Second Coming and the Millennial Kingdom.

Many verses contain the prophetic gap. Even the Apostles of Jesus Christ could not see the gap as we read in Acts following the Lord's resurrection.

"When they therefore were come together, they asked of him, saying, Lord, ***wilt thou at this time restore again the kingdom to Israel?"*** *- Act 1:6 KJV.*

The Apostles had no clue there would an extended gap known as the Church Age. They were expecting Jesus at that time to fulfill all prophecy concerning Israel, especially now that He had risen from the dead, proving beyond any shadow of a doubt, He is the Son of God equal with the Father. But the timing of the restoration of Israel was not for them to know. There was coming, a Prophetic Gap wherein the Lord Jesus Christ would build His Church, the body of Christ.

These are but a few popular scriptures wherein the gap of the Church Age was hidden when written but now apparent to us. So, if we apply the prophetic gap to Nebuchadnezzar's image, everything perfectly fits into the symbolism and harmonizes with history. The gap in Nebuchadnezzar's image logically would be between the brass belly and thighs being Greece and the legs of iron representing the last days Middle Eastern kingdom. But currently, there is no kingdom ruling over the Middle East. Turkey is trying to revive the Caliphate, and Iran is seeking regional hegemony. Perhaps the two legs of iron have yet to arrive on the world scene. Or maybe the two legs of iron are Sunni and Shia Islam.

The feet and ten toes, ten kings, will be the final Kingdom that rules the Middle East. It unifies the legs and feet of iron and clay, taking us up to and through the 7-year Tribulation culminating with the Second Coming of Jesus Christ, the stone kingdom. If you view the image from the head down, then the three kingdoms of Babylon, Media/Persia, and Greece are easily depicted. If you consider the image from the feet up including the "stone kingdom," then the end times Antichrist kingdom blends nicely into the two legs of iron. The only way for these two views to harmonize is with a gap, the Church Age, between the brass belly and thighs (Greece), and the legs of iron (Antichrist Kingdom).

Timeframe

When the Prophet Daniel stood before king Nebuchadnezzar to interpret his dream, here is what he said.

*"But there is a God in heaven that revealeth secrets, and maketh known to the king Nebuchadnezzar what shall be in the **latter days**. Thy dream, and the visions of thy head upon thy bed, are these;"* - Daniel 2:28 KJV.

There is proof that the focus of Nebuchadnezzar's dream is the "latter days," the Second Coming of Jesus Christ. He will destroy the Gentile Kingdoms and set up His Stone Kingdom, the Millennial Kingdom.

Briefing

Point of interest:
a) Middle East Confederacy of 10 nations soon to rise to power.

Timeline:
a) Gentile Nations rule the Middle East (present time).
b) 10 Nation Kingdom Arises in the Middle East (Future Caliphate or Muslim Confederacy?)
c) Jesus destroys the 10 Nation Confederacy at his second coming (future).
d) The Millennial Kingdom - Stone Kingdom – thousand-year reign of Jesus Christ (future).

Discussion:

The End Times kingdom that rules the world is a 10-nation Confederacy. Many groups and leaders are trying to establish a ruling authority over the earth, the European Union, the United Nations, the Islamic Caliphate, and now a New World Order with a Global Reset promoted by the World Economic Forum. President Erdogan of Turkey wants to reestablish the Ottoman Empire with him as the ruling Caliph. The Muslim Brotherhood, founded in 1928 to revive the Ottoman Caliphate. So, keep your eyes looking east. That's where Bible prophecy will be fulfilled. You will not get relevant news about the Middle East from the mainstream, fake news, media. Seek some alternate Middle East news sources.

WILD BEASTS

As we continue to build our Prophetic roadmap of God's Plan for the Last Days, our next stop is not the Twilight Zone, but the Book of Daniel chapter 7, wherein Daniel restates chapter 2 with different symbolism and greater detail about the Fourth Kingdom. Please read the entirety of Daniel chapter 7 before continuing with our study.

The Lion, the Bear, and the Leopard

*"Daniel spake and said, I saw in my vision by night, and, behold, the four winds of the heaven strove upon the great sea. And **four great beasts** came up from the sea, diverse one from another. **The first was like a lion**... And behold another beast, a **second, like to a bear**... After this I beheld, and lo **another, like a leopard**. "- Dan 7:2-6 KJV.*

The lion, the bear, and the leopard align perfectly with the gold, silver, and brass of Nebuchadnezzar's image in Daniel chapter 2. The Lion symbolizes ancient Babylon. The bear with uneven shoulders is Media/Persia, Persia being the stronger of the two. The Leopard is Greece under Alexander the Great who's armies were known for their speed and stamina.

The Fourth Beast

*"After this I saw in the night visions, and behold a **fourth beast**, dreadful and terrible, and strong exceedingly; and it had **great iron teeth**: it devoured and brake in pieces, and stamped the residue with the feet of it: and it was **diverse from all the beasts** that were before it; and **it had ten horns**." - Daniel 7:7 KJV.*

The fourth beast has "great iron teeth," linking it with the iron legs and feet of Nebuchadnezzar's great image. It is "diverse from all the other beast kingdoms before it. This kingdom was not just another earthly kingdom like Babylon, Persia, or Greece. The fourth beast is not Rome as Rome was not diverse from previous kingdoms as it retained much from the Greek Empire. Here again, a hidden gap exists between the third and fourth beasts. Greco-Roman is defined as Rome being greatly influenced by Greek culture in art, architecture, and even wrestling. Rome does not fit the context of the "dreadful and terrible" beast "diverse" from all the others.

Diverse in Greek means to be changed, altered, or transformed. So, this fourth kingdom will not be just another kingdom but something that has been changed, altered, or transformed. Could this mean that it is not entirely human? Going back to Daniel Chapter 2, we read:

*"And whereas thou sawest iron mixed with miry clay, **they** shall mingle themselves with the **seed of men**: but **they** shall not cleave one to another, even as iron is not mixed with clay." - Daniel 2:43 KJV.*

Who are "they" that try to mingle with the "seed of men?" The "seed of men" are human beings. For some reason, "they" cannot mix with human beings, just as iron does not mix with clay. Another interesting note is that "they" are identified with "miry clay." Miry clay is identified with the pit:

*"He brought me up also out of an **horrible pit**, out of the **miry clay**, and set my feet upon a rock, and established my goings." - Psalm 40:2 KJV.*

So, do "they" come from the pit, the bottomless pit? In Revelation, we read:

*"The beast that thou sawest was, and is not; and **shall ascend out of the bottomless pit,** and go into perdition:" - Revelation 17:8 KJV.*

What are we looking at here? A kingdom of aliens led by a fallen angel. A kingdom of "trans" beings, hybrid humans, trans-humans, or whatever horror "science" will come up with next? Time will tell, but I want you to be aware of these verses because just when you think you have seen everything, something strange our way comes.

The fourth beast has ten horns, just as Nebuchadnezzar's image has feet with ten toes. Horns are symbolic of power, so these ten horns are ten kings. But something strange happens as Daniel is gazing upon the horns.

*"I considered the horns, and, behold, **there came up among them another little horn**, before whom there were three of the first horns plucked up by the roots: and, behold, in this horn were eyes like the **eyes of man**, and a **mouth speaking great things**." - Daniel 7:8 KJV.*

A "little horn," another king, arises from among the ten kings (horns). That is a new revelation that we did not see in Daniel Chapter 2. We will get to the interpretation shortly but let finish the vision first.

Just as Daniel was trying to digest the ten-horned beast with the "little horn" rising among the ten, the Lord God Almighty makes a spectacular fiery entrance.

*"I beheld till the thrones were cast (set) down, and **the Ancient of days did sit**, whose garment was white as snow, and the hair of his head like the pure wool: his throne was like the **fiery flame**, and his wheels as burning fire. A **fiery stream** issued and came forth from before him: thousand thousands ministered unto him, and ten thousand times ten thousand stood before him: **the judgment was set, and the books were opened**." - Daniel 7:9-10 KJV.*

Wow, it's hard to imagine such a scene. Poor Daniel must have been in complete shock and awe. God Almighty comes in a fiery procession and sits in judgment. You can talk about the wind, rain, snow, sleet, and hail. But fire—that's in a category by itself. So how does the fourth Beast and the little horn fare in judgment from the Almighty? Need you to ask?

*"I beheld then because of the voice of the great words which the horn spake: I beheld even till the **beast was slain**, and **his body destroyed**, and **given to the burning flame**." - Daniel 7:11 KJV.*

The little horn, the Antichrist, and his kingdom are cast into the burning flame, the lake of fire—precisely what happens in the Book of Revelation as the Antichrist, the False Prophet, and later, Satan himself, are finally cast in the lake of fire. In Daniel Chapter 2, we saw that the "stone" comes and destroys the final kingdom symbolized by the feet with ten toes (kings).

So, let's back up for a minute and analyze what we have read so far.
- The ten horns on the fourth beast are a confederacy of 10 kings or nations.
- The "little horn" that arose from among the ten horns is the Antichrist.
- The "Ancient of days" pronounces judgment on the Antichrist and his kingdom (followers), sentencing them to the burning fire.
- The Antichrist and his Beast kingdom are destroyed by the Lord Jesus Christ when He returns to earth.

Soon after the Ancient of Days (God the Father) passing judgment, another fascinating event happens.

*"I saw in the night visions, and, behold, one like **the Son of man came with the clouds of heaven, and came to the Ancient of days**, and they brought him near before him. And there was **given him dominion, and glory, and a kingdom**, that all people, nations, and languages, should serve him: **his dominion is an everlasting dominion**, which shall not pass away, and his kingdom that which shall not be destroyed." - Daniel 7:13-14 KJV.*

The Lord Jesus Christ appears in the clouds and goes to the Father, where He is given a kingdom and dominion over the entire earth. That happens first in heaven, where Jesus is given the kingdom and inaugurated as King of Kings and Lord of Lords. John records the proclamation in Revelation chapter 11.

*"And the seventh angel sounded; and there were great voices in heaven, saying, **The kingdoms of this world are become the kingdoms of our Lord, and of his Christ; and he shall reign for ever and ever**." - Revelation 11:15 KJV*

The judgment and proclamations in Daniel chapter 7 are from the Ancient of Days, God the Father. But the execution of those mandates is performed on the earth by Jesus Christ at His Second Coming. That is the fulfillment of Psalm 110.

"The LORD said unto my Lord, Sit thou at my right hand, until I make thine enemies thy footstool." - Psalm 110:1 KJV.

God the Father is telling God the Son to sit at His right hand until He makes all the enemies of Jesus Christ His footstool. That is where Jesus is seated at the time of this writing. That is where Stephen saw Jesus as he was being martyred. Jesus stands because had the rulers of Israel accepted Stephens' testimony of Jesus, the Messiah of Israel, the 7-year tribulation would have soon started with Jesus taking the 7-sealed scroll from the Father.

*"But he, being full of the Holy Ghost, looked up stedfastly into heaven, and saw the glory of God, and **Jesus standing on the right hand of God**" - Acts 7:55 KJV*

Jesus is now seated at the right hand of God, building the body of Christ, the church through the Holy Spirit. At the Rapture, the ministry of the Holy Spirit will cease. Jesus will begin His judgment upon a Christ-rejecting Israel and godless world. We will talk about that soon.

Daniel is given the interpretation of the dream as follows.

*"Thus, he said, The fourth beast shall be the fourth kingdom upon earth, which shall be **diverse** from all kingdoms, and shall devour the whole earth, and shall tread it down, and break it in pieces." - Dan 7:23 KJV.*

That is reminiscent of what we read in Chapter 2 about the legs of iron being diverse from previous kingdoms. The Fourth beast is also dissimilar from the preceding three beasts. Rome cannot be the fourth beast as it was not diverse from the previous empire of Greece. This final evil world empire will be Satanic to the core, unlike anything the world has ever seen.

*"And the ten horns out of this kingdom are **ten kings** that shall arise: and **another shall rise after them;** and he shall be **diverse** from the first, and he shall subdue three kings. And he shall **speak great words against the most High** and shall wear out the saints of the most High, and think to change times and laws: and **they shall be given into his hand until a time and times and the dividing of time**." - Daniel 7:24-25 KJV.*

This verse shows the ten horns are ten kings (kingdoms), and the "little horn" will arise after them. The "little horn" blasphemes God. The "little horn" is the Antichrist. We are also told that the Antichrist will rule for "**a time and times and the dividing of time**." A time is one year, times is two years, and half a time is six months. So, the Antichrist will rule the world for 3 ½ years. This time duration is also stated in the Book of Revelation.

*"And there was given unto him a mouth speaking great things and blasphemies; and **power was given unto him to continue forty and two months.**" - Revelation 13:5 KJV.*

Forty-two months equals 3 ½ years. The fourth Beast with the "little horn" is yet future since the Antichrist arises with the ten horns already in power. We have not seen a ten-nation confederacy appear in the Middle East. The fourth Beast is strictly limited to the Last Days. This Beast kingdom will arise during the first half of the 7-year Tribulation, giving the Antichrist time to rise to power and rule for the last 3 ½ years.

The following interpretation given to Daniel validates what we stated earlier about the judgment from God and the coming kingdom of Jesus Christ.

*"But **the judgment** shall sit, and they shall **take away his dominion**, to **consume and to destroy** it unto the end. And the **kingdom and dominion**, and the greatness of the kingdom under the whole heaven, shall be **given to the people of the saints of the most High,** whose kingdom is an **everlasting kingdom**, and **all dominions** shall serve and obey him." - Daniel 7:26-27 KJV.*

The Antichrist and his Beast kingdom are destroyed. Jesus Christ receives dominion over the whole earth, and His saints inherit an everlasting kingdom.

The Prophetic Gap

It's easy to see the prophetic gap preceding the Fourth Beast. As the Fourth Beast rises to power with the ten horns in place, it cannot immediately follow the Leopard kingdom of Greece defeated around 160 B.C. in the Maccabean Revolt. No ten-nation kingdom arose to replace Grecian (The Seleucid dynasty) hegemony in the Middle East. The Fourth Beast with ten horns (ten kings) and the little horn (Antichrist) are entirely relegated to the Latter Days, quite possibly being specifically reserved for the 7-year Tribulation period. The little horn Antichrist rules during the last half of the Tribulation with the approval of the ten kings. I believe that the Fourth Beast, a ten-nation Islamic Caliphate, will rise shortly after the beginning of the 7-year Tribulation.

Of course, I do not rule out a European confederacy as the EU could morph into such a kingdom. The UN could also be a significant player in the Tribulation. But since the Middle East is already under the control of Islam, they would be the most likely pick. I can't foresee Islam losing control over the Middle East anytime soon, short of a nuclear war.

Briefing

Point of interest:
  a) Middle East Confederacy of 10 nations.
  b) Jesus Christ sets up his kingdom on earth and reigns for a thousand years.

Person of interest:
  a) political leader: aka antichrist: little horn: rules the world for 3 ½ years.
  b) son of man, Jesus Christ returns to defeat the antichrist, destroy his kingdom.

Timeline:
  a) Gentile Nations rule the Middle East (The Present)
  b) The Antichrist Beast Kingdom–10 Nation Confederacy (Future).
  c) The Antichrist reigns for 3 ½ years, the Last Half of the 7-year Tribulation (Future).
  d) Second Coming of Jesus Christ–Jesus destroys the Beast kingdom (Future).
  e) The Millennial Kingdom – 1000-year reign of Jesus Christ (Future).

This chapter affirms our briefing from the previous chapter Heavy Metal. A 10-nation Confederacy is coming to the Middle East. From that 10-nation alliance will arise the Antichrist. He will come to the forefront of Middle East politics on a peace platform, confirming a covenant with Israel. That will be his vehicle to capture the hearts of the masses. He will do remarkable things. The people and other political leaders will admire him and his diplomatic success. He will use peace to establish his power base and, at the midpoint of the 7-year Tribulation attack Israel, breaking his peace covenant. The stage is set for his arrival.

THE TRIBULATION DEFINED

I have mentioned the 7-year Tribulation several times in the previous chapters. Upon examination, we will see that this period immediately precedes the Second Coming of Jesus Christ and follows the Rapture of the Church. Defining this dreadful period will enable us to understand its purpose and those involved. That knowledge is critical to our understanding of end times Prophecy. This 7-year period has several names in Scripture; the Tribulation, the Great Tribulation, the Day of the Lord, the Time of Jacob's Trouble, and the 70th Week of Daniel's Prophecy, just to name a few. Let's begin our study with the Bible's first mention of this terrible period.

First Mention

*"I call heaven and earth to witness against you this day, that ye shall soon **utterly perish from off the land** whereunto ye go over Jordan to possess it; ye shall not prolong your days upon it but shall **utterly be destroyed**. And the LORD shall **scatter you among the nations**, and ye shall be left few in number among the heathen, whither the LORD shall lead you. When thou art in **tribulation**, and all these things are come upon thee, even in **the latter days**, if thou turn to the LORD thy God, and shalt be obedient unto his voice; (For the LORD thy God is a merciful God;) **he will not forsake thee**, neither destroy thee, nor forget the **covenant of thy fathers** which he sware unto them." Deuteronomy 4:30-31.*

The Lord gives essential instructions to the Jews about what will happen to them if they disobey His commands. They had left Egypt in the Exodus and are about to cross over the Jordan River into the Promised Land. The Lord God gives the Jews a startling prophecy of their fate if they forsake Him and follow other gods.

Text Passage	Timeframe
"utterly perish from the land"	Roman invasion of 70 A.D.
"utterly be destroyed"	Jerusalem and Temple destroyed 70 A.D.
"scatter you among the nations"	Scattered after the Roman invasion 70 A.D.
Prophetic Gap	Gap between the "scattering" among the nations and the tribulation of the "latter days"
"tribulation – in the latter days"	Coming 7-year Tribulation.
"he will not forsake thee"	If they repent and turn to the Lord during the 7-year Tribulation.
"covenant of thy fathers"	God will remember the covenant of Abraham and King David. He will restore the Jews back to their land and Kingdom

The first part of the Prophecy was fulfilled in 70 A.D. by the Roman invasion of Judah and Jerusalem. The Roman legions destroyed the Temple and much of Jerusalem, drove the people from the land, and scattered them among the nations where many of their descendants remain even today. The subsequent fulfillment will be the "tribulation" that occurs in the "latter days." The phrase "latter days" means the "last days" or the "end days," not simply a vague, imprecise time in the future. It is a reference to the 7-year Tribulation. The coming Tribulation of the "latter days" is spoken of many times in the Prophetic Scriptures. Here are a few startling texts.

The Worst Time in all History

*"And at that time shall Michael stand up, the great prince which standeth for the children of thy people: and there shall be **a time of trouble, such as never was since there was a nation even to that same time:** and at that time thy people shall be delivered, every one that shall be found written in the book."* - Daniel 12:1 KJV.

*"Alas! for that **day is great, so that none is like it** it is even the **time of Jacob's trouble**; but he shall be saved out of it."* - Jeremiah 30:7 KJV

*"For then shall be **great tribulation, such as was not since the beginning of the world to this time, no, nor ever shall be.** And except those days should be shortened, there should no flesh be saved: but for the elect's sake those days shall be shortened."* - Matthew 24:21-22 KJV.

*"And one of the elders answered, saying unto me, What are these which are arrayed in white robes? and whence came they? And I said unto him, Sir, thou knowest. And he said to me, **These are they which came out of great tribulation**, and have washed their robes, and made them white in the blood of the Lamb."* - Rev 7:13-14 KJV.

The above Scriptures refer to the same period as there can be only one "worst" period in all of history. They refer to the coming 7-year Tribulation. Interestingly, Jeremiah refers to this as "the time of Jacob's trouble." In Genesis Chapter 32, we read,

*"And he said, **Thy name shall be called no more Jacob, but Israel**: for as a prince hast thou power with God and with men, and hast prevailed."* - Genesis 32:28 KJV.

Jacob's name was changed to Israel. So, the Tribulation is a time of Israel's trouble. Here we begin to see that the Tribulation is a time for Israel, the Jewish people, not the church. Remember, all the tribes of Israel came out of Jacob. He is the patriarch of the nation of Israel.

So, how do we know this Tribulation is seven years? We have already read Scriptures referring to a 3 ½ year period. That is the duration of the Antichrist's rule over the end-time beast kingdom in the Middle east. But where does the 7-year period originate? It originates in the Book of Daniel, Chapter 9 verses 24 through 27. That is Daniel's 70 weeks Prophecy. Daniel knows from reading Jeremiah that the captivity in Babylon will last for 70 years.

*"And this whole land shall be a desolation, and an astonishment; and these nations shall serve the king of Babylon **seventy years**."* - Jer 25:11 KJV.

Daniel Chapter 9 opens with Daniel praying to the Lord, asking what is to follow the captivity. During his prayer, the angel Gabriel interrupts him with the answer. The 70 Weeks Prophecy is the answer to Daniel's prayer. Let's examine those four verses as they are critical to a correct understanding of Bible Prophecy.

The 70-Weeks Prophecy

*"**Seventy weeks** are determined upon **thy people and upon thy holy city**, to finish the transgression, and to make an end of sins, and to make reconciliation for iniquity, and to bring in everlasting righteousness, and to*

seal up the vision and prophecy, and to anoint the most Holy. Know therefore and understand, that from the going forth of the commandment to restore and to build Jerusalem unto the Messiah the Prince shall be **seven weeks, and threescore and two weeks**: *the street shall be built again, and the wall, even in troublous times. And after threescore and two weeks shall Messiah be cut off, but not for himself: and the people of the prince that shall come shall destroy the city and the sanctuary; and the end thereof shall be with a flood, and unto the end of the war desolations are determined. And he shall confirm the covenant with many for* **one week**: *and in the midst of the week he shall cause the sacrifice and the oblation to cease, and for the overspreading of abominations he shall make it desolate, even until the consummation, and that determined shall be poured upon the desolate." - Daniel 9:24-27 KJV.*

Since this passage is paramount for students of Bible Prophecy, I will break down each verse and phrase. As you will see, this passage takes us from the rebuilding of Jerusalem after the Babylonian captivity up to the end of the 7-year Tribulation. Let's begin with verse 24.

*"****Seventy weeks*** *are determined upon* **thy people and upon thy holy city**, *to finish the transgression, and to make an end of sins, and to make reconciliation for iniquity, and to bring in everlasting righteousness, and to seal up the vision and prophecy, and to anoint the most Holy." - Daniel 9:24 KJV.*

- "Seventy weeks" – This prophecy is 70 weeks long. But what is meant by "weeks"? The word for weeks means a heptad, a period of seven days or years. In this case, we know from history the timeline is 70 heptads of years or 490 years. Also, the Lord told Israel that if they did not repent and turn back to the Lord after their punishment in Babylon, then subsequent punishment would be seven times worse. We read this in Leviticus Chapter

26. "*And if ye will not yet for all this hearken unto me, then I will punish you seven times more for your sins.*" - *Lev 26:18 KJV.* Seventy years of Babylonian captivity times seven equals 490. Hence Daniel's Prophecy is for 490 years.

- The entire 490-year prophecy is for "thy people and upon thy holy city." Who were Daniel's people? That's right, the Jews. And what was Daniel's holy city? You got it, Jerusalem. It amazes me that many so-called prophecy experts can't see that the entire prophecy is focused on Israel and Jerusalem. That is a crucial point as it defines the who and where of the prophecy. The importance of this fact will become apparent when we examine verse 27.

- Before the completion of the 490 years prophecy, six proclamations must be fulfilled.
    - "to finish the transgression."
    - "make an end of sins."
    - "make reconciliation for iniquity."
    - "bring in everlasting righteousness."
    - "seal up the vision and prophecy."
    - "Anoint the Most Holy (Place)."

- Have these six things already happened concerning Israel? NO, Israel is still in the transgression of rejecting their Messiah. Is there an "end of sin" in Israel today? Have they been "reconciled" back to God? Is there "everlasting righteousness" in Israel? Have the "vision and prophecy" been fulfilled concerning Israel? Lastly, has the "Most Holy" Place been anointed? Currently, there is no Most Holy Place, so how could it be anointed. None of these proclamations have been fulfilled to date, and they will not be fulfilled until Jesus, Israel's Messiah, returns in power and glory at the end of the Tribulation.

- Since there is unfulfilled Scripture within the prophecy, we can conclude that the 490 years have not been fulfilled, there must be some time remaining for its completion.

"Know therefore and understand, that from the going forth of the **commandment to restore and to build Jerusalem unto the Messiah the Prince shall be seven weeks, and threescore and two weeks:** *the street shall be built again, and the wall, even in troublous times." - Daniel 9:25 KJV.*

- The "commandment to restore and build Jerusalem" was given to Nehemiah in Chapter 2 of his book. *"And I said unto the king, If it pleases the king, and if thy servant have found favour in thy sight, that thou wouldest* **send me unto Judah, unto the city of my fathers' sepulchres, that I may build it.** *And the king said unto me, (the queen also sitting by him,) For how long shall thy journey be? and when wilt thou return? So, it pleased the king to send me; and I set him a time. ... Then said I unto them, Ye see the distress that we are in, how* **Jerusalem lieth waste, and the gates thereof are burned with fire: come, and let us build up the wall of Jerusalem,** *that we be no more a reproach".* - Nehemiah 2:5-6, 17 KJV. Nehemiah was permitted by Artaxerxes, king of Persia to do precisely what Daniel's prophecy states, "restore and build Jerusalem" and rebuild "the wall."
- The date of this commandment given by Artaxerxes to Nehemiah was March 14, 445 B.C.
- "seven weeks, and threescore and two weeks" equals 69 weeks or 483 prophetic years. That is almost the entire prophecy, short only one week, seven years. 69 x 7 = 483 years.
- So, 483 years after the commandment given to Nehemiah, the Messiah would appear in Jerusalem. Zechariah tells us that the Messiah would ride into Jerusalem on a donkey. Jesus fulfilled

this on Palm Sunday when He rode into Jerusalem on a young donkey.

- So, here is the math for the fulfillment of verse 25. We must convert the prophecy to days as the prophecy was based on the lunar calendar (360 days), and history is based on the Gregorian calendar or solar calendar (365.25 days).
  - 483 prophetic years * 360 days per prophetic lunar year = **173,880 days in the first 69 weeks.**
  - Jesus rode into Jerusalem on April 6, 32 A.D. Palm Sunday.
  - 445 B.C to 32 A.D. = 445 + 32 − 1 = 476 years (subtract 1 year because there is no zero year between B.C. and A.D) in the Gregorian calendar.
  - 476 years * 365 days = 173,740 days (Gregorian calendar)
    - 173,740 days + 24 days (March 14 to April 6 inclusive) + 116 days for leap years = **173,880 days**
    - "The Gregorian reform modified the Julian calendar's scheme of leap years as follows: Every year that is exactly divisible by four is a leap year, except for years that are exactly divisible by 100, but these centurial years are leap years if they are exactly divisible by 400. For example, the years 1700, 1800, and 1900 are not leap years, but the years 1600 and 2000 are leap years as they are divisible by 400." Introduction to Calendars. (15 May 2013). United States Naval Observatory.
    - To determine the number of leap years in our timeline, divide 476 by 4, giving 119 leap years. Then subtract 3 for years 100, 200, and 300 B.C. as they are centurial years not divisible by 400. That gives 116 leap years for our calculation.

- Palm Sunday, April 6, 32 A.D. was precisely 173,880 days from the commandment given to Nehemiah on March 14, 445 B.C. to rebuild Jerusalem after the Babylonian captivity.
- The first 69 weeks, or 483 years, or 173,880 days of this prophecy were fulfilled precisely to the day by Jesus on Palm Sunday almost 2000 years ago!
- Did Jesus mentioned this critical prophecy? *"And when he was come near, he beheld the city, and wept over it, Saying,* **If thou hadst known, even thou, at least** <u>**in this thy day**</u>**, the things which belong unto thy peace!** *but now they are hid from thine eyes. For the days shall come upon thee, that thine enemies shall cast a trench about thee, and compass thee round, and keep thee in on every side, And shall lay thee even with the ground, and thy children within thee; and they shall not leave in thee one stone upon another; because* **thou knewest not the** <u>**time of thy visitation**</u>*". - Luke 19:41-44 KJV.*
- Wow! What a powerful Scripture. Jesus spoke those words shortly after arriving in Jerusalem. The Jews missed their Messiah because they did not know Bible Prophecy. Don't you make the same mistake.

Jewish Lunar Calendar	Gregorian Calendar
483 years' times 360 days per year =	445 B.C. to 32 A.D = 476 years
173,880 days	476 years' times 365 days per year = 173,740 days
	March 14 to April 6 inclusive = 24 days
	Leap years = 116 days
	173,740 + 24 + 116 = **173,880 days**

*"And after threescore and two weeks shall **Messiah be cut off,** but not for himself: and the people of the **prince that shall come shall destroy the city and the sanctuary,** and the end thereof shall be with a flood, and unto the end of the war desolations are determined." - Daniel 9:26 KJV.*

- After completing the 69 weeks, the first 483 years of the prophecy, the Messiah will "be cut off."
- That is precisely what happened a few days after Jesus rode into Jerusalem. He was crucified.
- Notice that happened after 69 weeks but not in the 70th week, which has yet to be defined in the text.
- Another event happens after the 69th week—the destruction of the city, Jerusalem, and the sanctuary, the Temple. That was a historical event that occurred in 70 A.D., 38 years after the crucifixion of Jesus Christ.
- "the prince that shall come" is a reference to someone that "shall come" later. He is not the one that destroys the city and the

sanctuary, but his people did. Who destroyed the Temple? The 10th Roman legion comprised primarily of Arabs, Turks, and Syrians. Local "people" from nearby cities, not Roman citizens from Italy.

- Jesus' crucifixion, Jerusalem's and the Temple's destruction happened in the Prophetic Gap between the 69th and 70th weeks of Daniel's Prophecy.
- As we will soon see, we are still in this Prophetic Gap as the final week has not been fulfilled.

The 7-year Tribulation

*"And **he** shall confirm the covenant with many for **one week**: and in the midst of the week he shall cause the sacrifice and the oblation to cease, and for the overspreading of abominations he shall make it desolate, even until the consummation, and that determined shall be poured upon the desolate." - Daniel 9:27 KJV.*

- The pronoun "he" refers to the previous noun, "the prince that shall come."
- He makes or confirms a treaty or covenant for "one week," the last seven years. This covenant is with Israel and surrounding nations. This confirmation of the covenant begins the clock ticking for the 70th week of Daniel's 70 Weeks Prophecy, the 7-year Tribulation.
- This "prince that shall come" is the Antichrist.
- He stops the "sacrifice and the oblation" in the Temple, so a third Temple must be built. I believe the Temple will be rebuilt in the early months of the Tribulation. The "sacrifice and the oblation" are the daily morning and evening sacrifices to the Lord God performed by the priests in the Temple.

- He breaks his covenant with Israel in the "midst," the middle of the seven years.
- He perpetrates the "Abomination of Desolation" spoken by Jesus, the Apostle John, and the Apostle Paul. The Abomination of Desolation occurs when the Antichrist sets up his image in the Temple, and everyone is required to worship it or die. That is an "abomination" unto the Lord, and the Temple becomes "desolate" of the presence of God. This desolation continues "until the consummation," the end of the seven years. "That determined shall be poured out upon the desolate" means the plagues and destructions in the Book of Revelation will be poured out upon the Antichrist, his kingdom, and his followers during the Tribulation.
- That is the foundational verse that sets the length of the Tribulation at seven years.
- As we shall see, Jesus returns at the end of the seven years at the Battle of Armageddon.

Remember from verse 24 that the entire 70 weeks' prophecy is for the Jew and Jerusalem. That includes the last seven years, the Tribulation. It is for the Jew and Jerusalem. It is not for the Church; we are not invited.

I want to add a word about the phrase "confirm the covenant." The word confirm means to "enforce, re-establish or strengthen an existing covenant." I believe that part of the Antichrist's peace plan is to confirm the covenant of Moses. That will allow the Jews to rebuild the Temple, re-institute the Priesthood, and commence animal sacrifices. The Jews will be elated as they finally have their Temple to observe and follow the Torah. Without a Temple, that was impossible. But the Antichrist has a sinister ulterior motive. He wants to sit in the Temple as God before the Lord Jesus returns. The

Antichrist wants to rule and reign for a thousand years in his evil kingdom. He will do everything in his power not to relinquish control of this world to Jesus Christ upon His return at the Battle of Armageddon.

"Who opposeth and exalteth himself above all that is called God, or that is worshipped; so that <u>he as God sitteth in the temple of God, shewing himself that he is God</u>." - 2Thessalonians 2:4 KJV

The Day of the Lord

In the opening paragraph of this chapter, I mentioned "the Day of the Lord." Let's look at a few verses to get the flavor of that day.

- *"For the **day of the LORD** of hosts shall be upon every one that is proud and lofty, and upon every one that is lifted up; and he shall be **brought low**. ... And the loftiness of man shall be bowed down, and the haughtiness of men shall be made low: and the LORD alone shall be exalted in that day." - Isaiah 2:12, 17 KJV.*
- *"Howl ye; for the **day of the LORD** is at hand; it shall come as a **destruction from the Almighty**." - Isaiah 13:6 KJV.*
- *"Behold, the **day of the LORD** cometh, cruel both with **wrath and fierce anger**, to lay the land **desolate**: and he shall **destroy** the sinners thereof out of it." - Isaiah 13:9 KJV.*
- *"Blow ye the trumpet in Zion, and sound an alarm in my holy mountain: let all the inhabitants of the land tremble: for the **day of the LORD** cometh, for it is nigh at hand; A **day of darkness and of gloominess, a day of clouds and of thick darkness**." - Joel 2:1-2 KJV*
- *"Shall not the **day of the LORD** be **darkness**, and not light? even very dark, and no brightness in it? - Amos 5:20 KJV.*
- *"The great **day of the LORD** is near, it is near, and hasteth greatly, even the voice of the day of the LORD: the mighty man shall cry there bitterly.*

*That day is a day of **wrath**, a day of **trouble and distress**, a day of*
***wasteness and desolation**, a day of **darkness and gloominess**, a*
*day of **clouds and thick darkness**," - Zephaniah 1:14-15 KJV.*

I think you get the picture. The "Day of the Lord" is a time of
destruction, calamity, and darkness, both spiritual and physical. This
day is synonymous with the 7-year Tribulation. But there is great
hope for the true Church as we read.

 *"But ye, brethren, are **not in darkness, that that day should overtake***
***you as a thief.** Ye are all the children of light, and the children of the day:*
*we are not of the night, **nor of darkness**. Therefore, let us not sleep, as do*
others; but let us watch and be sober." - 1Thessalonians 5:4-6 KJV.

We will not partake of God's wrath and darkness. Since we are "not
in darkness," the Day of the Lord will not overtake us "as a thief."
How does the Lord save us from "that day?" We are Raptured before
the 7-year Tribulation. We escape the judgment coming upon the
earth.

*"Much more then, being now justified by his blood, **we shall be saved***
***from wrath through him**." - Romans 5:9 KJV*

"And to wait for his Son from heaven, whom he raised from the dead, even
*Jesus, **which delivered us from the wrath to come**." - 1 Thessalonians*
1:10 KJV

*"**For God hath not appointed us to wrath**, but to obtain salvation by our*
Lord Jesus Christ," - 1 Thessalonians 5:9 KJV

Day of Vengeance

My objective in this chapter is to define the 7-year Tribulation. It is paramount that you understand the purpose of the Tribulation: to redeem Israel and destroy the Antichrist. A remnant of Israel will be saved. The Antichrist, his kingdom, and all that follow him are destroyed.

As we progress in our study, it will become increasingly clear that the tribulation's purpose is to bring Israel to repentance through judgment, just as God had done many times in the Old Testament. When Jesus returns at the Second Coming, He will fulfill what we read in Isaiah Chapter 63.

"For the **day of vengeance** is in mine heart, and the **year of my redeemed** is come." - Isaiah 63:4 KJV.

The Tribulation is a "day of vengeance" for all the world, including Israel. But the time of Israel's redemption has come. The Apostle Paul writes:

"Esaias also crieth concerning Israel, Though the number of the children of Israel be as the sand of the sea, **a remnant shall be saved.**" - Romans 9:27 KJV

"Brethren, my heart's desire and prayer to God for Israel is, **that they might be saved.**" - Romans 10:1 KJV

"And so **all Israel shall be saved:** as it is written, there shall come out of Sion the Deliverer, and shall turn away ungodliness from Jacob:" - Romans 11:26 KJV

Briefing

Point of interest:
   a) A 7-year period called the tribulation is the worst period in all history.
   b) The Tribulation begins with a peace covenant brokered by the Antichrist between Israel and surrounding nations.
   c) The Temple is rebuilt in Jerusalem.
   d) The Antichrist enters the Temple at the tribulation midpoint declaring himself "god".

Person of interest:
   a) At the end of the 7-year tribulation, Jesus Christ returns to destroy the antichrist and set up His Millennial Kingdom.
   b) A political leader, the Antichrist, confirms a covenant (treaty)

Timeline:
   a) Gentile Nations rule the Middle East - The Present Time
   b) The Antichrist Confirms the Covenant of Moses starting the countdown for the 7-year Tribulation.
   c) The Antichrist Beast Kingdom, a 10 Nation Confederacy.
   d) The Antichrist Breaks his Covenant at the middle of the 7-year Tribulation.
   e) The Antichrist reigns over the earth for 3 ½ years, the last half of the 7-year Tribulation.
   f) Second Coming of Jesus Christ - Jesus destroys the Antichrist Kingdom at the end of the 7-year Tribulation.
   g) A Remnant of Israel Saved - Jesus Redeems and Restores Israel at the end of the 7-year Tribulation.

h) The Millennial Kingdom - the 1000-year reign of Jesus Christ after the 7-year Tribulation.

Calm down, take a deep breath. The 7-year Tribulation is not for us, the Church, the Body of Christ. We are not destined for the wrath of God. That has already been paid in full on our behalf by Jesus Christ on the Cross. The 7-year Tribulation is for the redemption of Israel and the judgment of the ungodly (Antichrist and his followers). In the next chapter, that point will become clear. Be a faithful witness for Jesus Christ so we can bring as many with us as possible by the saving power of the gospel of grace.

THE RAPTURE

Over the previous three chapters, we have discovered God's Plan for the Latter Days. The obvious question is, how does the Rapture of the Church fit into God's timeline? In this chapter, we will answer several questions like; What exactly is the Rapture? What is the purpose of the Rapture? And did Jesus ever mention the Rapture? Before we jump into those questions, let's lay some groundwork. We frequently hear someone say that the Rapture is not Biblical because the word "rapture" is not in the Bible.

The word "rapture" is taken directly from the Middle French word "rapture," which is derived from the Medieval Latin word "raptura," which originates in the Latin word "raptus" as stated in the Westminster Dictionary of Theological Terms. The word means to seize, to kidnap, to snatch away by force. So, if you had a French Bible or a Latin Bible, the word "rapture" would surely be in your Bible.

The original Greek word is "harpazo" and has the same meaning, to catch away by force. In the KJV, the translation is "caught up." Even though the word "rapture" is not in English Bibles, the concept certainly is, and that is what's important.

The Church
Since the Rapture pertains solely to the Church, the body of Christ, it would benefit us here to define what the Church is and is not.
- The Church is NOT a continuation of the Jewish dispensation (Old Testament believers) under a new name.
- The Church is NOT the Kingdom that was promised to Israel. Kingdom Theology is error and has many names such as Latter Rain Movement, Manifest Sons of God, Restorationism,

Reconstructionism, New Apostolic Reformation, Kingdom Now, Dominionism, Word of Faith, Third Wave Movement, and Joel's Army, to name a few. Nowhere in Scripture is the Church charged with setting up or ushering in the Kingdom of the Lord Jesus Christ. He will do that upon His return to earth. He needs no one's help.

- The Church in Scripture is spoken of as a "House," a "Temple," a "Body," but NEVER a Kingdom.
- Jesus Christ is the "Head" of the body of believers, the Church.
- Jesus is never spoken of as King concerning the Church.
- The Kingdom of Messiah was well known in the OT. But the Church was a mystery revealed by the Apostle Paul.
- The "Mystery" was that God was going to do a complete "NEW THING," composed of both Jew and Gentile called "the body of Christ, the church."
- The Church is a "Called Out" Body.
- The Church was "chosen before the foundation of the world" Ephesians 1:4-5, but the Jewish nation was descendant from Abraham, Isaac, and Jacob.
- The Church is the "Body of Christ."
- The Church began with the apostle Paul's conversion on the road to Damascus and will close at the Rapture.
- The mission of the Church is to take the gospel of grace to the world and make disciples, not to establish a kingdom.

Even with this cursory review of the Church, it is easy to see that the Church is unique in God's Plan for the Ages. Many people are confused about Bible Prophecy because they muddy the waters between the Church and Israel. They want to put the Church in prophecies concerning Israel. Robbing Israel of God's promises and covenants is a grievous error.

The Church is not Israel, and the Church has not replaced Israel. Roman Catholicism and many mainline Protestant denominations believe that God is through with the Jews since they crucified their Messiah. They believe God replaced Israel with the Church and all the promises to Israel now apply to the Church. That is called Replacement Theology or Supersessionism, introduced by Augustine in the 5th century A.D. The idea that the Church has replaced Israel and will establish an earthly kingdom for Christ is utterly contrary to Scripture. If you were a 5th century Catholic Priest working for the Pope and Caesar, it makes sense to tell them that their kingdom will last forever and conquer the world; after all, they are paying your salary.

What is the Rapture?

Let's examine the primary Rapture passages to begin answering this question. We begin with 1st Thessalonians chapter four. The issue in the church of Thessalonica was that several believers had died, and they asked Paul to explain their fate. Early believers felt the Lord Jesus Christ would soon return, but when believers started dying of old age or natural causes, they questioned Paul about the fate of those who have passed. Therefore, the apostle Paul wrote chapter four verses 13-18 in his first letter to the Thessalonians to address that issue.

*"But I would not have you to be ignorant, brethren, concerning **them which are asleep**, that ye sorrow not, even as others which have no hope. For if we believe that Jesus died and rose again, even so **them also which sleep in Jesus will God bring with him**. For this we say unto you by the **word of the Lord**, that we which are alive and remain unto the coming of the Lord shall not prevent them which are asleep. **For the Lord himself shall descend from heaven with a shout, with the voice of the**

archangel, and with the trump of God: and the dead in Christ shall rise first: Then we which are alive and remain shall be caught up together with them in the clouds, to meet the Lord in the air: and so shall we ever be with the Lord. Wherefore comfort one another with these words." - *1Thessalonians 4:13-18 KJV*

Let's analyze this passage phrase by phrase.

- *"But I would not have you to be ignorant, brethren, concerning them which are asleep, that ye sorrow not, even as others which have no hope."* - This opening statement reflects Paul's concern regarding the believers at Thessalonica. The question concerns the destiny of believers that had passed. Paul encourages them not to overly grieve or be excessively saddened at the death of a Christian. Those that die without Christ are to be greatly grieved as they have no hope.

- *"For if we believe that Jesus died and rose again, even so them also which sleep in Jesus will God bring with him"* – Those that sleep (die) in Christ are coming back at the Rapture. Jesus will bring their soul and spirit with Him when He returns. Their soul and spirit will be reunited with a newly resurrected incorruptible glorified body. Just as Jesus died and rose again, so will believers that die in Christ rise again at the Rapture.

- *"For this we say unto you by the word of the Lord, that we which are alive and remain unto the coming of the Lord shall not prevent them which are asleep."* - Paul states that he received this teaching directly from the Lord Jesus Christ after his Damascus Road conversion. He did not receive it from Peter, James, or John. The living saints will not precede the dead saints in the Rapture. Those believers that died in Christ are dealt with first.

- *"For the Lord himself shall descend from heaven with a shout, with the voice of the archangel, and with the trump of God."* - The Rapture begins with a shout from the heavens unlike any ever heard.

Perhaps this shout pertains to the dead in Christ, calling their bodies to prepare for resurrection. The next sound is the voice of the archangel. That could be the call to those that are alive. The shout and voice will be distinctive for true believers in Christ, but it might sound like thunder for the lost world as it did when God the Father spoke at Jesus' baptism. The trump of God calls us to leave this earth and gather in the air to meet the Lord.

- *"and the dead in Christ shall rise first:"* – This is the resurrection of those saints that sleep (are dead) in Christ. They are resurrected first and given an incorruptible glorified body fit for eternity.
- *"Then we which are alive and remain shall be caught up together with them in the clouds, to meet the Lord in the air"* – Next, the living saints, we that are alive at the Rapture, will be changed and caught up with the resurrected saints to meet the Lord Jesus Christ in the clouds in the atmosphere. As Jesus was received into the clouds at His ascension, we will be caught up in the same fashion.
- *"and so shall we ever be with the Lord."* – All the Church saints will then have new glorified bodies. The dead have been raised, and the living changed. We are now fit for eternal life with Jesus Christ. Our salvation is now complete, soul, spirit, and body.
- *"Wherefore comfort one another with these words."* – These are comforting words for the saints alive at the Rapture as we will not see death. Comforting also for the families of the dead in Christ as their loved ones will be resurrected to eternal life at the Rapture, having victory over the grave.

There are two significant aspects to the Rapture of the Church Saints. One, the resurrection of those believers that have died. The resurrected saints have new glorified bodies fit for eternity. Two, the changing of the living believers into glorified bodies, enabling them also to enter eternity. A new glorified body is necessary as a "flesh and blood" body cannot enter the kingdom of heaven.

"Now this I say, brethren, that flesh and blood cannot inherit the kingdom of God; neither doth corruption inherit incorruption." - 1Corinthians 15:50 KJV.

The other primary Scripture passage on the Rapture is found in 1 Corinthians Chapter 15.

*"Now this I say, brethren, that **flesh and blood cannot inherit the kingdom of God**; neither doth corruption inherit incorruption. Behold, **I shew you a mystery**; We shall not all sleep, but **we shall all be changed**, In a moment, in the twinkling of an eye, at the last trump: for the trumpet shall sound, and the **dead shall be raised incorruptible**, and **we shall be changed**. For this corruptible must put on incorruption, and this mortal must put on immortality. So when this corruptible shall have put on incorruption, and this mortal shall have put on immortality, then shall be brought to pass the saying that is written, **Death is swallowed up in victory. O death, where is thy sting? O grave, where is thy victory?** The sting of death is sin; and the strength of sin is the law. But thanks be to God, which giveth us the victory through our Lord Jesus Christ. Therefore, my beloved brethren, be ye steadfast, unmovable, always abounding in the work of the Lord, forasmuch as ye know that your labor is not in vain in the Lord." - 1Corinthians 15:50-58 KJV.*

Let's also analyze this passage phrase by phrase.

- *"Now this I say, brethren, that flesh and blood cannot inherit the kingdom of God; neither doth corruption inherit incorruption."* - "flesh and blood" refers to the living saints. In our "flesh and blood" bodies as we now have, we cannot enter heaven, the eternal realm of God. After Jesus' resurrection, His body was flesh and bones. "Behold my hands and my feet, that it is I myself:

handle me, and see; for a spirit hath not **flesh and bones**, as ye see me have.' – Luke 24:39 KJV. Jesus shed His blood on the Cross for our sin. So, we, the living, must be changed into a new body fit for eternity with Christ, a glorified flesh and bones body like His. Corruption refers to the dead in Christ. Their bodies have corrupted, disintegrated in the grave. That body inherits nothing of its own power as it returns to dust. The only possible way for that dead, corrupted body to inherit incorruption, eternal life, is through the resurrection power of Almighty God.

- *"Behold, I shew you a mystery"* – This is a critical point of understanding. The Apostle Paul refers to the Rapture doctrine as a "***mystery***." A MYSTERY IN SCRIPTURE IS SOMETHING HERETOFORE UNKNOWN. The principle of the Rapture was unknown to everyone before the apostle Paul. He began teaching it on his first missionary trip to Thessalonica. It's important to understand that the Old Testament Prophets knew nothing about the Church and the Rapture. They knew that God would save the Gentiles at some time, but they did not see how that would happen.

- *"We shall not all sleep, but we shall all be changed,"* – Here Paul begins explaining the mystery. We shall not all sleep. In other words, not all saints will die. There will be many saints living when Jesus returns for His Church at the Rapture. Whether you are living or dead at that time, we, all the Church saints that have ever lived, will be changed, changed into our new glorified bodies.

- *"In a moment, in the twinkling of an eye, at the last trump: for the trumpet shall sound, and the dead shall be raised incorruptible, and we shall be changed."* – Instantaneously, at the last trump, all Church saints will be changed. The last trump referred to the trumpet blasts when Israel wandered in the desert for 40 years after the Exodus. The first trump was the call to prepare to move the camp. The last trump was to move out to a new destination. That is precisely what we will do at the Rapture. We will move out, leave this earth for our new destination in heaven with Jesus. The Feast of Trumpets could also fulfill this passage as the trumpet is blown one hundred times at the sighting of the new moon. The last long blast is also known as the "last trump."

- *"For this corruptible must put on incorruption, and this mortal must put on immortality."* – Hear we find a clear distinction between the dead and living saints. The dead (corruptible) put on incorruption. The living (mortal) saints put on immortality. The resurrected dead saints and the living saints both get new glorified bodies.

- *"So when this corruptible shall have put on incorruption, and this mortal shall have put on immortality, then shall be brought to pass the saying that is written, Death is swallowed up in victory. O death, where is thy sting? O grave, where is thy victory?"* – After we receive our new glorified bodies, those alive at the Rapture will say, "O death, where is thy sting?" They cheated death as they were changed from mortal to immortal. The resurrected dead will say, "O grave, where is thy victory?" as they have risen from the dead, and the grave can no longer hold them. They have the final victory over death and the grave.

- *"The sting of death is sin; and the strength of sin is the law."* – The wages of sin is death, eternal separation from God. Sin is defined in God's law. Violate God's law, and you are a sinner worthy of death. The law gave strength to sin because no one, except Jesus, could ever keep the law.

- *"But thanks be to God, which giveth us the victory through our Lord Jesus Christ."* – But thanks be to God that we have victory over sin, victory over death and victory over the law through the grace and mercy of our Lord Jesus Christ. *"But if ye be led of the Spirit, ye are **not under the law.**"* – Galatians 5: 18 KJV.

- *"Therefore, my beloved brethren, be ye steadfast, unmovable, always abounding in the work of the Lord, forasmuch as ye know that your labor is not in vain in the Lord."* – In other words, hang in there, keep the faith, continue doing what the Lord has assigned you because your work will be rewarded in heaven. "But lay up for yourselves treasures in heaven, where neither moth nor rust doth corrupt, and where thieves do not break through nor steal:" – Matthew 6:20 KJV. The treasures are the good works that the Lord has for you to do. These good works are not for salvation but reward.

From these two classic Rapture Scriptures, we can draw some conclusions about the details of the Rapture. There are two distinct groups of believers participating in this spectacular event.

Dead Saints	Resurrected at the Rapture, given glorified bodies
Living Saints	Changed into glorified bodies
Both Caught Up	Snatched by force from the earth
Meet the Lord Jesus	We all meet Him in the clouds in the air
Ever be with Him	We will be with the Lord Jesus Christ for all eternity

Did Jesus Ever Mention the Rapture?

The Rapture is a profound, startling, almost unbelievable prophecy. Millions of people suddenly snatched from the face of the earth. Many dead people coming out of their graves. The one thing this outrageous prophecy has going for it is that it's true; it's in your Bible. But, did Jesus ever mention it? No, Jesus never mentioned any of the mystery doctrines of the Church, the Body of Christ during His earthly ministry. He revealed the doctrine of the Rapture to the apostle Paul, and Paul revealed it to the church.

The Apostle Paul gives the main points of the Rapture doctrine in 1 Thessalonians Chapter 4. The Lord Jesus Christ gave Paul the revelation. The Apostle Paul gave us the mechanism of how the gathering of the saints would happen. This event cannot be the Second Coming of Jesus at the end of the Tribulation because in 1 Thess. 4, he comes **FOR** His saints. At the second coming, Jesus returns **WITH** His angels to make war against the Antichrist and his armies. In Revelation Chapter 19, we see Jesus returning with His angels to make war. That is not the stated purpose of the rapture.

*"And I saw heaven opened, and behold a **white horse**, and he that sat upon him was called **Faithful and True**, and in righteousness he doth **judge and make war**. His eyes were as a flame of fire, and on his head were many crowns; and he had a name written, that no man knew, but he himself. And he was clothed with a vesture dipped in blood: and his name is called The Word of God. **And the armies which were in heaven followed him upon white horses, clothed in fine linen, white and clean.**"* - *Revelation 19:11-14 KJV.*

*"For the Son of man shall come in the glory of his **Father with his angels**; and then he shall reward every man according to his works."* - *Matthew 16:27 KJV*

*"When the Son of man shall come in his glory, **and all the holy angels with him**, then shall he sit upon the throne of his glory:"* - *Matthew 25:31 KJV*

Jesus' Second Coming at the end of the 7-year Tribulation is for judgment upon the Antichrist and a Christ-rejecting world (along with the redemption of Israel). The Rapture is the coming of the Lord for His Saints before the 7-year Tribulation. This distinction is clear from scripture.

What is the Purpose of the Rapture?

There are several scenarios for the timing of the Rapture, as listed below. There are some that claim there is no Rapture, that the Rapture is just a myth, or a false doctrine started by John Darby in the 19th century. Well, we just looked at the Scriptures that define the Rapture, so the "no Rapture" teaching is a complete error. That doctrine is a false doctrine. Notice that the four popular Rapture scenarios are all juxtaposition to the 7-year Tribulation.

Rapture Scenario	Timeframe
Pre-tribulation Rapture	Before the 7-year Tribulation
Mid-tribulation Rapture	At the middle of the 7-year Tribulation
Post-tribulation Rapture	At the end of the 7-year Tribulation
Pre-wrath Rapture	About 5 ½ years into the 7-year Tribulation

Only one scenario can be correct as they are mutually exclusive. But why so much confusion and misunderstanding about the timing of the Rapture? Well, I believe the confusion stems from two sources. One, misunderstanding the purpose of the Tribulation. Two, not realizing the uniqueness of the Church. We have already noted that the Tribulation is the "time of Jacob's trouble," a time of trouble for Israel. Daniel proclaims these 7 years, the 70th week of his 70 weeks' prophecy, is distinctly for the Jew and Jerusalem (Dan 9:24). Once you understand that the 7-year Tribulation is NOT for the perfecting of Church saints but the redemption of Israel, it becomes clear that the Church is not involved in the 7-year Tribulation. We have already been redeemed by the blood of Jesus Christ shed on the Cross for our sin. Israel is still in unbelief and continues to reject Jesus as their Messiah as of this writing. They need redemption; we already have it.

The second misunderstanding about the timing of the Rapture concerns the uniqueness of the Church. Roman Catholics and mainstream Protestant denominations believe the Church has replaced Israel because they crucified their Messiah. If the Church has replaced Israel, then Israel's promises now fall upon the Church, and Israel's curses also. One of those curses is the 7-year Tribulation. So, if you believe the error of Replacement Theology, then logically, the Church will go through the 7-year Tribulation since the Church has replaced Israel in God's plan for the ages. However, the Church has not replaced Israel. Once we understand the Church's uniqueness in God's prophetic plan, it becomes clear that the Church has no part in the 7-year Tribulation. The whole purpose of the Rapture is to keep the Church out of the Tribulation as that is a time of judgment for Israel to bring them to national repentance to be saved. If that's not the case, then the Rapture is superfluous.

These Scriptures bear repeating:
*"Esaias also crieth concerning **Israel,** Though the number of the **children of Israel** be as the sand of the sea, **a remnant shall be saved.**"* - Romans 9:27 KJV

*"Brethren, my heart's desire and prayer to God **for Israel** is, **that they might be saved.**"* - Romans 10:1 KJV

"And so **all _Israel_ shall be saved** as it is written, there shall come out of **Sion** the Deliverer, and shall turn away ungodliness from **Jacob:**" - Romans 11:26 KJV

When Paul wrote these words around 60 A.D., the salvation of Israel was yet future. Even today, it is yet future. The salvation of the remnant of Israel happens during the 7-year Tribulation. Again, the purpose of the 7-year Tribulation is to save Israel by bringing judgment upon them so they will repent. The purpose of the Rapture is to remove the Church before the commencement of that judgment.

"Because thou hast kept the word of my patience, **I also will keep thee from the hour of temptation, which shall come upon all the world,** to try them that dwell upon the earth". - Revelation 3:10 KJV.

So, let me state this as clearly as I can. The Rapture of the Church occurs BEFORE the 7-year Tribulation. That is the Pre-Tribulation Rapture doctrine. The Rapture's purpose is to keep the Church out of the Tribulation as the Tribulation is for the redemption of Israel, not the Church.

Us and Them

Another exciting passage concerning those taken in the Rapture and those left behind is found in 1 Thessalonians Chapter 5. I have underlined several essential words and phrases. The pronouns are capitalized, so a clear distinction can be made between "US" and "YE" believers and "THEY" and "THEM," the unbelievers left to endure the 7-year Tribulation.

*"But of the times and the seasons, brethren, **YE** have no need that I write unto you. For yourselves know perfectly that the <u>day of the Lord</u> so cometh as a <u>thief in the night</u>. For when **THEY** shall say, <u>Peace and safety</u>; then <u>sudden destruction</u> cometh upon **THEM**, as travail upon a woman with child; and **THEY** <u>shall not escape</u>. But **YE**, brethren, are <u>not in darkness, that that day should overtake you as a thief</u>. **YE** are all the children of light, and the children of the day: **WE** are not of the night, nor of darkness. Therefore let **US** not sleep, as do others; but let **US** watch and be sober. For **THEY** that sleep sleep in the night; and **THEY** that be drunken are drunken in the night. But let **US**, who are of the day, be sober, putting on the breastplate of faith and love; and for an helmet, the hope of salvation. For <u>God hath not appointed **US** to wrath, but to obtain salvation</u> by our Lord Jesus Christ, Who died for **US**, that, whether **WE** wake or sleep, **WE** should live together with him. Wherefore <u>comfort yourselves</u> together, and edify one another, even as also **YE** do." - 1Thessalonians 5:1-11 KJV. Emphasis mine*

The crux of this passage is that we believers are not in darkness, separated from God, so the day of the Lord will not "overtake you as a thief." We are of the light (God is Light). Unbelievers are of the darkness, the night, the day of the Lord. We will be taken out of this world before the 7-year Tribulation "for God hath not appointed us to wrath, but to obtain salvation (deliverance)." (Strongs; G4991, *soteria*; deliverance, preservation, safety, salvation; deliverance from the molestation of enemies). We are to be delivered from the 7-year Tribulation, the wrath of God. We "obtain" this deliverance at the Rapture. The Rapture event will complete our salvation by changing our mortal human bodies into an eternal glorified body. The blood of Christ has redeemed our soul. Our spirit is a new creation in Christ. The only part left is the body which will be changed at the Rapture. An additional meaning of "salvation" from Strongs is: "future salvation, the sum of benefits and blessings which the Christians, redeemed from all earthly ills, will enjoy after the visible return of

Christ from heaven in the consummated and eternal kingdom of God." Below is a summary in table form that clearly shows the distinction between "us" and "them.

US	Them
Not in darkness	In darkness, of the night
Not overtaken as a thief	Overtaken by God as a thief in the night
Children of light	Children of darkness
Watch and be sober	Sleep and are drunken
Not appointed to wrath	Receive wrath and destruction
Escape the wrath of God	Overtaken by God's wrath and destruction
Comfort with these words	?

"They" are in darkness. The 7-year Tribulation will overtake unbelievers as a thief in the night. They sleep and are not ready for the Lord's return. They will not escape the wrath of God and the destruction to come. However, "we," the faithful saints, are not in darkness, the Tribulation. The Tribulation does not overtake us. The "Day of the Lord" is a day of darkness, thick darkness as we read previously. We are children of light, not darkness. We are not appointed to wrath as "they" are. We escape the coming wrath of God; this is comforting to us.

The Great Apostasy or Departure?
One more primary Rapture Scripture we need to examine before we move on to other prophecy topics is 2nd Thessalonians Chapter 2.

Much controversy engulfs this scripture with strong feelings on every side. The text is long, so I will break it down verse by verse.

"Now we beseech you, brethren, by the coming of our Lord Jesus Christ, and by our gathering together unto him, That ye be not soon shaken in mind, or be troubled, neither by spirit, nor by word, nor by letter as from us, as that the day of Christ is at hand. Let no man deceive you by any means: for that day shall not come, except there come a falling away first, and that man of sin be revealed, the son of perdition; Who opposes and exalts himself above all that is called God, or that is worshipped; so that he as God sits in the temple of God, shewing himself that he is God. Remember ye not, that, when I was yet with you, I told you these things? And now ye know what withholds that he might be revealed in his time. For the mystery of iniquity doth already work: only he who now restrains will restrain, until he be taken out of the way. And then shall that Wicked be revealed, whom the Lord shall consume with the spirit of his mouth, and shall destroy with the brightness of his coming: Even him, whose coming is after the working of Satan with all power and signs and lying wonders, And with all deceivableness of unrighteousness in them that perish; because they received not the love of the truth, that they might be saved. And for this cause God shall send them strong delusion, that they should believe a lie: That they all might be damned who believed not the truth, but had pleasure in unrighteousness." - 2Thessalonians 2:1-12 KJV

To analyze this passage, I will use the following outline.
* Context – verse 1
* Issue – verse 2
* Resolution – verse 3
* Discussion – verse 4-12

Context

"*Now we beseech you, brethren, by the coming of our Lord Jesus Christ, and by our gathering together unto him,*" – *2 Thessalonians 2:1 KJV*. At first glance, one might think there are two topics here, "the coming of the Lord" and "our gathering together unto him." But that is not the case. We see this construct many times in the KJV, where two phrases are connected with an "and" or the word "even." The first phrase defines the topic, and the second phrase gives a descriptive characteristic of the topic. The "coming of the Lord" is for us "gathering together unto him." That is one event, the Rapture. That is the only future event where the Lord comes, and we believers, the Church, are gathered to meet Him. So, the context of the passage is set in verse 1 as the Rapture of the Church. Then we would logically expect Paul to mention the Rapture somewhere in the subsequent verses. Stating the context and not mentioning it again would be illogical and flawed literary style, something someone of Paul's education and intelligence would never do. Not to mention that the Holy Spirit, the Spirit of Truth, would never leave the reader with a vague, confusing, and incomplete concept.

Issue

"*That ye be not soon shaken in mind, or be troubled, neither by spirit, nor by word, nor by letter as from us, as that the day of Christ is at hand.*" - *2Thessalonians 2:2 KJV*. The believers in Thessalonica were shaken up. They were upset and troubled because they were told the Day of the Lord (the 7-year Tribulation) had begun. That was contrary to what Paul taught; otherwise, there would be no reason for them to be troubled. We do not know how they received this erroneous information, but it must have come from a somewhat credible source for them to write to Paul for clarification. It could have come by revelation from a demon spirit, or by word of mouth, or by a forged letter allegedly from the Apostle Paul himself. Either way, they were upset and wanted some clarification on the Rapture timeline.

Resolution

"Let no man deceive you by any means: for that day shall not come, except there come a falling away first, and that man of sin be revealed, the son of perdition;" - 2Th 2:3 KJV. The verse opens with a stern warning, "let no man deceive you." In other words, if any man comes to you with a different Rapture scenario than the scenario Paul is about to give, he is a deceiver. That was true in Paul's day and still valid today. In our modern world, deception can come from many sources and in different forms. There are a great many "means" available for the devil's minions to perpetrate mass deception upon the Church. What the Thessalonians had heard about being in the Day of the Lord was a deception.

Paul clearly states an event must come "first" before the beginning of the Day of the Lord, the 7-year Tribulation, wherein the Antichrist, the son of perdition, is revealed. Remember, the Antichrist is revealed when he confirms the 7-year covenant that begins the Tribulation (Daniel 9:27). The 7-year Tribulation and the Day of the Lord in this context are synonymous. But what exactly is this "first" event that precedes the Tribulation?

The Greek word is *"apostasia."* It is rendered as "a falling away" in the KJV and most all modern Bibles. But was that the original intended meaning? As you can see in the table below, all the English Bibles (Wycliffe to Geneva) before the King James Version translated *"apostasia"* as "departing."

Year	Bible	Translation
382	Jerome's Latin Vulgate	Departure First
1384	Wycliffe Bible	Departynge First
1526	Tyndale Bible	Departynge First
1535	Coverdale Bible	Departynge First
1539	Crammer Bible	Departing First
1576	Breeches Bible	Departing First
1583	Beeza Bible	Departing First
1608	Geneva Bible	Departing First
1611	King James Bible	Falling Away

House, When the Trumpet Sounds, p. 270

- *"Let no one deceive you in any way. For it will not be, unless **the departure comes first**, and the man of sin is revealed, the son of destruction,"* - *2Thess 2:3 HNV*. Here in the modern Hebrew Names Version the word "apostasia" is translated as "the departure."
- How's your Latin? "ne quis vos seducat ullo modo quoniam nisi venerit **discessio primum** et revelatus fuerit homo peccati filius perditionis" – 2Th 2:3 VUL. The phrase "discessio primum" means "departure first," St. Jerome's Latin Vulgate, 382 A.D. Since the earliest writings, "apostasia" had been translated as "departing" or "departure."
- The Greek word "*apostasia*" is a combination of "apo," meaning "from" and "istemi," meaning "stand." It means to stand away from or departure. The word's context in our passage under investigation has nothing to do with falling away from the faith as the object departed from is not in the word meaning.
- The Greek has the definite article before "*apostasia*" adding emphasis as "the departure" or "the departing." That means it

is a reference back to a previous mention or teaching. If this were the first occurrence of this teaching, Paul would have used the indefinite article as "a departure." "the apostasia" is, therefore, a definitive event previously taught by Paul, the rapture from verse 1.

- "Since the Greek language does not need an article to make the noun definite, it becomes clear that with the usage of the article, reference is being made to something in particular. In **2 Thessalonians 2:3,** the word *apostasia* is prefaced by the definite article, which means that Paul is pointing to a particular type of departure known to the Thessalonian church." <small>Daniel K. Davey, "The *Apostasia* of II Thessalonians 2:3," Th.M. thesis, Detroit Baptist Theological Seminary, May 1982, p. 47.</small>
- Paul is not introducing new teaching in verse 3 about a "spiritual departure," i.e., a falling away from the faith. He refers to a "physical departure" previously taught by him during his missionary visit to Thessalonica and in his first epistle to those believers.
- "the departure" MUST be an event; otherwise, it would be impossible to know when it happened. A spiritual departure, a falling away from the faith, is not an event. It is a process, one that has been ongoing since the first century. There have always been areas falling away from the faith for various reasons and, at the same time, revivals happening elsewhere. It is impossible to date the starting and ending of a spiritual departure from the faith. The process is too indefinite and ambiguous. However, the Rapture is a specific event that happens very quickly, easily observable as a singular event.
- Another point that needs to be made here is that Paul is not giving the primary teaching in this text. The direct instruction was given to the Thessalonian believers while Paul was with them. We are reading a second or follow-up conversation on the topic of the Rapture and the Day of the Lord in this passage. That is why Paul

uses more common or familiar language because he references something he has already taught. He is using everyday words to refer to the primary teaching given while present with them. Words like "the departure" and "he who now restrains" are concepts previously taught by Paul, so he does not elaborate on them as he expects the believers in Thessalonica to remember his teachings and reference those words back to his primary teaching. We know this is the case as Paul states: *"Remember ye not, that, when I was yet with you, I told you these things?"* - *2Thessalonians 2:5 KJV*

There are three rules for acquiring a piece of real estate, whether for business or personal residence: location, location, location. Similarly, there are three rules for correct Bible interpretation: context, context, context. I can't stress this enough. If you depart from the context, you will fall into error. It is interesting and valuable to examine the Greek words and notice how the text was handled historically. Still, the passage's context is paramount and must be followed for any interpretation to be valid. In verse one, we noted that the passage's context is the Rapture of the Church, not a falling away from the faith. Therefore, the departure, the "apostasia," must refer to the Rapture, the physical departure of the Church. There is no other word in the passage that would refer to the Rapture context of verse one. Paul clearly states that the Rapture comes first, then the man of sin is revealed, which begins the Day of the Lord, the 7-year Tribulation. Here is a paraphrase of verse 3. "Let no man deceive you by any means: for the Day of the Lord, the 7-year Tribulation will not come, except there comes the departure, the Rapture first, and then that man of sin, the Antichrist is revealed, the son of perdition."

V. 4 – *"Who opposes and exalts himself above all that is called God, or that is worshipped; so that he as God sits in the temple of God, shewing himself that he is God."* – The Antichrist, the man of sin, not only opposes God but exalts himself above all that is Godly. That is pride and arrogance supreme. It sounds like what Lucifer states in Isaiah Chapter 14.

*"How art thou fallen from heaven, O Lucifer, son of the morning! how art thou cut down to the ground, which didst weaken the nations! For thou hast said in thine heart, **I will** ascend into heaven, **I will** exalt my throne above the stars of God: **I will** sit also upon the mount of the congregation, in the sides of the north: **I will** ascend above the heights of the clouds; **I will** be like the most High. Yet thou shalt be brought down to hell, to the sides of the pit. They that see thee shall narrowly look upon thee, and consider thee, saying, Is this the man that made the earth to tremble, that did shake kingdoms;"* - Isaiah 14:12-16 KJV.

These are the five "I will's" of Satan (Lucifer). They are in complete agreement with "opposes and exalts himself above all that is called God" in verse 4. The Antichrist wants to "be like the Most High" and sit in God's temple, "showing himself that HE is God." The Antichrist perpetrates this event in the middle of the 7-year Tribulation. That is the "abomination of desolation" spoken of by Jesus in Matthew Chapter 24, the Olivet discourse.

*"When ye therefore shall see the **abomination of desolation**, spoken of by Daniel the prophet, stand in the holy place, (whoso readeth, let him understand:) ... For then shall be great tribulation, such as was not since the beginning of the world to this time, no, nor ever shall be."* - Matthew 24:15, 21 KJV

The passages in the Book of Daniel are as follows:

"And he shall confirm the covenant with many for one week: and in the midst of the week he shall cause the sacrifice and the oblation to cease, and for the overspreading of **abominations he shall make it desolate***, even until the consummation, and that determined shall be poured upon the desolate."* - Daniel 9:27 KJV

"And arms shall stand on his part, and they shall pollute the sanctuary of strength, and shall take away the daily sacrifice, and they shall place the **abomination that maketh desolate***."* - Daniel 11:31 KJV

"And from the time that the daily sacrifice shall be taken away, and the **abomination that maketh desolate** *set up, there shall be a thousand two hundred and ninety days."* - Daniel 12:11 KJV

The "abomination of desolation" occurs when the Antichrist sets up his image in the newly rebuilt temple in Jerusalem, declaring himself God. This event marks the midpoint of the 7-year Tribulation.

V. 5 – *"Remember ye not, that, when I was yet with you, I told you these things?"* Again, Paul is not giving the primary teaching in this letter. He referred back to his teachings when he was present with the believers at Thessalonica. 2 Thessalonians Chapter 2 is a review of Paul's primary teaching.

V. 6 – *"And now ye know what withholdeth that he might be revealed in his time."* Paul is again referencing his previous teaching, stating that the saints should know or remember what is restraining the Antichrist from being revealed. He is to be revealed at the appropriate time and not before. Something or someone is restraining the revelation of the Antichrist until the proper time in God's prophetic timeline.

V. 7 – "*For the mystery of iniquity doth already work: only he who now letteth will let, until he be taken out of the way.*" – The "mystery of iniquity" is already at work. What is the "mystery of iniquity?" Just as the mystery of godliness was God manifest in the flesh through the man Jesus Christ, Satan will be manifest in the flesh through the person of the Antichrist. Since Satan is not omniscient, he does not know when the Tribulation might begin, so he has always had someone waiting in the wings to fill this role when called upon. The one restraining the revelation of the Antichrist is referred to as "he." The old English word "let" means to restrain. Someone is restraining the mystery of iniquity on a global scale. Since the only member of the Trinity on earth currently is the Holy Spirit, He is restraining as He is the only one powerful enough for the task. The Holy Spirit will continue to restrain the hideous evil of the Antichrist until He is "taken out of the way." That happens at the Rapture as the Holy Spirit's earthly dwelling is in the soul and spirit of believers. We are the "temple" of the Holy Spirit. When the Church leaves, so does the Holy Spirit's restraint, and then all hell breaks loose.

V. 8-9 – "*And then shall that Wicked be revealed, whom the Lord shall consume with the spirit of his mouth, and shall destroy with the brightness of his coming: Even him, whose coming is after the working of Satan with all power and signs and lying wonders,*" – As soon as the restrainer, the Holy Spirit, is taken out of the way "that Wicked," the Antichrist, is revealed. His revealing begins the 7-year Tribulation. He is revealed when he confirms a peace covenant with Israel and surrounding nations. He is a deceiver, a false Christ doing many lying signs and wonders empowered by Satan. These "signs and lying wonders" are real. They are "lying" as they are not from God but intended to deceive many into following the Antichrist. The Lord Jesus Christ destroys him, his kingdom and his followers at His return at the end of the 7-year Tribulation.

V. 10 – *"And with all deceivableness of unrighteousness in them that perish; because they received not the love of the truth, that they might be saved."* – Those that follow the Antichrist are wholly deceived. They love their unrighteous, sinful deeds and evil thoughts because they have no love for the truth. Having no love for the truth, they do not seek the truth of God, so they perish. Had they had a passion for the truth, they might have been saved.

V. 11-12 – *"And for this cause God shall send them strong delusion, that they should believe a lie: That they all might be damned who believed not the truth, but had pleasure in unrighteousness."* – Because the followers of the Antichrist had no love for the truth, God will seal their fate. He sends them a "strong delusion" so they fully embrace the lie. The big lie is probably that the Antichrist is God. For this they are all damned because they had no love for the truth and even took pleasure in sinful, perverted acts. We read in Revelation the following: *"Neither repented they of their murders, nor of their sorceries, nor of their fornication, nor of their thefts."* - *Revelation 9:21 KJV*

In these verses 4-12 we see the following:
- The true Anti-God nature of the Antichrist is revealed at the midpoint of the 7-year Tribulation by committing the abomination of desolation.
- The removal of the restrainer, the Holy Spirit, allows the Antichrist to come to power at the beginning of the 7-year Tribulation and be fully revealed at the mid-point.
- The Antichrist is destroyed at the Second Coming of Jesus Christ by His Word and His brightness, His glory.
- The deception and delusion that befalls the followers of the Antichrist.

- The damnation of the followers of the Antichrist because they had no love for the truth.

UFO's and Aliens

Most people by now have heard of aliens and UFOs. Some think it just nonsense or fantasy. Others have had experiences with aliens, seen UFO's or even been abducted. They know it's not all fantasy or hallucination. The Internet is saturated with fake UFO-related info, but there is a core of actual UFO data that cannot be dismissed. Sightings have been made by credible people such as pilots, law enforcement, military, and government officials.

An interesting aspect of UFOs is they are never tracked in outer space. They just appear in our atmosphere and disappear just as quickly. They travel at high speed and perform seemingly impossible maneuvers. They are not from other star systems or galaxies far, far away. They are fallen angel/demon entities that have always been here, existing in a higher dimension. They appear in our 3-dimensional world for a short time and then leave. They are trans-dimensional malevolent beings.

These powers of darkness, evil spirits, and entities would like to come to the earth's surface and stay, but they are restrained from doing so. They were here on earth before and after Noah's flood. Fallen angels cohabitating with human women lived among man and gave birth to the giants (Genesis 6:4). These were destroyed during the flood, but only the body was destroyed; souls and spirits are eternal. These evil spirits have always been with us and are posing as intelligent alien entities from space. They are deceivers.

They would love to return to the earth's surface and pick up where they left off. But they are restrained from doing so. The Holy Spirit is restraining that from happening. However, we just read that at the Rapture; He is "taken out of the way." The restrainer is removed, and the alien/demon/fallen angel powers of darkness will be allowed to return to the surface and interfere once again with humanity. Let's look at some scripture that proves this hypothesis.

In Daniel chapter two we read:

*"And whereas thou sawest iron mixed with miry clay, **they** shall mingle themselves with the seed of men: but **they** shall not cleave one to another, even as iron is not mixed with clay." - Daniel 2:43 KJV*

Daniel is prophesying about the latter days, the end times in which we live. "They," symbolized by the miry clay, come from the pit. The "seed of men" are regular human beings. These two groups are unable to cohabitate. "They" are not genetically human even though they may look human. "They" are non-human powers of darkness that have come once again to destroy humankind. That begins once the restrainer, the Holy Spirit, is taken away at the Rapture. Daniel predicted "they" would return in the latter days. They are buzzing around in our atmosphere even now, waiting for their day. Remember, Satan is the prince and the power of the air. "They" are his demonic powers soon to return. You do not want to be here after the Rapture. Get right with Jesus Christ while you still have time.

Summary
This passage shows that Paul has given us the timeline for the Rapture and the 7-year Tribulation.

Event	The Rapture comes first.	v. 3
Event	The man of sin, the Antichrist, confirms a covenant with Israel. That begins the 7-year Tribulation.	v. 3
Event	The Antichrist enters the newly rebuilt Temple proclaiming to be God at the mid-point of the Tribulation.	v. 4
Explanation	The Holy Spirit is restraining the man of sin until the appropriate time. He is initially revealed when he confirms a covenant with Israel that begins the 7-year Tribulation.	v. 6
Explanation	At the proper time, the Holy Spirit's restraint is removed. The restraint from the Holy Spirit is removed at the Rapture.	v. 7
Explanation	Then the Antichrist's true identity is fully revealed at the mid-point when He enters the Temple in Jerusalem proclaiming himself God.	v. 8
Event	The Antichrist is destroyed at the Second Coming of Jesus Christ.	v. 8
Explanation	Many follow the Antichrist being deceived by his lying signs and wonders.	v. 9
Explanation	His followers have no love for the truth of God but love ungodliness.	v. 10
Explanation	His followers are given a strong delusion to believe the Antichrist.	v. 11
Event	They are damned to hell as they love sin and hate the truth.	v. 12

To be concise: 1. The Rapture, 2. The Tribulation, 3. The Second Coming of Jesus Christ, in that order.

OOPS, I Missed the Rapture

What do you do if you miss the Rapture? Many will miss the Rapture for a variety of reasons, all centered upon unbelief. What you do at that point is critical. Your next move will determine your eternal destiny.

Since you missed the Rapture, it is apparent that you are not a faithful follower of Jesus Christ. Oh yes, you may have attended Church on Sunday occasionally, but you never received Jesus Christ as your Lord and Savior. You never truly gave Jesus your life and followed Him. You may have viewed him as a great person or moral example. You could have believed that Jesus was a unique historical figure and a great teacher. You could have accepted Jesus intellectually but never repented of your sin and received Him as your Savior.

Well, this is now your **NUMBER ONE** priority. Receiving Jesus as Lord and Savior will determine whether you receive eternal life with Him or spend eternity in the lake of fire. In the final analysis, there are only two destinations for man: eternal life or eternal damnation. In other words, it's heaven or hell; the choice is yours.

*"Marvel not at this: for the hour is coming, in the which all that are in the graves shall hear his voice, And shall come forth; they that have done good, unto the **resurrection of life**; and they that have done evil, unto the **resurrection of damnation**." John 5:28-29 KJV*

You can choose heaven by receiving Jesus as your Lord and Savior. Or you can select hell simply by doing nothing and going along with the world's lies. Believe the media propaganda, follow the Antichrist, and your fate in hell is sealed. Decide in your mind right now to seek the truth of God.

What is the truth? What is the true gospel of Jesus Christ? In a nutshell, the true gospel centers on the death, burial, and resurrection of Jesus Christ (1st Corinthians 15:1-4). Jesus Christ died on the cross shedding His blood as God's holy sacrifice for sin. His atoning death on the cross provided the means for you and me to be in right standing with God. He took upon himself the judgment we deserve. He paid the price for our sin with His own blood. For without the shedding of blood, there is no forgiveness of sin. Jesus was buried in a new tomb showing that he did indeed die. Three days later, Jesus rose from the dead validating that He was and is the Son of God, God in the flesh.

If you are not a Christian and you miss the Rapture, then you will be very confused. When this makes sense to you, pray a simple prayer like this, **"Lord Jesus, I believe you are the Son of the living God, the Savior of the world; I believe you died on the cross for my sin and rose from the dead the third day; I repent of my sin; Cleanse me from all sin by your blood. I give you my life and receive you as my Lord and Savior, Amen."** Or, if that is too much, then just cry out, **"HELP ME JESUS."** Either way, Jesus knows your heart and will respond to you. If you can find a Bible read the New Testament and the Old Testament prophets. Start your Bible reading with Hebrews through Revelation as those books apply to the time in which you live.

Now that you have given your life to the Lord Jesus Christ, he is your testimony. Your testimony is that you believe in Jesus Christ as your

Lord and Savior; He is your King and no other. That is very important as you will need to walk out this testimony over the 7-year Tribulation period. Remember, your eternal destiny is at stake; you are not playing church. It's not about joining a religion. It's about a personal relationship with Jesus Christ that determines your eternal home.

*"And they overcame him (antichrist) by the **blood of the Lamb** (Jesus), and by the **word of their testimony**, and they loved not their lives unto the death."* Revelation 12:11 KJV (emphasis mine)

"But he that shall endure unto the end, the same shall be saved." Matthew 24:13 KJV

The testimony of Jesus Christ will cost many their lives, as you have read above. Better to die for Jesus and go to heaven than to renounce Him and be cast into hell. You will only overcome, by the blood of Jesus and the word of your testimony. Jesus said:

*"For whosoever will **save** his life to himself shall **lose** it: and whosoever will **lose** his life for my sake shall find it."* Matthew 16:25 KJV (emphasis mine)

I realize this is heavy stuff, but you are living in heavy times, and that was the most serious decision you will ever make. Ok, I think you get the point.

If you are a churchgoer and your pastor did not preach on Bible topics like sin, repentance, and the second coming of Jesus, then next Sunday, ask him why. Ask him why he did not preach the true Gospel of Jesus Christ and His Second Coming prophecies. After all, had he preached the truth, you might have gone in the Rapture and would not need to endure the coming Tribulation.

Let him know his judgment will be severe for not preaching the truth of the Word of God. If he tries to make excuses instead of repenting, leave and find a group of true believers. The Apostle Paul stated in his letter to Timothy:

*"Now the Spirit speaketh expressly, that **in the latter times some shall depart from the faith,** giving heed to seducing spirits, and doctrines of devils."*

Be sure you associate yourself with a group that stresses the truth of God's Word, the Bible. The Word of God is your only source of truth for these last days.

Deception and lies are the order of the day for those clinging to the world for answers. Separate yourself from them and stick to the Word of God and the Lord Jesus Christ. Oh, forget about the modern Bible translations; get a King James Version because the prophetic scriptures are easier to follow. The textual links are much clearer and more accessible to reference similar verses. If you are new to the Bible, then study Hebrews through Revelation in the New Testament. When you feel comfortable, then study the prophetic Scriptures found throughout this book. Your increased understanding of coming end times events will give you confidence in the Lord when the hearts of others are failing for fear. Keep the faith in love.

*"Watch ye therefore, and pray always, that ye may be **accounted worthy to escape all these things that shall come to pass,** and to stand before the Son of man." Luke 21:36 KJV*

It's better to be a doorman in God's Kingdom than to reign with the wicked.

"For a day in thy courts is better than a thousand (elsewhere). I had rather be a doorkeeper in the house of my God, than to dwell in the tents of wickedness." Psalm 84:10 KJV Parenthesis mine

If you would like more on missing the Rapture, get my ebook by clicking the link below. This book is ideal for family and friends who are not saved and miss the Rapture if it happened today.

https://www.amazon.com/So-You-Missed-Rapture-Tribulation/dp/0982995415

CONFIDENTIAL

Briefing

Point of interest:
   a) the rapture of the church: Millions suddenly Missing, possible FALSE FLAG alien abduction, worldwide chaos.
   b) cemetery operators around the world baffled as many graves disrupted and bodies missing.
   c) the rapture removes the righteous from the earth so the judgments of God can begin.
   d) THE 7-year tribulation COMMENCES SHORTLY AFTER THE RAPTURE.
Person of interest:
   a) the Almighty: JESUS CHRIST RETURNING IN THE ATMOSPHERE FOR HIS CHURCH SAINTS, THE BODY OF CHRIST
Discussion:

The next event on God's prophetic timeline is the Rapture of the Church, where Jesus Christ comes to rescue His Church (dead and living saints) before the 7-year Tribulation. The Church does not participate in the 7-year Tribulation. The Rapture is coming soon, so be a faithful witness for the Lord Jesus Christ no matter what happens. Could things get nasty in the west before the Rapture? Sure, they could. They are already bad for Christians in most of the world. Every day Saints are imprisoned or killed for their faith. If that comes to America, we must be ready by having a strong relationship with Jesus Christ. Sadly, most Christians in America are lukewarm. They are not spiritually prepared for suffering for Christ. So, get ready now!

The Antichrist could explain away the Rapture as a massive alien abduction. We have been programmed for decades to accept an intelligent alien race coming to our world to save us from ourselves. Finally, those conservative Christians are gone so the world can build their socialist utopian paradise, the New World Order. The push for a global government will be unstoppable. Nimrod tried to create his new world order, his one-world government, Babel. But God intervened by confounding their languages. God will again intervene in the last days destroying the new world order with the return of Jesus Christ. He will defeat the Antichrist and set up His new world order, the Millennial Kingdom.

THE TRIBULATION-MATTHEW 24

In a previous chapter, we defined the Tribulation as having a twofold purpose. One, to judge and redeem Israel. Two, to bring judgment upon the Antichrist, his kingdom, and followers. Another critical aspect of the Tribulation is that this period is discussed in several Old and New Testament passages. The one we will consider in this chapter is the Olivet Discourse, Matthew Chapters 24 and 25.

Jesus has arrived in Jerusalem for the final week of his life (Matthew 21:1-11). His crucifixion is only a few days away. As He and the disciples are gazing at the beautifully renovated Temple, Jesus utters these startling words:

"See ye not all these things? verily I say unto you, There shall not be left here one stone upon another, that shall not be thrown down." - Matthew 24:2 KJV.

I am sure this prophecy by Jesus caught the disciples by surprise. The Temple had stood for four centuries; how could it possibly be destroyed. As Jesus moved up to the Mount of Olives, the disciples came to him concerned about the future of the temple.

"And as he sat upon the mount of Olives, the disciples came unto him privately, saying, Tell us, when shall these things be? and what shall be the sign of thy coming, and of the end of the world?" - Matthew 24:3 KJV.

The disciples ask two questions. One, "when shall these things be", when will the Temple be destroyed? Two, "what shall be the sign of thy coming, and of the end of the world?". Thus begins the Olivet Discourse.

The Beginning of Sorrows

*"And Jesus answered and said unto them, **Take heed that no man deceive you.** For many shall come in my name, saying, I am Christ; and shall deceive many. And ye shall hear of **wars and rumours of wars:** see that ye be not troubled: for all these things must come to pass, but **the end is not yet.** For **nation shall rise against nation,** and kingdom against kingdom: and there shall be **famines,** and **pestilences,** and **earthquakes,** in divers places. All these are the beginning of sorrows."* - Matthew 24:4-8 KJV.

"Take heed that no man deceive you." That is the most prominent warning in the New Testament. Jesus, His disciples, and Paul gave this warning more than any other. Deception is the true cancer of the Church as there are many frauds, fakes, and charlatans. But Jesus is giving this warning to His disciples in a private briefing on the Mount of Olives. It is not directed at the Church specifically, as the Church had not yet begun. **This is a Jewish Messiah giving a briefing to His Jewish disciples concerning events for the Jews.** Jesus is warning the Jews not to be deceived as He will instruct them in the truth.

"For many shall come in my name, saying, I am Christ; and shall deceive many." There have been many Jews claiming to be the Messiah. Most we have never heard of except for Simon bar Kokhba, who led the second Jewish-Roman war in 135 A.D. He also claimed to be the Jewish Messiah and was followed by many Jews. The Jews are looking for someone to deliver them from their enemies. Anyone that can do that and bring peace, they will accept as Messiah. This prophecy will culminate in the Antichrist, who simultaneously poses as Christ and opposes God. As we have seen, the Antichrist deceives many people and the entire nation of Israel, at least for the first 3 ½ years of the 7-year Tribulation, as he brings peace and lets them rebuild the Temple.

"And ye shall hear of wars and rumors of wars: see that ye be not troubled: for all these things must come to pass," Over the centuries, we have seen wars and rumors of wars. Recently there was WW1, WW2, the Korean War, the Vietnam War, and several wars in Israel. In this century, there have been wars and rumors of wars too many to count—Wars in Iraq, Afghanistan, Libya, Somalia, Egypt, and Syria. Since the time of Jesus, there have been only about 200 years of real peace on earth. Every day since the Bush Administration, we have been at war somewhere in the Middle East. Jesus tells His disciples that wars will happen, but don't be troubled as war is not the last days' primary sign of the end.

"but the end is not yet" That does not refer to the end of the world or the end of time. "end" – *telos* – means the end of some act or state, the last in succession or series, that by which a thing is finished, its close, the end of a purpose or aim. The "end" refers to the end of Satan's dominion upon the earth and Gentile control over Jerusalem. With these passages, the 7-year Tribulation is just beginning, so the "end" is several long years away.

"For nation shall rise against nation, and kingdom against kingdom:" Nation refers to Gentile nations or nationalities waring with each other. We see this battle emerging between the nation-state and globalism. The global elite waring against the will of the people who desire freedom and independence. Brexit and the election of Donald Trump as President are good examples. The international elite love socialism and communism as those political structures put them in control of everyone's daily life, especially their money and resources. These elitists have front groups like the Council on Foreign Relations, The Trilateral Commission, The World Economic Forum, The World Health Organization, and The Federal Reserve, just to name a few.

There are many more around the world seeking to implement a one-world government.

"and there shall be famines, and pestilences, and earthquakes, in diverse places" Even with high food production, famines are prevalent in today's modern world. You would think by now we would have conquered this malady, but not so. War generally brings starvation, and famine brings pestilence and disease. Here are some WHO statistics:

Famines–deaths	Diseases (Pestilence)–deaths per year
1990's – Somalia	Malaria – 3 million
1950-60's – China – 30 million	Influenza – 20,000
1996 – North Korea – 3 million	Measles – 240,000
1947 – Soviet – 1.5 million	Meningitis – 10,000
1943 – Bengal – 3 million	Rotavirus – 600,000 (viral gastroenteritis)
1932 – Ukraine – 7 million	Schistosomiasis – 200M – 20 million (flukeworm)
1998-2000– Sudan/Ethiopia–100,000's	Shigellosis – 600,000 (bacillary dysentery)
1998-2004 – Congo famine – 3.8 million	Tuberculosis – 2 million
2011-2012–East Africa – 10's of thousands	Typhoid – 2 million
Global	HIV/AIDS – 1.7 million

"*All these are the beginning of sorrows.*" Jesus references the beginning years of the 7-year Tribulation and not history in general. The "beginning of sorrows" refers to a woman in or about to be in labor. The phrase "woman in travail" is also used frequently to describe this period. The fact that Jesus is referring to the 7-year Tribulation will become obvious as we continue to examine the text.

Gospel of the Kingdom

"*Then shall they deliver you up to be afflicted, and **shall kill you**: and ye shall be hated of all nations for my name's sake. And then shall many be offended, and shall betray one another, and shall hate one another. And many **false prophets shall rise**, and shall **deceive many**. And because iniquity shall abound, the love of many shall wax cold. **But he that shall endure unto the end, the same shall be saved. And this gospel of the kingdom shall be preached in all the world for a witness unto all nations; and then shall the end come**.*" - Matthew 24:9-14 KJV

"*Then shall they deliver you up to be afflicted, and shall kill you: and ye shall be hated of all nations for my name's sake.*" Those that choose to follow Jesus Christ during the 7-year Tribulation will have a tough go of it. The government and apostate church authorities aligned with the Antichrist will be seeking them out for death. Saints will be hated by all the nations that follow the Antichrist, and no one can be trusted. There will be no safe place to hide. Believers in Jesus Christ will be labeled as radicals or domestic terrorists unwilling to conform to the demands of the new world order. That has already begun in many countries, including America.

"*And then shall many be offended, and shall betray one another, and shall hate one another*" Many will be offended by the gospel of the kingdom because it will require a decision to follow Jesus and put your life at risk. Most people are cowards and compromisers, not willing to make that decision. Instead, they will align themselves with the authorities and betray the faithful saints of Jesus Christ. They will hate the true Saints of Christ as they are living evidence of their fate in the lake of fire. The true saints are humble and righteous. Those offended are proud haters of God and love their sin. Those that betray the saints will seek recognition and favor from the authorities, just as in the days of Hitler and Stalin. Citizens were ratting out other citizens to gain favor and approval from an evil regime.

"And many false prophets shall rise, and shall deceive many." Many fakes and frauds, "false prophets," will be aligned with the Antichrist regime touting how great he is and how his government will solve the world's problems. They will laud his peace-making successes in the Middle East and his humanitarian efforts worldwide to relieve the social ills of humanity. He will be promoted as the savior of the world. Indeed, he will be Time Magazine's Man of the year. But it will all be a deception, and sadly many will fall for it, especially those unfamiliar with Scripture. They will be "easy pickins" for this master of deceit who not only lies but has great signs and wonders to back up his lies.

"And because iniquity shall abound, the love of many shall wax cold." Sin will abound as never before. Those that want to do good will be severely oppressed. Their love for doing right will "wax cold" as everything in the world is working against them. They will be like Lot in Sodom. He wanted to do right but was vexed by the sin and perversion of the people surrounding him.

I want to pause here and do a quick comparison of these Scriptures and Revelation Chapter 6, the opening characteristics of the 7-year

Tribulation. Both the Olivet Discourse of Matthew Chapter 24 and Revelation Chapter 6-19 concern the same 7-year Tribulation period.

Matthew 24	Revelation 6
v. 5 False Christ's (spirit of antichrist)	1st Seal – White horse, antichrist revealed
v. 6 Wars and rumors of wars	2nd Seal – Red horse – power to make war
v. 7 Famine	3rd Seal – Black horse - famine
v. 7 Pestilences, earthquakes	4th Seal – Pale horse - death
v. 9 Saints killed for Jesus' name's sake	5th Seal – Martyred souls under the alter
v. 14 Gospel of the Kingdom preached	Chapter 14:6-7, Chapter 7
v. 15 Abomination of desolation	Chapter 13
v. 29-31 King Jesus returns	Chapter 19

"But he that shall endure unto the end, the same shall be saved." This verse reflects the fact that the Church Age is over. We in the Church do not have to continue to the end of anything to know we are saved. Paul tells us, *"For the wages of sin is death; but the gift of God is eternal life through Jesus Christ our Lord." - Romans 6:23 KJV.* We know we have eternal life when we receive Jesus Christ as Savior and are filled and sealed by the Holy Spirit. However, during the 7-year Tribulation, that will not be the case. If a believer recants his testimony for Jesus and takes the mark of the beast, he is doomed to the lake of fire. A believers' testimony must be lived out each day until death or the end of the Tribulation. Only then will they be saved.

"To him that **overcometh** will I grant to sit with me in my throne, even as I also overcame, and am set down with my Father in his throne." - Revelation 3:21 KJV. "And they **overcame him (Antichrist)** by the blood of the Lamb, and by the word of their testimony; and **they loved not their lives unto the death.**" - Revelation 12:11 KJV parenthesis mine.

The Tribulation Saints must endure until the end to be saved, the end of their life or the end of the 7-year Tribulation, whichever comes first.

"And this gospel of the kingdom shall be preached in all the world for a witness unto all nations; and then shall the end come." The gospel of the kingdom is unique and time sensitive as we only hear about the gospel of the kingdom in Matthew's gospel. John the Baptist introduces the gospel of the kingdom in Chapter 3.

"In those days came John the Baptist, preaching in the wilderness of Judaea, And saying, Repent ye: for the kingdom of heaven is at hand." - Mat 3:1-2 KJV.

When Jesus began His ministry in Galilee, He also preached the gospel of the kingdom.

"From that time Jesus began to preach, and to say, Repent: for the kingdom of heaven is at hand." - Matthew 4:17 KJV.

The gospel of the kingdom is a simple gospel calling men to repentance as the King and His Kingdom are "at hand." Jesus, the King, was present among them. Again, we read:

"And Jesus went about all Galilee, teaching in their synagogues, and preaching the **gospel of the kingdom**, and healing all manner of sickness and all manner of disease among the people." - Matthew 4:23 KJV. In Matthew Chapter 9 we read a similar verse. "And Jesus went about all the cities and villages, teaching in their synagogues, and preaching the **gospel of the kingdom**, and healing every sickness and every disease among the people." - Matthew 9:35 KJV.

Jesus then sends out the twelve disciples to preach the gospel of the kingdom.

"These twelve Jesus sent forth, and commanded them, saying, Go not into the way of the Gentiles, and into any city of the Samaritans enter ye not: But go rather to the lost sheep of the house of Israel. And as ye go, preach, saying, **The kingdom of heaven is at hand**." - Matthew 10:5-7 KJV.

But something interesting happens in Matthew Chapter 12. The rulers of Israel reject Jesus, and His miracles attributed to Beelzebub, lord of the devils, Satan.

"But when the Pharisees heard it, they said, This fellow doth not cast out devils, but by Beelzebub the prince of the devils." - Matthew 12:24 KJV.

No longer does Jesus or the disciples preach the gospel of the kingdom. Since the King has been rejected and cursed, the offer of the visible, earthly kingdom is soon to be withdrawn and postponed. Even Jesus' teaching style has changed to speaking in parables so that the spiritual truths would be hidden. That is quite bizarre but clearly stated in the following passage.

"And the disciples came, and said unto him, **Why speakest thou unto them in parables**? He answered and said unto them, **Because it is given unto you to know the mysteries of the kingdom of heaven**, but to them it is not given. For whosoever hath, to him shall be given, and he shall *have more abundance: but whosoever hath not, from him shall be taken away even that he hath. Therefore speak I to them in parables: because they **seeing see not**, and **hearing they hear not**, neither do they understand. And in them is fulfilled the prophecy of Esaias, which saith, By hearing ye shall hear, and shall not understand; and seeing ye shall see, and shall not perceive: For this people's heart is waxed gross, and their ears are dull of hearing, and their eyes they have closed; lest at any time they should see with their eyes, and hear with their ears, and should understand with their heart, and should be converted, and I should heal them. **But blessed are your eyes, for they see: and your ears, for they hear.** For verily I say unto you, That many prophets and righteous men have desired to see those things which ye see, and have not seen them; and to hear those things which ye hear, and have not heard them." - Matthew 13:10-17 KJV*

So, the preaching of the "gospel of the kingdom" diminished in Matthew chapter 12, but Jesus clearly states that it will again be preached during the 7-year Tribulation. It will be preached as a "witness" that the kingdom is once again "at hand," coming soon. Then it will matter not who likes it or who does not. Jesus is returning at the end of the 7-year Tribulation, and He is not seeking anyone's approval or permission. The phrase "and then the end shall come" refers to Satan's rule on earth, the end of the evil, corrupt worldly systems. The end of Antichrist's new world order, the end of God's wrath being poured out upon the earth.

Abomination of Desolation

*"When ye therefore shall see the **abomination of desolation**, spoken of by Daniel the prophet, **stand in the holy place,** (whoso readeth, let him understand:) Then let them which be in Judaea flee into the mountains: Let him which is on the housetop not come down to take any thing out of his*

house: Neither let him which is in the field return back to take his clothes."
- Matthew 24:15-18 KJV

"When ye therefore shall see the abomination of desolation, spoken of by Daniel the prophet, stand in the holy place, (whoso readeth, let him understand:)" That event, the Abomination of desolation, is a milestone in the 7-year Tribulation as it occurs at the 3 ½ year midpoint. Jesus references the prophet Daniel and adds the condition "whoso readeth, let him understand," meaning that if you are not familiar with the abomination of desolation, go study the Book of Daniel. We have already looked at verses making a direct reference to the abomination of desolation. Remember, the abomination of desolation is distinctly Jewish as it takes place in their Temple; that has nothing to do with the Church, the body of Christ.

*"And he shall confirm the covenant with many for one week: and in the midst of the week he shall cause the sacrifice and the oblation to cease, and for the overspreading of **abominations** he shall make it **desolate**, even until the consummation, and that determined shall be poured upon the desolate." - Daniel 9:27 KJV*

*"And from the time that the daily sacrifice shall be taken away, and the **abomination that maketh desolate** set up, there shall be a thousand two hundred and ninety days." - Daniel 12:11 KJV.*

3 ½ years equals 1260 days. The 1290 days have 30 extra days, most likely for the judgment of the nations at Christ's return.

The Abomination of Desolation occurs when the Antichrist enters the Temple in Jerusalem proclaiming to be God. He erects an image of himself and, with the help of the false prophet, demands all people worship his image or suffer death.

*"Then let them which be in **Judaea flee into the mountains**: Let him which is on the housetop not come down to take anything out of his house: Neither let him which is in the field return back to take his clothes."* When the Jews in Jerusalem see the Antichrist's abomination of desolation, they must run and run quickly. Don't take time to grab your to-go bag or clothes. Just get out of Judaea as soon as possible. Here again, we are specifically referencing the region of Judaea in Israel. That is not a warning to the folks in Paris, London, or New York. Once more, a distinctly Jewish command. Are you starting to get the idea that the Olivet discourse pertains to the Jews and not the Church? I hope so.

*"And woe unto them that are with child, and to them that give suck in those days! But pray ye that your flight be not in the winter, neither on the **sabbath day**. For then shall be **great tribulation, such as was not since the beginning of the world to this time, no, nor ever shall be**. And except those days should be shortened, there should **no flesh be saved**: but for the elect's sake those days shall be shortened."* - Matthew 24:19-22 KJV

More warnings to those that witness the Abomination of Desolation. Interesting that Jesus commands them to *"pray ye that your flight be not in winter."* It does snow in Jerusalem, which would make a speedy exit from the region difficult. He also instructs them to pray that their escape is not "on the Sabbath day." That is yet another distinctly Jewish characteristic of the 7-year Tribulation. Travel distance is restricted on the Sabbath day, making a complete escape from Jerusalem to the mountains impossible. The Sabbath is Saturday and has no relevance to the Church.

*"Let no man therefore judge you in meat, or in drink, or in respect of a holyday, or of the new moon, or of the **Sabbath**:"* - Colossians 2:16 KJV.
The Sabbath is for the Jew, not the Gentile Church.

*"For then shall be **great tribulation**, such as was not since the beginning of the world to this time, no, nor ever shall be."* At this point in the 7-year Tribulation, we are at the midpoint. Jesus declares the last 3 ½ years to be the "great tribulation'. Here again He refers to the "worst" period in all human history. There has never been, nor will ever be, a 3 ½ year period like it. It's also named the time of Jacob's trouble.

*"Ask ye now, and see whether a man doth travail with child? wherefore do I see every man with his hands on his loins, as a **woman in travail**, and all faces are turned into paleness? **Alas! for that day is great, so that none is like it: it is even the time of Jacob's trouble;** but he shall be saved out of it." - Jeremiah 30:6-7 KJV.*

Remember, that period is the time of Jacob's (Israel's) trouble, not the Church.

Frequently in Scripture, the 7-year Tribulation is characterized by a woman in travail or labor about to give birth. That is an interesting analogy as labor pains grow in intensity and frequency as the time of delivery nears. That is precisely how the 7-year Tribulation unfolds. It begins with peace and security for the Jews, but things start getting bad quickly as the Antichrist invades Israel at the midpoint. During the 7-year Tribulation, the seal, trumpet, and bowl judgments of the Book of Revelation unfold with increasing intensity and frequency.

"And except those days should be shortened, there should no flesh be saved: but for the elect's sake those days shall be shortened." This is a dire, ominous warning to those who must endure the 7-year Tribulation. Jesus states that if this period of Tribulation were extended beyond the seven years, "there should no flesh be saved." In other words, those in the last half of the Tribulation will experience **extinction-**

level events. Before modern times man was unable to cause his extinction. But today, with our vast arsenals of nuclear weapons, extinction is a distinct possibility. That is a warning from the Lord Jesus Christ of the massive, global death and destruction coming in the 7-year Tribulation, specifically during the second half.

Christ and Eagles

*"Then if any man shall say unto you, Lo, here is Christ, or there; believe it not. For **there shall arise false Christs, and false prophets, and shall shew great signs and wonders; insomuch that, if it were possible, they shall deceive the very elect**. Behold, I have told you before. Wherefore if they shall say unto you, Behold, he is in the **desert**, go not forth: behold, he is in the **secret chambers**, believe it not. For as the lightning cometh out of the east, and shineth even unto the west; so shall also the coming of the Son of man be. For wheresoever the carcase is, there will the eagles be gathered together." - Matthew 24:23-28 KJV*

"Then if any man shall say unto you, Lo, here is Christ, or there; believe it not. For there shall arise false Christs, and false prophets, and shall shew great signs and wonders; insomuch that, if it were possible, they shall deceive the very elect. Behold, I have told you before." As with any narrative, there is a pause in the chronological progression of the timeline to backfill some details. That is the purpose of verses 23-28. They backfill details about the false Christs from verses 5 and 11. Jesus is warning that people will proclaim that Christ is here or there but don't believe them. Some of these false Christs and false prophets will work "great signs and wonders." We are not talking about Las Vegas magic tricks or Hollywood special effects but real powerful signs and wonders. However, we read elsewhere they are "lying" signs and wonders. They are "lying" because their purpose is deception, not to bring praise and glory to God. Many will be

deceived. The deception will be so powerful that even the elect might be deceived if that were possible. Only those who follow Jesus and know the Prophetic Scriptures will have the necessary discernment to understand what is happening. Jesus is giving this warning beforehand, so believers can prepare for the coming deception, which I believe is already here.

"Wherefore if they shall say unto you, Behold, he is in the desert; go not forth: behold, he is in the secret chambers; believe it not." That is strange. Why would Christ be in the "desert"? If the false Christ was a Muslim proclaiming to be the Mahdi, he could easily be in the desert, at Mecca. Could it be that Jesus was aware of the Muslim hoards that would take over the Middle East? I think so. More on the Mahdi later. Some will also declare that Christ is in some secret chamber. Could this be the secret chambers of the Vatican or the Freemasons? Whatever it might be, don't believe it. Anyone coming from those venues is a fake.

"For as the lightning cometh out of the east, and shineth even unto the west; so shall also the coming of the Son of man be." Jesus is not going to show up on earth secretly exiting a secret chamber or palace. He is not going to appear walking out of the desert. He won't be doing cheesy signs and wonders good enough to fool the ignorant masses but not the true elect. His is coming as the Son of David, King of Kings, and Lord of Lords. His coming will be magnificent, spectacularly brilliant, and sudden as a bolt of lightning that blasts intense light and deafening thunder from horizon to horizon. He is coming in the clouds, and every eye will see Him. There will be no mistaking the second coming of Jesus Christ. This event will affect every living person on planet earth.

"For wheresoever the carcase is, there will the eagles be gathered together." That is another seemingly strange verse of scripture. Strange possibly to us, but not to the Holy Spirit. What could a carcass, a dead body, and eagles have to do with the second coming of Jesus Christ? When Jesus returns, He is not coming as a humble, compassionate, meek, and mild servant of God as He once did. He is returning in anger, vengeance, and wrath to make war. He is the Lord of Hosts, military hosts prepared for battle. The Middle East will be littered with carcasses when Jesus returns, and the fowls of the air will gather for the great supper of the day of the Lord.

Jesus will make war with the Antichrist, his armies, and followers when He returns. That is the Battle of Armageddon. It is a short campaign as these enemies of God are easily defeated. As a result of their defeat, massive numbers of dead bodies, carcasses will literate Israel's land. The "eagles gathered together" refers to the below verse that describes the Lord's victory at Armageddon.

*"And I saw an angel standing in the sun; and he cried with a loud voice, saying to all the **fowls that fly in the midst of heaven**, Come and gather yourselves together unto the **supper of the great God**; That ye may eat the flesh of kings, and the flesh of captains, and the flesh of mighty men, and the flesh of horses, and of them that sit on them, and the flesh of all men, both free and bond, both small and great." - Revelation 19:17-18 KJV*

*"And I saw heaven opened and behold a white horse; and he that sat upon him was called Faithful and True, and **in righteousness he doth judge and make war**." - Revelation 19:11 KJV*

Jesus is returning as the Son of David to sit on David's throne as prophesied. David was a mighty warrior that defeated Israel's enemies and brought the golden era to Israel. Jesus will do the same for a thousand years.

"Who is this that cometh from Edom, with dyed garments from Bozrah? this that is glorious in his apparel, travelling in the greatness of his strength? I that speak in righteousness, mighty to save. Wherefore art thou **red in thine apparel**, and thy garments like him that treadeth in the winefat? I have trodden the winepress alone; and of the people there was none with me: for **I will tread them in mine anger** and **trample them in my fury**, and their blood shall be sprinkled upon my garments, and I will stain all my raiment. For **the day of vengeance is in mine heart**, and the year of my redeemed is come." - Isaiah 63:1-4 KJV

Jesus' robes are stained with the blood of His enemies. The Battle of Armageddon is on.

"For they are the spirits of devils, working miracles, which go forth unto the kings of the earth and of the whole world, to gather them to the **battle of that great day of God Almighty**. Behold, I come as a thief. Blessed is he that watcheth, and keepeth his garments, lest he walk naked, and they see his shame. And he gathered them together into a place called in the Hebrew tongue **Armageddon**." - Revelation 16:14-16 KJV

Sign in Heaven
"**Immediately after the tribulation of those days** shall the sun be darkened, and the moon shall not give her light, and the stars shall fall from heaven, and the powers of the heavens shall be shaken: And **then shall appear the sign of the Son of man in heaven**: and then shall all the tribes of the earth mourn, and **they shall see the Son of man coming in the clouds of heaven with power and great glory**. And he shall send his angels with a great sound of a trumpet, and they shall gather together his

elect from the four winds, from one end of heaven to the other." - Matthew 24:29-31 KJV

"*Immediately after the tribulation of those days.*" – That is the last half of the 7-year Tribulation. Jesus defined this last half of the 7-years as the "great tribulation" in verse 21. So, the "tribulation of those days" closes the 7-year Tribulation. Immediately the sun is darkened, and the moon does not give its light. We see similar language in Isaiah:

"*Behold, the day of the LORD cometh, cruel both with wrath and fierce anger, to lay the land desolate: and he shall destroy the sinners thereof out of it.* **For the stars of heaven and the constellations thereof shall not give their light: the sun shall be darkened in his going forth, and the moon shall not cause her light to shine.** *And I will punish the world for their evil, and the wicked for their iniquity; and I will cause the arrogancy of the proud to cease, and will lay low the haughtiness of the terrible.*" - Isaiah 13:9-11 KJV.

Also, in the book of Joel:
"**The sun and the moon shall be darkened, and the stars shall withdraw their shining.** *The LORD also shall roar out of Zion, and utter his voice from Jerusalem; and the* **heavens and the earth shall shake:** *but the LORD will be the hope of his people, and the strength of the children of Israel.*" - Joel 3:15-16 KJV.

Matthew, Isaiah, and Joel describe the Day of the Lord, specifically the culmination of that day when the Lord Jesus Christ returns in power and great glory.

"sign of the Son of man in heaven" – This is the second coming of Jesus Christ. The Jewish remnant will "mourn" for Jesus because they are heartbroken that their ancestors crucified their Messiah.

Zechariah prophesied:

"And I will pour upon the house of David, and upon the inhabitants of Jerusalem, the spirit of grace and of supplications: and **they shall look upon me whom they have pierced, and they shall mourn for him***, as one mourneth for his only son, and shall be in bitterness for him, as one that is in bitterness for his firstborn." - Zechariah 12:10 KJV.*

Jesus is returning in the "clouds of heaven". The two angels at the ascension of Jesus after His resurrection told us so:

"And when he had spoken these things, while they beheld, **he was taken up; and a cloud received him out of their sight***. And while they looked stedfastly toward heaven as he went up, behold, two men stood by them in white apparel; Which also said, Ye men of Galilee, why stand ye gazing up into heaven? this same Jesus, which is taken up from you into heaven,* **shall so come in like manner as ye have seen him go into heaven***." - Acts 1:9-11 KJV.*

 Jesus left this earth in a cloud, so He will return in the clouds with power and great glory.

"And he shall send his angels with a great sound of a trumpet, and they shall gather together his elect from the four winds, from one end of heaven to the other." The angels will go from one end of the earth to the other, gathering His "elect." But who are they? They are Jews that survived the 7-year Tribulation. Many will still be scattered throughout the nations. Not all will be in Israel. The "elect" are the Jews that will enter the Millennial Kingdom.

*"Now learn a parable of the fig tree; When his branch is yet tender, and putteth forth leaves, ye know that summer is nigh: So likewise ye, when ye shall see all these things, know that it is near, even at the doors. Verily I say unto you, **This generation shall not pass**, till all these things be fulfilled. Heaven and earth shall pass away, but my words shall not pass away."* - Mat 24:32-35 KJV

Historically the fig tree is a type of Israel. Jesus is giving a parable: a short story designed to reveal spiritual truth. He states that when the branch gets tender and puts on leaves, summer is near. We see this type of spring growth arising from winter dormancy every year. Then Jesus likens that natural annual pattern of spring growth to the events preceding His return. Just as we see, summer is near when the fig tree grows new leaves. We can know that His second coming is near when we see the events in Matthew 24 begin to unfold and converge.

Jesus then tells us that "This generation shall not pass, till all these things be fulfilled." What does "this generation" mean? Well, it initially indicated the generation of the disciples. He could be referring to the Jewish nation, but that would be obvious because end-time prophecies could not be fulfilled if they passed. I believe Jesus is talking about those living in the last days, specifically when the nation of Israel is reborn. On November 29, 1947, the United Nations passed a resolution that called for establishing a Jewish State. On May 14th, 1948, Israel declared their Independence. That generation would not pass until all things Jesus spoke about in the Olivet Discourse were fulfilled. The 70th anniversary was in 2017-2018. Yet here we are in 2023. Jesus also said that by strength, the generation might be 80 years. That moves us forward to 2028. But that timeframe would include the 7-year Tribulation bringing us back to 2021. Interesting. The Bible repeatedly tells us that God's

Word will be fulfilled, it will "not pass away." Time is short. We are living at the end of the Church Age. We are living on borrowed time.

The Days of Noah

*"But of that day and hour knoweth no man, no, not the angels of heaven, but my Father only. **But as the days of Noe were, so shall also the coming of the Son of man be**. For as in the days that were before the flood they were **eating and drinking, marrying and giving in marriage**, until the day that Noe entered into the ark, And knew not until the flood came, and took them all away; so shall also the coming of the Son of man be. Then shall **two be in the field; the one shall be taken, and the other left**. Two women shall be grinding at the mill; the **one shall be taken, and the other left**. Watch therefore: for ye know not what hour your Lord doth come." - Matthew 24:36-42 KJV*

"But of that day and hour knoweth no man" is a passage frequently taken out of context. Many think this is a reference to the Rapture, but it is NOT! To what day is the passage referring? We need to look at the previous verses to know the context is the day the Lord returns, the second coming of Jesus Christ. No man at the time of Jesus' ministry on earth knew the day and hour of His return. No one before the beginning of the 7-year Tribulation knows the day and hour of His return either. The followers of Jesus Christ during the 7-year Tribulation should be able to calculate the day of Jesus' return as the Antichrist's rule is only 42 months. But certainly, no one before that time can know the day and hour.

"But as the days of Noe were, so shall also the coming of the Son of man be" – Jesus is making an analogy to the time of Noah's flood. There is some aspect of Noah's flood that will be repeated before the second coming of Jesus Christ. Many things can be said about the "days of

Noah" before the flood. There were Giants on the earth that had voracious appetites eating animals, man, and even each other.

"*For as in the days that were before the flood they were eating and drinking, marrying and giving in marriage, until the day that Noe entered into the ark,*" – Jesus is clearly stating that the days just before His second coming at the end of the 7-year Tribulation will be like the days before Noah's flood. Let's go back to Genesis to read about those days.

"*There were **giants in the earth** in those days; and also **after that,** when the sons of God came in unto the daughters of men, and they bare children to them, the same became mighty men which were of old, men of renown. And GOD saw that the **wickedness** of man was great in the earth, and that every imagination of the thoughts of his heart was **only evil continually.** ... The earth also was **corrupt** before God, and the earth was filled with **violence.** And God looked upon the earth, and, behold, it was **corrupt,** for all flesh had **corrupted** his way upon the earth. - Genesis 6:4-5, 11-12 KJV*

Before the flood, the earth was populated with giants. The book of Enoch tells us these giants were huge with voracious appetites. Their appetites were destroying life on earth as they ate everything, including humans. The fallen angels (Sons of God) cohabitated with human women (daughters of men), giving birth to a race of giants. This unnatural union was corrupting the human genome. That was Satan's plan to corrupt the human genome so the perfect human, the Son of God, Jesus Christ, could not be born.

But Noah found favor in God's eyes as he was "perfect in all his generations." Noah had no fallen angel DNA. His genome was perfectly human, not having been corrupted. He was an excellent candidate to perpetuate the human race after God destroys the corrupted hybrid-human giants with the flood.

Getting back to the New Testament, Jesus said the days before His second coming would be like the days of Noah. The earth would be filled with violence and wickedness. The fallen angel/demon entities would try once again to destroy humankind. That adds a new perspective to the following verse.

*"But as the days of Noe were, so shall also the coming of the Son of man be. For as in the days that were **before the flood** they were **eating and drinking, marrying and giving in marriage**, until the day that Noe entered into the ark," - Matthew 24:37-38 KJV*

A cursory reading would seem to indicate life as usual. Eating, drinking, and marrying are what people do all the time. But when you interpret this passage considering the giants and corruption of Noah's day, its meaning is quite different. The giants were eating human beings and even each other due to their destructive, voracious appetites. The giants were drinking the blood of animals and humans. The Giants were marrying human women who gave birth to more giants with a corrupted genome. That is not life as usual. That was a global disaster.

Now the Tribulation is only seven years long, so there is not enough time for giants to grow from babies. Many who research this phenomenon believe the giants are already living in underground facilities in remote areas waiting for their day to arrive. That day will arrive when the Restrainer is removed and the forces of hell, the powers of darkness, are again unleashed on planet earth. Something evil comes our way.

"And knew not until the flood came, and took them all away; so shall also the coming of the Son of man be." Here we see that the pre-flood humans and hybrids did not believe or understand what was happening "until the flood came." By then, it was too late, and the flood waters "took them all away." So, who exactly was "taken away" in the flood? The ungodly! Jesus said that's how it will be at the "coming of the Son of man." Upon Jesus' return at the end of the 7-year Tribulation, all the ungodly, be they man or some trans-human hybrid, are destroyed, taken from the face of the earth.

"Then shall two be in the field; the one shall be taken, and the other left. Two women shall be grinding at the mill; the one shall be taken, and the other left. Watch therefore: for ye know not what hour your Lord doth come." Jesus links this passage with the previous verse using the word "then." Just as the ungodly were "taken" in the flood. At His coming, the ungodly will be taken from the earth. Two working in the field, two grinding at the mill, one taken from the earth in judgment, and one left to enter the kingdom. Remember, the context is "the coming of the Son of man," not the Rapture.

This passage is not about one taken in the Rapture and the other left behind. The disqualifier for a Rapture interpretation is there is no mention or hint of a resurrection in the passage. The first phase of the Rapture is the resurrection of the dead saints. Without a resurrection, there can be no Rapture. The Rapture passages in 1st Thessalonians chapter 4 and 1st Corinthians chapter 15 both begin with a resurrection of the dead in Christ. No resurrection, No Rapture!

The one taken and the other left are also portrayed in the parable of the wheat and tares.

*"Another parable put he forth unto them, saying, The kingdom of heaven is likened unto a man which **sowed good seed** in his field: But while **men slept**, his **enemy** came and **sowed tares** among the wheat, and went his way. But when the blade was sprung up, and brought forth fruit, then appeared the tares also. So the servants of the householder came and said unto him, Sir, didst not thou sow good seed in thy field? from whence then hath it tares? He said unto them, An **enemy** hath done this. The servants said unto them, Wilt thou then that we go and gather them up? But he said, Nay; lest while ye gather up the tares, ye root up also the wheat with them. **Let both grow together until the harvest**: and in the time of harvest I will say to the **reapers, Gather ye together first the tares, and bind them in bundles to burn them: but gather the wheat into my barn**."* - Matthew 13:24-30 KJV.*

Jesus himself gives the interpretation of this parable, so there is no confusion about what it means.

"He answered and said unto them, He that soweth the good seed is the Son of man; The field is the world; the good seed are the children of the kingdom; but the tares are the children of the wicked one; The enemy that sowed them is the devil; the harvest is the end of the world; and the reapers are the angels. As therefore the tares are gathered and burned in the fire; so shall it be in the end of this world. The Son of man shall send forth his angels, and they shall gather out of his kingdom all things that offend, and them which do iniquity; And shall cast them into a furnace of fire: there shall be wailing and gnashing of teeth. Then shall the righteous shine forth as the sun in the kingdom of their Father. Who hath ears to hear, let him hear." - Matthew 13:37-43 KJV*

Let's itemize each of the points for clarity and see how this relates to what we have studied so far here in Matthew chapter 24.

The sower of the good seed is Jesus Christ
The good seed are those that believe in him
The field where the good seed is sown is the world
The tares are the children of the devil
The devil is the sower of the bad seed, the tares
The harvest is at the end of the world (age)
The reapers are angels
The tares are gathered and tossed into the fire (hell)
Again, this happens at the end of the world (age)
Everything that offends Jesus will be gathered and removed from His kingdom and cast into the fire (hell)
In hell, there will be weeping and gnashing of teeth
The righteous (good seed) will shine forth in God's kingdom, the Millennial Kingdom of Jesus Christ.

An interesting point here is that the angels are the reapers that gather the tares, the ungodly, at the harvest. Compare that to the below passages, one from the book of Joel and the other Revelation.

"*Let the heathen be wakened, and come up to the valley of Jehoshaphat: for there will I sit to judge all the heathen round about. **Put ye in the sickle, for the harvest is ripe**: come, get you down; for the press is full, the fats overflow; for their wickedness is great.*" - Joel 3:12-13 KJV

The harvest of the wicked account in Revelation.

"*And I looked, and behold a white cloud, and upon the cloud one sat like unto the Son of man, having on his head a golden crown, and in his hand a **sharp sickle**. And **another angel** came out of the temple, crying with a* loud voice to him that sat on the cloud, ***Thrust in thy sickle, and reap***: for the time is come for thee to ***reap***, for the ***harvest of the earth is ripe***. And he that sat on the cloud thrust in his ***sickle*** on the earth; and the ***earth was reaped***. And ***another angel*** came out of the temple which is in heaven, he also having a ***sharp sickle***. And ***another angel*** came out from the altar, which had power over fire; and cried with a loud cry to him that had the ***sharp sickle***, saying, ***Thrust in thy sharp sickle,*** and gather the clusters of the vine of the earth; for her grapes are ***fully ripe***. And the ***angel thrust in his sickle into the earth***, and ***gathered the vine*** of the earth, and cast it into the ***great winepress of the wrath of God.***" - Rev 14:14-19 KJV.

Four angels with sickles, a great harvest at the end of the age, the wrath of God poured out on the ungodly tares; it all works together. Remember, this is not about wheat, tares, and grapes. It is about the unrighteous people being subject to the wrath of God and punished in the fires of hell. The righteous saints (wheat) will enter the Kingdom.

Noah's Flood	Matthew 24	Parable	Revelation 14
Ungodly taken	One taken– ungodly	Tares gathered to the fire	Angel reapers, Ungodly taken from earth to the fire
Righteous saved	One left– righteous	Wheat enter the kingdom	Righteous shine forth in the kingdom on earth

Are you Ready?

"But know this, that if the goodman of the house had known in what watch the thief would come, he would have watched, and would not have suffered his house to be broken up. ***Therefore be ye also ready****: for in such an hour as ye think not the Son of man cometh." - Mat 24:43-44 KJV*

The message of the rest of Matthew Chapter 24 is to be ready. That encouragement is for those enduring the 7-year Tribulation but applies equally to us today. We should always be ready, for the Lord could come for His Church at any time. There are no events that must precede the Rapture. Are you Ready?

Summary

We see in the Olivet Discourse that Jesus gave His Jewish disciples a private briefing about the 7-year Tribulation. Jesus clearly states this period of destruction will be the worst period in earth's history. That aligns perfectly with the 70th week of Daniel's prophecy and the "time of Jacob's trouble." Jesus gives increasing illumination on the events of the Tribulation, supplying us with increasingly detailed descriptions of what the Jews and humankind, in general, are to expect during this "destruction from the Almighty."

Briefing

Points of interest:

a) war, famine, disease, mass casualties, Temple in Jerusalem rebuilt.

b) Global disasters: cosmic disturbances in the sun, moon, and stars: Bizarre creatures on earth, possible return of the giants of old.

c) MATTHEW CHAPTER 24, THE OLIVET DISCOURSE, DESCRIBES EVENTS THAT TRANSPIRE DURING THE 7-YEAR TRIBULATION

d) At the mid-point of the 7-year Tribulation, the antichrist sets up an image in the Temple in Jerusalem, forcing everyone to worship the image or suffer death.

Person of interest:

a) world leader, aka Antichrist, enters the Temple proclaiming himself god.

b) Jesus Christ returns at the end of the 7-year tribulation defeating God's enemies and the enemies of Israel.

Discussion:

Matthew Chapter 24, the Olivet Discourse, is a briefing given to Jesus' disciples about what will happen to the Jews in the latter days. Many prophecy buffs get in trouble when they try to put the Church into the text. The Church is not involved in the events of the Olivet Discourse. It is strictly for the Jews, so none of the sufferings of the Jews apply to the Church. Does the Church suffer? Sure, but not the wrath of God. That is reserved for the ungodly. During this 7-year Tribulation, there will be massive earthquakes and strange phenomena in the heavens. These events will get increasingly severe as time progresses. There will be some strange creatures on the earth also. Some might resemble humans, but they are hybrids. There will be others that are non-human.

The Antichrist perpetrates the abomination of desolation at the mid-point of the Tribulation. He desecrates the Jewish Temple by setting up an image of his kingdom in the Temple. Everyone is forced to worship the image or suffer death. Many will now realize the true nature of the Antichrist and refuse to worship him. Those refusing to worship him will be beheaded.

PSALM 83 WAR

Nearby Neighbors

There are two great wars depicted in Scripture as happening in the Last Days. Both are Middle Eastern wars centered around Israel and Jerusalem. These two are major wars, but there are other minor wars and skirmishes as we have seen over the past 60 years, including the continuing conflict with Hamas in Gaza and Palestinians in the West Bank and the Islamic State. Jesus said there would be "wars and rumors of wars" up to the time of His second coming, and that event will be at the battle of Armageddon.

The first war with Israel's neighboring nations is commonly referred to as the Psalm 83 war or the Zechariah 12 war. In Psalm 83, we read:

*"Keep not thou **silence**, O God: hold not thy **peace**, and be not **still**, O God. For, lo, thine enemies make a **tumult** and they that hate thee have **lifted up the head**. They have taken **crafty counsel** against thy people, and consulted against thy hidden ones." Psalm 83:1-3 KJV*

The psalmist is pleading with the Lord not to be still, to not be at peace but to rise and fight against the enemies of Israel. Israel's enemies are in a tumult, an uproar, against Israel. They are clamoring for and obsessed with the destruction of Israel, as we see daily in the news. They have "lifted the head" in prideful arrogance boasting about their false god Allah and blaspheming the God of the Bible. They take counsel among themselves and the UN, making plans to destroy Israel and the Jew.

*"They have said, Come, and let us **cut them off** from being a nation; that the name of Israel may be **no more in remembrance**. For they have consulted together with one consent: they are **confederate against thee**: The tabernacles of **Edom**, and the **Ishmaelite**; of **Moab**, and the **Hagarenes**; **Gebal**, and **Ammon**, and **Amalek**; the **Philistines** with the inhabitants of **Tyre**;" Psalm 83:4-7 KJV*

These nations want not only to destroy Israel but to wipe out any evidence that Israel ever existed. The confederation of countries against Israel begins with Edom and the Ishmaelites, southern Jordan, and western Saudi Arabia. Moab and Ammon are Jordan. The Hagarines is Egypt. Gebal in northern Lebanon. Amalek, the Philistines, and Tyre are the coastal regions from the Sinai to southern Lebanon.

"Assur also is joined with them: they have holpen the children of Lot. Selah. Do unto them as unto the Midianites; as to Sisera, as to Jabin, at the brook of Kison: Which perished at Endor: they became as dung for the earth. Make their nobles like Oreb, and like Zeeb: yea, all their princes as Zebah, and as Zalmunna:" Psalm 83:8-11 KJV

Assur is a reference to Assyria, which would include western Iraq and Syria. The children of Lot are Moab and Ammon (Gen 19:36-38). Assyria was their right arm of military strength (holpen).

Where are all these nations on a map of the Middle East? They are Israel's immediate neighbors, as seen on the following map.

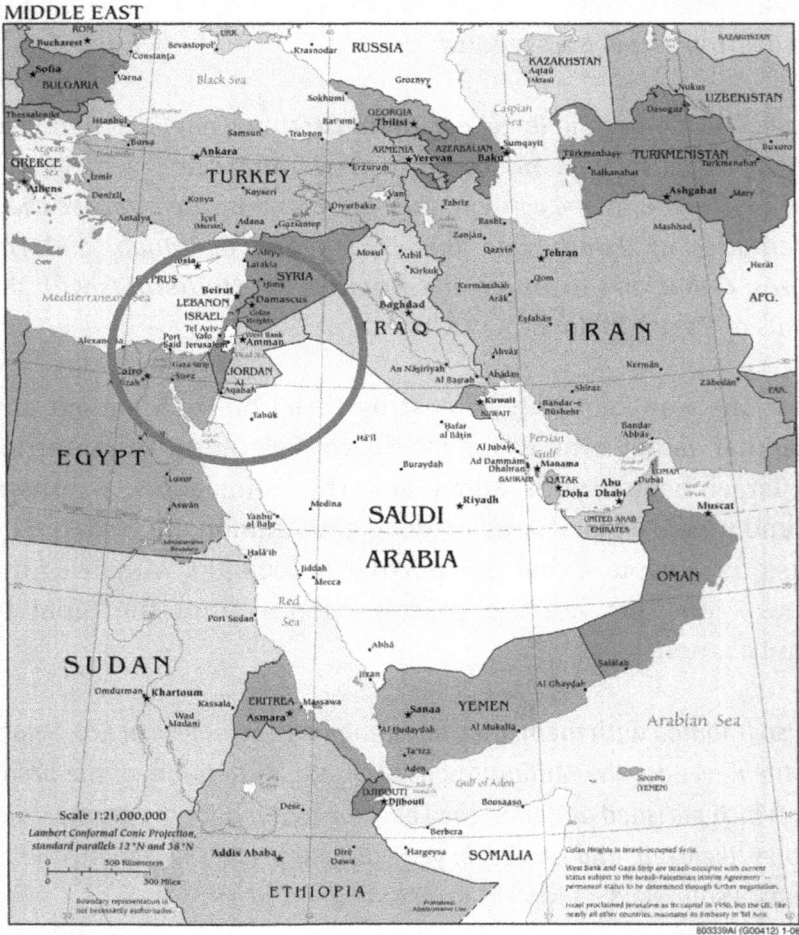

Psalm 83 war involves Jordan, Saudi Arabia, Egypt, Lebanon, Syria, and Iraq. These areas include regions controlled by the Palestinian

Authority, Hamas, Hezbollah, Kurds, Iran, Russia, Turkey, ISIS, and al Qaeda.

The psalmist asks the Lord to do unto those nations as He did unto the Midianites; Sisera, Jabin, Oreb, Zeeb, Zebah, and Zalmuna. These were kings of Midian, western Arabia. We read about these kings in the book of Judges, chapters 7 & 8, where Gideon defeated those kings after attacking Israel. An interesting side note is the kings of Midian are wearing crescent moon ornaments around their neck and on their camels. The worship of Allah, the moon god, predates Mohammad by many centuries. I'll talk more about that later.

Israel's Victory
This local war is also described in Zechariah Chapter 12:

*"Behold, I will make **Jerusalem a cup of trembling** unto all the people **round about**, when they shall be in the siege both against Judah and against Jerusalem. And in that day will I make Jerusalem a **burdensome stone** for all people: all that burden themselves with it shall be cut in pieces, though all the people of the earth be gathered together against it."* *Zechariah 12:2-3 KJV*

Jerusalem is a "cup of trembling" to those nations "round about," her nearby neighbors. During this war, those nations will tremble in fear over Jerusalem as they drink the cup of God's wrath poured out upon them. Jerusalem is also a "burdensome stone." Stones were used as boundary markers back then. Those that try to divide the city of Jerusalem or change the borders of Jerusalem or Israel will be "cut in pieces," destroyed by the Lord. That's exactly what is happening today. Many want to divide Jerusalem and make it an international city, not the capital of Israel. They also want Israel to return to the pre-1967 borders, which will make the nation indefensible.

*"In that day will I make the governors of Judah like an **hearth of fire** among the wood, and like a **torch of fire** in a sheaf; and **they shall devour all the people round about**, on the right hand and on the left: and Jerusalem shall be inhabited again in her own place, even in Jerusalem. ... In that day shall the LORD defend the inhabitants of Jerusalem; and he that is feeble among them at that day shall be as David; and the house of David shall be as God, as the angel of the LORD before them." Zechariah 12:6, 8 KJV*

Israel will be like a "hearth of fire," consuming her enemies as fire consumes wood. She will be a "torch of fire" to a sheaf, a bundle of dry corn stalks or straw. Israel will devour her nearby enemies as fire consumes dry wood and straw. Even the weak and feeble will be strong like David. The power of the Lord will strengthen them and guide their victory over the nations. Israel is victorious in this war but not so in the next. The 2nd great war is covered in the next chapter.

CONFIDENTIAL

Briefing

Point of interest:
    a) a regional war between Israel and neighboring countries
    b) victory for Israel
Discussion:

War is coming to Israel from her surrounding enemy nations. This war will be swift as Israel destroys these nations as wood and straw are consumed by fire. Defeated in this war are Syria (Iran proxy), Lebanon (Hezbollah), Gaza (Hamas), the Palestinian Authority in the West Bank, Jordan, Iraq, and Egypt. That war could be pre-Rapture and set the stage for the 7-year peace covenant confirmed by the Antichrist. Or it could be combined with the battle of Armageddon. Keep your eyes on Syria as that war gets closer to the Golan and borders of Israel.

Update:
The Psalm 83 war may have already been fulfilled. The battle of Israeli independence in 1948, the 6-day war in 1968, and the Yom Kippur war of 1973 could be the fulfillment. Israel was vastly outnumbered and out gunned, but somehow, with the Lord's help, they defeated the armies of their surrounding neighbors. They were victorious beyond anyone's expectations. Many thought the Arab armies would easily defeat them, but Israel reigned victorious.

Today, the nations of Jordan, Egypt, and Saudi Arabia are at peace with Israel. They are working together on trade deals, military equipment, regional peace, and stability. Many Middle Eastern nations, like Oman, for example, have realized that Israel is there to stay. They are building a cooperative relationship with Israel for the benefit of all. The atmosphere of war in those nations has subsided. But not so with other players in the region. Russia, Iran, Turkey, Syria, Iraq, and Lebanon are still very hostile towards Israel and seemingly getting worse. They will be the fulfillment of Ezekiel chapters 38 and 39.

GOG FROM MAGOG

Chief Prince of What?

The chronicle of Gog from Magog is found in the book of Ezekiel chapters 38 and 39. He depicts a vast invading army from the north swooping down on Israel as a mighty storm to cover the land. All seems hopeless, but GOD intervenes and destroys most of the invaders, leaving only a remnant driven back to a desolate place seemingly never to be heard from again. Let's pick up the account.

*"Son of man, set thy face against **Gog**, the land of **Magog**, the chief prince of **Meshech** and **Tubal**, and prophesy against him, And say, Thus saith the Lord GOD; Behold, I am against thee, O Gog, the chief prince of **Meshech** and **Tubal**: And I will turn thee back, and put hooks into thy jaws, and I will bring thee forth, and all thine **army**, horses and horsemen, all of them clothed with all sorts of armour, even a **great company** with bucklers and shields, all of them handling swords: **Persia**, **Ethiopia**, and **Libya** with them; all of them with shield and helmet: **Gomer**, and all his bands; the house of **Togarmah** of the north quarters, and all his bands: and **many people with thee**." - Ezekiel 38:2-6 KJV*

First, let's try to identify these names to determine who comprises this "great company" and where this "army" originates. Names like Persia are prominent being modern-day Iran. Ancient Ethiopia was directly south of Egypt, so this could include modern-day Sudan and Ethiopia. Libya is modern-day Libya. Those were easy, but where is Magog?

Josephus defined Magog as the Scythians in the southern part of Asia from the Black Sea to Mongolia. Groups of barbarians, aliens, and foreigners scattered throughout that region. They used the word

Scythians as we might use the word nomad, Bedouin, migrant, or refugee. Strong's gives the following. H4031, *magowg*, "land of Gog, the mountainous region between Cappadocia and Media and habitation of the descendants of Magog, son of Japheth and grandson of Noah." That seems much more definitive than Scythians. The below map locates the region of Magog.

The circle approximates the region between Cappadocia and Media, the area where Noah's Arc came to rest. In a modern map, most of this region is in Turkey, as shown below.

In looking at the ancient map again, we can see Meshech (Moschi) and Tubal. They are also located in modern-day Turkey, directly adjacent to the area of Magog.

There are two others mentioned, Gomer and Togarmah. We read the following in Genesis Chapter 10:

"The sons of Japheth; **Gomer**, and **Magog**, and **Madai(Media)**, and Javan, and **Tubal**, and **Meshech**, and Tiras. And the sons of **Gomer**; Ashkenaz, and Riphath, and **Togarmah**." - Genesis 10:2-3 KJV Parenthesis mine. This verse shows that the groups mentioned in Ezekiel Chapter 38 are all the sons and grandsons of Noah. It is a well-documented fact that the descendants of Japheth populated the region of Asia Minor then migrated west, north, and eastward. So, I think it is safe to say that Turkey is a significant player in this end-times invasion of Israel.

Here are some other interesting maps to consider. Joel Richardson, "Where is Magog, Meshech and Tubal?", Prophezine, Saturday, April 1, 2017.

http://www.prophezine.com/index.php?option=com_content&id=51 7:where-is-magog-meshech-and-tubal

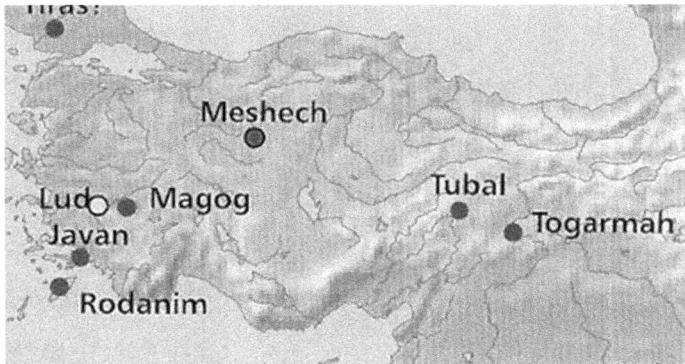

IVP Atlas of Bible History

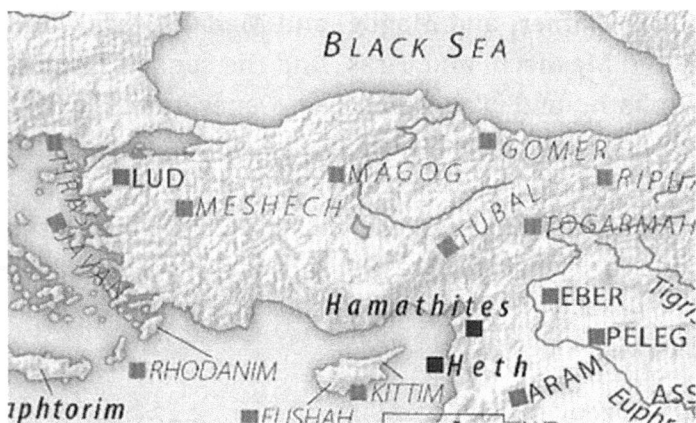
The New Moody Atlas of the Bible

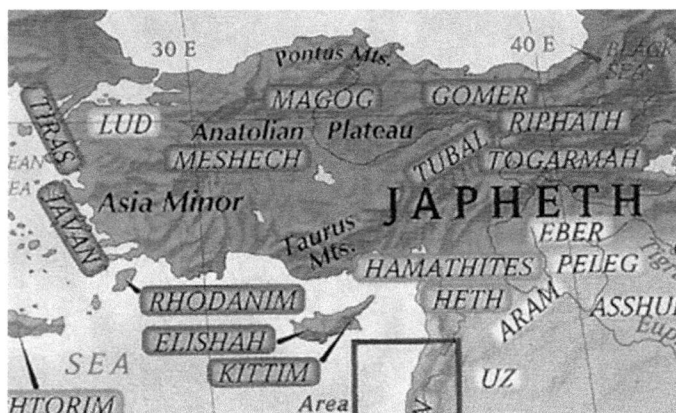
The Holman Bible Atlas

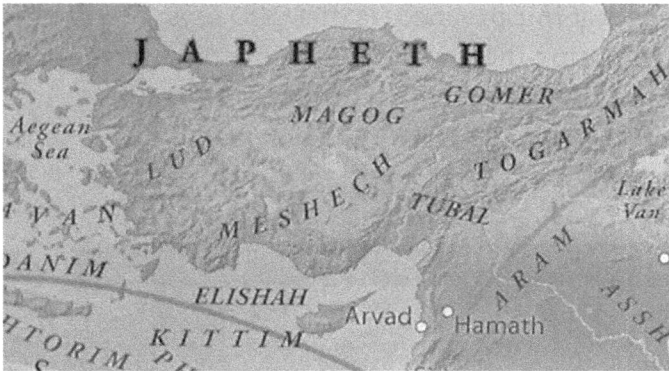
Zondervan Atlas of the Bible

Pinpointing the exact location of these ancient cities and regions is not possible without further archeological research. However, the area of Asia Minor (modern-day Turkey) is the probable locale for these ancient sites.

Some prophecy experts want to include Russia in the mix of nations. They translate the phrase "chief prince of Meshech and Tubal" as "Rosh prince of Meshech and Tubal," where Rosh refers to Russia. The Hebrew word "rosh" is only translated once in scripture as a proper name. In Genesis 46:21 we read that Rosh is a son of Benjamin. The word "rosh" is used 598 times, being translated mostly as head, chief, or top. If Russia is the correct interpretation, then the phrase would read "Russia(n) prince of Meshech and Tubal (Turkey). It sounds unlikely that a Russian would become the leader of Turkey as they have been longstanding enemies. But GOD works in mysterious ways, so I won't rule it out completely. But keep your eyes on the Turkey/Iranian alliance as they are undoubtedly major players. We already see Turkey, Iran, and Russia vying for a strategic position or even hegemony in the Middle East.

Another exciting aspect of this prophecy is that GOD says, "I will turn thee back" and "I will bring thee forth." God directly intervenes in world affairs, causing this great northern power to come against Israel, so He can defeat them and glorify His holy name.

So, here is what we have so far.

Entity	Location
Gog	The leader of this alliance
Land of Magog	Turkey
Meshech and Tubal	Turkey
Gomer and Togarmah	Turkey
Persia	Iran
Ethiopia	Sudan & Ethiopia
Libya	Libya
Rosh	Russia ???
Many peoples	Other smaller nations

The Latter Years

*"Be thou prepared, and prepare for thyself, thou, and all thy company that are assembled unto thee, and be thou a guard unto them. **After many days** thou shalt be visited: in the **latter years** thou shalt come into the land that is brought back from the **sword**, and is gathered out of **many people**, against the mountains of Israel, which have been always **waste**: but it is brought forth out of the nations, and they shall dwell safely all of them. Thou shalt ascend and come like a **storm**, thou shalt be like a **cloud** to cover the land, thou, and all thy bands, and many people with thee." - Ezekiel 38:7-9 KJV.*

Here we see the period for the fulfillment of this prophecy. It will be fulfilled "after many days" from when Ezekiel wrote the words. In the "latter years," when GOD's work on earth concerning humankind is nearing completion. That is the day in which we now live. The prophecy concerns His people "brought back from the sword." Interesting that for 1200 years, the land of Israel was in Muslim control, and one of their main symbols is the "sword." When the Jews started returning to their land around the late 19th century, they came out of "many people" or nations. They returned to the "mountains of Israel," the previously worthless "waste" land started blooming. GOD blesses the land of Israel when the Jews are in it. Today it is a garden paradise compared to the surrounding Islamic nations. The army that invades Israel will cover the land like a great "storm" cloud, as hurricane Katrina covered southern Louisiana. How can the Jews possibly escape?

*"Thus saith the Lord GOD; It shall also come to pass, that at the same time shall things come into thy mind, and thou shalt think an **evil thought**: And thou shalt say, I will go up to the land of **unwalled villages**; I will go to them that are at **rest**, that dwell **safely**, all of them dwelling **without walls**, and having neither **bars nor gates**, To take a **spoil**, and to take a **prey**; to turn thine hand upon the desolate places that are now inhabited, and upon the people that are **gathered out of the nations**, which have gotten cattle and goods, that dwell in the midst of the land. **Sheba, and Dedan**, and the merchants of **Tarshish**, with all the **young lions** thereof, shall say unto thee, Art thou come to take a spoil? hast thou gathered thy company to take a prey? to carry away silver and gold, to take away cattle and goods, to take a **great spoil**?" - Ezekiel 38:10-13 KJV*

Just before this latter-day invasion of Israel, Gog is going to have an "evil thought." Many today have evil thoughts about Israel. The mainstream media loves showing radical individuals and groups obsessed with their hatred for Israel. But Gog's evil thought will drive him to invade. He obsesses over Israel and its newfound wealth.

Israel today is a land of "unwalled villages." Sure, there is a wall and fence by Jerusalem, but the rest of the country is "unwalled." They have an occasional terrorist incident but are generally at rest and live in safety. Currently Israel is at war with Hamas. Will that fighting escalate to the Gog Magog war? Time will tell.

With the recent discoveries of gas and oil, Israel is quickly becoming a land of great wealth and resources. Gog knows this and wants Israel's resources for a spoil and her people for prey.

But as Gog begins his invasion, some speak out against him. "Sheba and Dedan" refers to Saudi Arabia. They protest Gog's invasion of Israel. Joining them are the "merchants of Tarshish." Tarshish is southern Europe but could reference the European Union. The "young lions" could reference the independent colonies of Europe, which includes the Americas. So, many nations protest Gog's military action against Israel. But it is only a verbal protest. No one comes to Israel's aid militarily. Just a lot of noise and saber-rattling from weak nations. They will meet at the UN and pass another meaningless resolution.

Peace and Security

There is an interesting correlation here with Daniel 8:24-25.

*"And his power shall be mighty, but not by his own power: and he shall **destroy wonderfully**, and **shall prosper**, and **practise**, and shall destroy the mighty and the holy people. And **through his policy also he shall cause craft to prosper** in his hand; and he shall magnify himself in his heart, and **by peace shall destroy many**: he shall also **stand up against the Prince of princes**, but he shall be broken without hand." - Daniel 8:24-25 KJV*

We read in Daniel Chapter 9 that the Antichrist comes to power and prominence via a peace covenant (Daniel 9:27). Through that covenant, he will bring prosperity to the Middle East, at least for a brief time. Through "his policy" of peace and "craft," business will prosper. By his peace treaty, he will destroy many. He will lull Israel into complacency with "peace and security," then he will turn on them. The recent pandemic was a compliance test for governments to see how far they could push citizens into compliance with masks, social distancing, lockdowns, forced closures, and an experimental vaccine. Those not in compliance were arrested and jailed, sending a message to everyone that compliance is mandatory, even if illegal and unconstitutional.

*"For when they shall say, **Peace and safety**, then **sudden destruction cometh upon them**, as travail upon a woman with child; and **they shall not escape**." - 1 Thessalonians 5:3 KJV*

If Gog is the Antichrist as many claim, he knows that Israel is at "rest," dwelling safely in "unwalled villages" enjoying their "peace and security." He was the one that brokered the "peace and safety." So, the timing of Gog's invasion is the middle of the 7-year Tribulation. That war could culminate in the Battle of Armageddon at the end of the 7-years. Remember, the second seal judgment is the red horse rider of war (Revelation 6:4).

The Latter Years cont'd

*"Therefore, son of man, prophesy and say unto Gog, Thus saith the Lord GOD; In that day when my people of Israel dwelleth safely, shalt thou not know it? And thou shalt come from thy place out of the **north parts**, thou, and many people with thee, all of them riding upon **horses**, a great*

*company, and a mighty army: And thou shalt come up against my people of Israel, as a cloud to cover the land; it shall be in the **latter days**, and I will bring thee against my land, that the **heathen may know me**, when I shall be **sanctified** in thee, O Gog, **before their eyes**. Thus saith the Lord GOD; Art thou he of **whom I have spoken** in old time by my servants the prophets of Israel, which prophesied in those days many years that I would bring thee against them?" - Ezekiel 38:14-17 KJV*

This passage restates that Gog will come from the "north parts" with a great army. The reference to them "riding upon horses" could be symbolic of a fast-moving mechanized army of tanks, artillery, and armored personnel carriers. Again, we are told this will happen in the "latter days." GOD's desired result of this invasion is that the "heathen may know me." GOD will glorify His Holy Name through the supernatural defeat of Gog and his armies. It will be evident to the world that GOD defeated the northern army, not Israel. GOD's name is "sanctified" by this miraculous defeat of Gog that happens right "before their eyes." All the nations that were protesting but doing nothing will be shocked, entirely in awe of what GOD has done in the destruction of Gog's war machine. GOD always has the last word, and that word brings glory and honor to Him, always.

Next, Ezekiel makes an exciting statement. He states that Gog has been "spoken in old time by my servants the prophets." Wow, the only one spoken by the prophets that could fit the bill is the man we label the Antichrist. So, is Gog the Antichrist? He could be, but other verses may show him to be someone else. I believe Gog is the Antichrist. After all, how many great wars can you have in only seven years? As we go through these passages, you will notice there are still many questions that have no definitive answers. But as the time of this war grows near, the pieces of the puzzle will fall into place.

Fire and Brimstone

*"And it shall come to pass at the same time when Gog shall come against the land of Israel, saith the Lord GOD, that **my fury shall come up in my face**. For in my jealousy and in the **fire of my wrath** have I spoken, Surely in that day there shall be a **great shaking** in the land of Israel; So that the fishes of the sea, and the fowls of the heaven, and the beasts of the field, and all creeping things that creep upon the earth, and all the men that are upon the face of the earth, **shall shake at my presence**, and the mountains shall be **thrown down**, and the steep places shall **fall**, and every wall shall fall to the ground. And I will call for a sword against him throughout all my mountains, saith the Lord GOD: every man's sword shall be **against his brother**. And I will plead against him with **pestilence** and with **blood**; and I will rain upon him, and upon his bands, and upon the many people that are with him, an overflowing **rain**, and **great hailstones**, **fire**, and **brimstone**. Thus will I **magnify myself, and sanctify myself**, and I will be known in the eyes of many nations, and they shall know that **I am the LORD**."* - Ezekiel 38:18-23 KJV

When this invasion of Israel by Gog happens, GOD will be furious. He will be jealous for His people Israel and pour out His wrath as fire upon Gog. There will be a "great shaking" in Israel; a great earthquake so that everything, including Gog and his armies, the fish, the birds, mammals, and every living thing, will "shake at my presence." Everything will know that Almighty God is intervening in this battle in a glorious way. Gog's defeat is imminent. That earthquake will be so powerful that mountains will fall, and walls will crumble. There will be mass confusion within the armies of Gog. They will begin fighting each other. Since this alliance of Gog is comprised of both Sunni and Shia nations, infighting will be the norm as they have been fighting each other for centuries.

GOD has many weapons at His disposal. Here He uses "pestilence and blood." Pestilence is a biological disease but could also include biological and chemical warfare. Perhaps Gog has plans to use such weapons, but GOD turns these maladies back upon Gog's armies. GOD also uses "an overflowing rain, and great hailstones, fire, and brimstone." These are some of GOD's favorite weapons as He has used them many times in the Old Testament to defeat Israel's enemies. Here are just a few passages.

*"Then the LORD rained upon Sodom and upon Gomorrah **brimstone and fire** from the LORD out of heaven; - Genesis 19:24 KJV"*

*"Upon the wicked he shall rain snares, **fire and brimstone**, and an horrible tempest: this shall be the portion of their cup." - Psalm 11:6 KJV*
*"And the streams thereof shall be turned into pitch, and the dust thereof into **brimstone**, and the land thereof shall become **burning pitchapter"***
- Isaiah 34:9 KJV

*"But the same day that Lot went out of Sodom it rained **fire and brimstone from heaven**, and destroyed them all. - Luke 17:29 KJV*

That is bad. You do not want to be on planet earth when that happens. Don't miss the Rapture flight. It only comes once, no late-night red-eye flights.

God frequently uses fire and brimstone to execute His judgment and pour out His wrath upon the ungodly. Hard to imagine fire and brimstone falling from the sky, creating such destruction, death, and chaos. But it's coming; just as sure as I am looking out the window at this beautiful day, it is coming.

The Lord will do all these things to "magnify myself and sanctify myself" in the eyes of the world. These events that bring the defeat and destruction of Gog will come from GOD, not the UN and not the armies of nations. Everyone will know that the GOD of heaven has defeated Gog. Whether they believe in GOD or not, the power and glory of Almighty GOD will be undeniable.

Fire on Magog

Ezekiel continues in chapter 39, describing the massive defeat of Gog and his armies.

*"Therefore, thou son of man, prophesy against Gog, and say, Thus saith the Lord GOD; Behold, I am against thee, O Gog, the chief prince of Meshech and Tubal: And I will turn thee back, and leave but the **sixth part of thee**, and will cause thee to come up from the north parts, and will bring thee upon the mountains of Israel: And I will smite thy bow out of thy left hand, and will cause thine arrows to fall out of thy right hand. **Thou shalt fall upon the mountains of Israel**, thou, and all thy bands, and the people that is with thee: I will give thee unto the **ravenous birds** of every sort, and to the **beasts of the field** to be devoured. Thou shalt fall upon the open field: for I have spoken it, saith the Lord GOD." - Ezekiel 39:1-5 KJV*

This chapter opens with Ezekiel restating GOD's judgment upon Gog. 5/6 or 83% of Gog's armies are destroyed. GOD will crush the weapons of this massive army symbolized by the "arrows" and the "bow." Interesting that the Arrow missile system is the most advanced missile defense systems in the world. What a coincidence. The destruction will happen on the "mountains of Israel," known as the West Bank, comprising ancient Samaria and Judea. Gee, another coincidence, right. ☺ The dead bodies of this massive army will be given to "ravenous birds" and to "beasts of the field" to be devoured.

We will look at this phenomenon shortly. These events will happen precisely as the passage describes, for "I have spoken it, saith the Lord GOD."

*"And I will send a **fire on Magog**, and among them that dwell **carelessly in the isles**: and they shall know that I am the LORD. So will I make my holy name known in the midst of my people Israel; and I will not let them pollute my holy name any more: and the heathen shall know that I am the LORD, the **Holy One in Israel**. Behold, it is come, and it is done, saith the Lord GOD; this is the day whereof I have spoken." - Ezekiel 39:6-8 KJV*

We determined in a previous section that Magog is modern-day Turkey. GOD is going to send fire on Magog. Could this be a limited nuclear response from Israel on the primary invading country? A map of Turkey reveals "the isles" in the Mediterranean.

http://www.greek-islands.us/map-greece/

Indeed, a tactical nuclear response from Israel would wreak havoc on the Greek isles. There is no mention of Greece being involved in this war, but they are dangerously close to the action. Again, GOD will magnify His Holy Name in Israel, and all will know that GOD is winning the war, not the IDF.

GOD states that He will *"make my holy name known in the midst of my people Israel; and I will not let them pollute my holy name any more."* The member of the Godhead that is not known or rejected in Israel is Jesus Christ. Jesus will make himself known to Israel as their true Messiah, and they will no longer pollute the name of Jesus through unbelief. Also, the heathen will know that Jesus Christ is Lord. Whether they choose to repent, follow, and obey the Lord Jesus Christ is another question, most will not.

GOD proclaims the He is "the Holy One in Israel." That is the only place in scripture where the phrase "holy one IN Israel" is used. Everywhere else, the term "holy one of Israel" is used. The Lord GOD, Jesus Christ, is in Israel at the culmination of this battle. Indicating that this great war is synonymous with the Battle of Armageddon at the end of the 7-year Tribulation. GOD states, "it is come" and "it is done." We read these two verses in the Book of Revelation that make the same proclamation.

*"And the seventh angel poured out his vial into the air; and there came a great voice out of the temple of heaven, from the throne, saying, **It is done**."* – Revelation 16:17 KJV

*"And he said unto me, **It is done**. I am Alpha and Omega, the beginning and the end. I will give unto him that is athirst of the fountain of the water of life freely."* – Revelation 21:6 KJV

Previously we read that Gog was someone spoken of by the Prophets, which gives credence to the possibility that he and the Antichrist are the same person. In this passage, the Lord states, "this is the day whereof I have spoken," indicating the day of Gog's defeat was also spoken of by the Prophets. That day could be the day of the great Battle of Armageddon.

*"And they that dwell in the cities of Israel shall go forth, and shall **set on fire and burn the weapons**, both the shields and the bucklers, the bows and the arrows, and the handstaves, and the spears, and they shall burn them with fire **seven years**. So that they shall take no wood out of the field, neither cut down any out of the forests; for they shall burn the weapons with fire: and they shall spoil those that spoiled them, and rob those that robbed them, saith the Lord GOD." - Ezekiel 39:9-10 KJV*

Israel will burn weapons and take whatever material is useful from the defeated northern army. It will take seven years to consume the materials and clean up after this massive destruction. Some give this as reasoning why this great war must be before or at the beginning of the 7-year Tribulation stating that the cleanup could not go past the Second Coming of Jesus Christ and into the Millennial Reign. But why not? I don't think that upon Jesus' return, He will wave a magic wand, and instantly, the earth will be a pristine paradise. Since man has made a mess of the world, man will have the opportunity to participate in its cleanup. Granted, there are things we can't clean up, like the region around Chernobyl. That will take the hand of God.

The massive radiation damage to the Pacific Ocean done by the Fukushima Daiichi reactor disaster will require a supernatural cleanup. This global cleanup will begin after the inauguration of the Millennial Kingdom of Jesus Christ. Both men and angels will participate in this effort. What man cannot do will be completed by the Lord's angels. Everything that offends the Lord Jesus Christ, both human beings and material objects, will be removed from the earth by His angels.

*"The Son of man shall send forth his angels, and they shall gather out of his kingdom **all things that offend**, and them which do iniquity;" - Mat 13:41 KJV*

Call the HAZMAT Team

*"And it shall come to pass in that day, that I will give unto Gog a place there of graves in Israel, the valley of the passengers on the **east of the sea**: and it shall stop the noses of the passengers: and there shall they bury Gog and all his multitude: and they shall call it The valley of Hamongog. And **seven months** shall the house of Israel be burying of them, that they may cleanse the land. Yea, all the people of the land shall bury them; and it shall be to them a renown the day that I shall be glorified, saith the Lord GOD." - Ezekiel 39:11-13 KJV*

God establishes a massive graveyard east of the Dead Sea in the region of ancient Moab and Edom (how fitting). The dead bodies will be so numerous they will stink to the high heavens. The stench will be unbearable for many miles. It will take seven months to bury the dead from Gog's armies. The valley of the graves is Hamongog, meaning the multitude of Gog. Gog's multitude seemed so strong and powerful. They stormed the land of Israel with a sure victory in their eyes. But GOD intervened, making their defeat sure. Their once-powerful multitude is now stinking and rotting on the battlefield. GOD is vindicated. Gog is vanquished.

*"And they shall **sever out men of continual employment**, passing through the land to bury with the passengers those that remain upon the face of the earth, **to cleanse it**: after the end of seven months shall they*

*searchapter And the passengers that pass through the land, when any seeth a **man's bone**, then shall he set up a **sign by it**, till the **buriers** have buried it in the valley of Hamongog. And also the name of the city shall be Hamonah. Thus shall they cleanse the land." – Ezekiel 39:14-16 KJV*

Here we see the HAZMAT team swing into action. They are "men of continual employment" that go through the land of Israel to cleanse it. If someone finds a "bone" or a body part, they mark it and call the disposal team. The HAZMAT team (buriers) will come and properly dispose of the body part in the valley of Hamongog. There will be a city in the region named Hamonah where the HAZMAT teams will be located. That has a particular connotation that the remains being handled are radioactive. Much care is described by Ezekiel in the 6th century B.C., describing the handling of the dead. That would only be a big deal if the remains were radioactive and hazardous. That is further evidence that this war will involve nuclear weapons. We know that nuclear war is coming. It just a matter of when. Man has never built a weapon he did not use.

*"And, thou son of man, thus saith the Lord GOD; Speak unto every **feathered fowl**, and to every **beast of the field**, Assemble yourselves, and come; gather yourselves on every side to my sacrifice that I do sacrifice for you, even a great sacrifice upon the mountains of Israel, that ye may eat flesh, and drink blood. Ye shall eat the flesh of the mighty, and drink the blood of the princes of the earth, of rams, of lambs, and of goats, of bullocks, all of them fatlings of Bashan. And ye shall eat fat till ye be full, and drink blood till ye be drunken, of **my sacrifice** which I have sacrificed for you. Thus ye shall be filled at my table with horses and chariots, with mighty men, and with all men of war, saith the Lord GOD." - Ezekiel 39:17-20 KJV*

The predators, both fowl, and beast are invited to the carnage served up by GOD from this horrific battle. Evil, ungodly men's carcasses being consumed by unclean animals only seems fitting. The terms "of rams, of lambs, and of goats, of bullocks" depict the leaders and commanders of the fallen armies. All those in this sacrifice of the Lord are "fatlings of Bashan." Bashan is the greater region of the Golan Heights in northeast Israel. Such devastation boggles the mind.

*"And I will set my glory among the heathen, and all the heathen shall see my judgment that I have executed, and my hand that I have laid upon them. So the house of Israel shall know that **I am the LORD their God from that day and forward.**" - Ezekiel 39:21-22 KJV*

GOD again proclaims His glory among the nations by this massive defeat of Gog's armies. The nations will see the swift and righteous judgment of GOD. There will be no doubt as to what has happened. From Gog's defeat, Israel will know the Lord God, Jesus Christ from "that day and forward," implying that they were in unbelief before this great war.

*"And the heathen shall know that the house of Israel went into **captivity** for their iniquity: because they trespassed against me, therefore hid I my face from them, and gave them into the hand of their enemies: so fell they all by the sword. According to their uncleanness and according to their transgressions have I done unto them, and hid my face from them. Therefore thus saith the Lord GOD; Now will I **bring again the captivity of Jacob**, and have **mercy upon the whole house of Israel**, and will be jealous for my holy name; After that they have borne their shame, and all their trespasses whereby they have trespassed against me, when they dwelt safely in their land, and none made them afraid." - Ezekiel 39:23-26 KJV*

There is one more captivity coming for Israel. After Gog attacks Israel, he has some success and takes Jerusalem captive for a short time. We read this also in Zechariah.

*"Behold, the day of the LORD cometh, and thy spoil shall be divided in the midst of thee. For **I will gather all nations against Jerusalem to battle**; and the city shall be taken, and the houses rifled, and the women ravished; and **half of the city shall go forth into captivity**, and the residue of the people shall not be cut off from the city. **Then shall the LORD go forth, and fight against those nations, as when he fought in the day of battle**." - Zechariah 14:1-3 KJV*

After the coming captivity, the Lord will fight the invading armies as He has many times in the Old Testament. The Jews fall into captivity because of their unbelief and iniquity. Because of their sin, GOD says, "I will hide my face from them." After their captivity has satisfied the judgment of GOD, He will pour out His mercy on them and defeat the northern army.

"When I have brought them again from the people, and gathered them out of their enemies' lands, and am sanctified in them in the sight of many nations; Then shall they know that I am the LORD their God, which caused them to be led into captivity among the heathen: but I have gathered them unto their own land, and have left none of them any more there. Neither will I hide my face any more from them: for I have poured out my spirit upon the house of Israel, saith the Lord GOD." - Ezekiel 39:27-29 KJV

Finally, Israel will be saved and know that Jesus Christ is Lord. The apostle Paul proclaims:

*"Esaias also crieth concerning Israel, Though the number of the children of Israel be as the sand of the sea, **a remnant shall be saved**." - Rom 9:27 KJV*

*"Brethren, my heart's desire and prayer to God for Israel is, that **they might be saved**." - Rom 10:1 KJV*

*"**And so all Israel shall be saved**: as it is written, There shall come out of Sion the Deliverer, and shall turn away ungodliness from Jacob:" - Rom 11:26 KJV*

Briefing

Point of interest:
    a) massive invasion of Israel from the north, coalition of Turkey, Iran and other nations in the middle east and Africa.
    b) invading armies defeated, cleanup from nuclear blast takes 7 years.
    c) High probability this war corresponds with the final battle of Armageddon at the end of the 7-year Tribulation.

Person of interest:
    a) leader named Gog, ruler of Turkey.

Discussion:

There are many clues to the timing of this great war, but none are 100% conclusive. However, we see the stage set and the players ready for the grand opening. Turkey, Iran, Libya, and Russia have a loose alliance. All that's needed is a trigger event to firm up this evil coalition and bring them to bear against Israel. Keep your eyes on these players, especially Hezbollah, as they are simply a proxy of

Iran. Hezbollah reportedly has thousands of missiles, including anti-ship arms. They could be the trigger that brings this prophecy to bear on Israel.

THE BOOK OF REVELATION

John's Greeting

The Book of Revelation is quite a work. The Apostle John must have been overwhelmed with awe and sorrow upon seeing these visions. Such magnificence and such destruction, quite a dichotomy. The Book is the Revelation of Jesus Christ, the revealing or unveiling of the Lord Jesus Christ. In the gospels, we have the revelation of Jesus Christ as the Son of Joseph, the suffering Savior, meek and humble. In the Book of Revelation, we have the revealing of Jesus Christ as the Son of David, the victorious King extracting judgment on His enemies, King of Kings and Lord of Lords.

The Apostle John receives this revelation while on the small island of Patmos in the Aegean Sea off the coast of western Turkey. Today this island is a tourist stop but in John's day, most likely a fishing village. The date of John's writing is unknown. Most premillennialists place the date around 95 A.D., but I believe John wrote Revelation much earlier as he does not reference the destruction of Jerusalem nor the Temple in 70 A.D and also makes no reference to the apostle Paul's ministry and the gospel of grace.

*"**The Revelation of Jesus Christ**, which God gave unto **him**, to shew unto his servants things which must shortly come to pass; and he sent and signified it by **his angel** unto his **servant John. Who bare record of the word of God, and of the testimony of Jesus Christ, and of all things that he saw**." - Revelation 1:1-2 KJV*

John states the revelation was given to the Lord Jesus Christ by the Father ("which God gave unto him"). This revelation will "shortly come to pass," which is why I believe it was written before 70 A.D. How could John make such a statement if he knew the Temple was destroyed, Jerusalem ransacked, and the people slaughtered? Jesus gives the vision to His angel, and the angel provides the vision to John. John asserts that he recorded the "word of God," the testimony of Jesus Christ, and all that he saw in the visions. He was an eyewitness to the unfolding of the last days, specifically the 7-year Tribulation and subsequent events.

*"**Blessed is he that readeth**, and they that hear the words of this prophecy, and keep those things which are written therein: for the time is at hand." - Revelation 1:3 KJV*

Revelation is the only book of the Bible that promises a blessing for the reader and hearer if they keep the instructions written therein. That will only be possible for those living in the 7-year Tribulation. For us today, no part of the book pertains to the Church, the body of Christ. John states that the "time is at hand." It will be a time for Israel. Always remember, John is an apostle to Israel, not the church (Galatians 2:6-9)

*"John to the **seven churches which are in Asia**: Grace be unto you, and peace, from him which is, and which was, and which is to come; and from the **seven Spirits** which are before his throne; And from **Jesus Christ**, who is the faithful witness, and the **first begotten of the dead**, and the prince of the kings of the earth. Unto him that loved us, and **washed us from our sins in his own blood**, And hath **made us kings and priests** unto God and his Father; to him be glory and dominion for ever and ever. Amen." - Revelation 1:4-6 KJV*

Wow, what a greeting. I don't think you could pack more theology in one sentence if you tried. John declares the book of Revelation is for the **"seven churches which are in Asia."** Asia was a Roman province in central Asia Minor, modern-day Turkey.

John extends the familiar greeting of grace and peace from "him which is, and which was, and which is to come." That can only be the Lord Jesus Christ. The "seven Spirits before the throne" is probably a reference to the seven characteristics of the Holy Spirit found in scripture: the Spirit of Wisdom and Understanding, the Spirit of Counsel and Might, the Spirit of Knowledge, the Spirit of the Fear of the Lord, the Spirit of Grace and Mercy, the Spirit of Judgment and Truth, the Spirit of Life in Christ Jesus. The greeting is also from the Lord Jesus Christ himself. Jesus is the "faithful witness" of all things, including what was given to John in this revelation. Jesus is the "first begotten of the dead" in that He is the "first fruits" of the resurrection of the just. No one was resurrected before Jesus Christ. He is the first fruit of many brethren. Some were brought back to life only to die again, like Lazarus. But no one before Jesus was resurrected to eternal life. He is the "first fruit."

"But now is Christ risen from the dead, [and] become the firstfruits of them that slept." - 1 Corinthians 15:20 KJV

Notice that Jesus is called the "prince of the kings of the earth" in Revelation chapter one because He has not yet been coronated King of Kings and Lord of Lords, which happens later. Jesus has "washed us from our sins in His own blood." He is the savior, and only His blood can cleanse sin. He has made Israel a nation of "kings and priests." They will rule and reign with Him in the Millennial Kingdom. Don't forget that the book of Revelation is about Israel's redemption, not ours, the Church, the body of Christ.

All glory and dominion are given to the Lord Jesus Christ for His willingness to do the Father's will, redeeming humankind and the world by His substitutionary death on the cross.

Jesus' second coming will be as He left, in the clouds coming to the Mount of Olives.

*"Behold, he **cometh with clouds**, and every eye shall see him, and they also which pierced him: and all kindreds of the earth shall wail because of him. Even so, Amen." - Revelation 1:7 KJV*

The Prophet Daniel saw the same thing.

*"I saw in the night visions, and, behold, one like the Son of man **came with the clouds of heaven**, and came to the Ancient of days, and they brought him near before him." - Daniel 7:13 KJV*

Jesus told the disciples in a private briefing.

*"And then shall appear the sign of the Son of man in heaven: and then shall all the tribes of the earth mourn, and they shall see the **Son of man coming in the clouds of heaven** with power and great glory." - Matthew 24:30 KJV*

"Every eye shall see him" at His second coming. Everyone on planet earth will know when Jesus returns. When He came the first time nearly 2000 years ago, only a limited group of people saw Him. Perhaps 12,000 to 15,000 people total. His ministry was localized to the land of Israel. Not so with the second coming. Everyone will see Him. I don't know how He does this, but He does not need CNN or some other fake news agency to cover it as He is God Almighty. Those that "pierced" Him are the Jews. They will weep and wail because they have been suffering so long in unbelief knowing their forefathers crucified Israel's Messiah will weigh heavy on their hearts.

"I am **Alpha and Omega**, the **beginning** and the **ending**, saith the Lord, which is, and which was, and which is to come, the **Almighty**." - Revelation 1:8 KJV

What a powerfully majestic verse of scripture. Jesus is the beginning and the end of all things about humanity and this universe. He was God, He is God, and He's coming back soon. He is the Almighty, Almighty God.

"In the beginning was the Word, and the Word was with God, and **the Word was God**. The same was in the beginning with God. **All things were made by him; and without him was not any thing made that was made**... And the Word was made flesh, and dwelt among us, (and we beheld his glory, the glory as of the only begotten of the Father,) full of grace and truth." - John 1:1-3, 14 KJV

Everything in Revelation from chapter 1 verse 10 through the end of the book **FOLLOWS THE RAPTURE** and applies to Israel enduring the seven-year tribulation and beyond!

The Seven Churches

"I John, who also am your brother, and companion in tribulation, and in the kingdom and patience of Jesus Christ, was in the isle that is called **Patmos**, for the word of God, and for the testimony of Jesus Christ. I was **in the Spirit on the Lord's day**, and heard behind me a **great voice**, as of a **trumpet**, Saying, I am **Alpha and Omega**, the **first** and the **last**: and, What thou seest, **write in a book**, and send it unto the **seven churches** which are in Asia; unto Ephesus, and unto Smyrna, and unto Pergamos, and unto Thyatira, and unto Sardis, and unto Philadelphia, and unto Laodicea." - Revelation 1:9-11 KJV

John's vision opened when he was "in the Spirit" on the Lord's day. The Lord's day refers to "the day of the Lord," not Sunday. That is the context of much of the Book. Immediately John hears a "great voice" sounding like a "trumpet." That is in stark contrast to the "still small voice" of the Holy Spirit today. If you look at an orchestra, there may be a dozen violins but generally only one trumpet. The loud trumpet voice declares, "I am Alpha and Omega, the first and the last." That can only be the Lord Jesus Christ talking with John. Jesus is the Alpha and the Omega. Those are the first and last letters of the Greek alphabet. He is the "first and the last," meaning He is all in all.

Jesus instructs John to write what he will see in a book and send that book to seven specific churches in the region of Asia, in Asia Minor. These churches were actual churches in John's day, as shown on the below map from BibleStudy.org. They are not grace churches as we have today, but law churches; Jewish believers in Jesus Christ as Messiah keeping Moses' commandments. That will become clear as we progress.

THRACE
The Seven Churches
of Revelation

ASIA

AEGEAN
SEA

Pergamum
Thyatira
Smyrna
Sardis
Philadelphia

Ephesus
Laodicea

Athens

PATMOS

GALATIA

RHODES

MEDITERRANEAN SEA

BibleStudy.org

*"And I turned to see the voice that spake with me. And being turned, I saw **seven golden candlesticks**; And in the midst of the seven candlesticks one like unto the **Son of man**, clothed with a **garment** down to the foot, and girt about the paps with a **golden girdle**. His head and his hairs were white like wool, as **white as snow**; and his eyes were as a **flame of fire**; And his feet like unto **fine brass**, as if they burned in a furnace; and his voice as the sound of **many waters**." - Revelation 1:12-15 KJV*

John turns to see who is talking with him and notices "seven golden candlesticks." Walking among the candlesticks is someone that looks like Jesus, the Son of man. John had only seen Jesus once in a glorified state on the mount of transfiguration with Peter and James. It probably took a few seconds for the magnitude of the moment to sink in. He is standing in the presence of the Almighty. His garment "down to the foot" symbolic of His righteousness. The "golden girdle" royalty as God the Son. His hair "white as snow" wisdom and truth. His eyes as a "flame of fire" holiness. His feet as "fine brass" justice and judgment. His voice as "many waters" powerfully speaking the Word of God.

"And he had in his right hand **seven stars**: and out of his mouth went a **sharp twoedged sword**: and his countenance was as the **sun** shineth in his strength. And when I saw him, **I fell at his feet as dead**. And he laid his right hand upon me, saying unto me, Fear not; I am the first and the last: **I am he that liveth, and was dead; and, behold, I am alive for evermore**, Amen; and have the **keys of hell and of death**." - Revelation 1:16-18 KJV

Jesus explains the "seven stars" and the "golden candlesticks" in a subsequent verse. The "sharp two-edged sword" is the Word of God, Jesus' Word as He is God. His glory shines like the sun, and when John finally realizes what has happened to him and whose presence he is in, he falls at Jesus' feet "as dead." John's mortal body and mind cannot take the Glory of the Most High God. But Jesus touches John and enables him to find courage for what he is about to witness. Jesus identifies himself again to John as one that "lives" but was "dead" and now lives for "evermore." John knows this could only be the Lord Jesus Christ. Having been resurrected from the dead, Jesus has the "keys of hell and of death." His resurrection gave Him victory over hell and death, so He now has the "keys," giving Him authority over what once was the devil's domain.

"Write the **things which thou hast seen**, and the **things which are**, and the **things which shall be hereafter**; The mystery of the seven stars which thou sawest in my right hand, and the seven golden candlesticks. **The seven stars are the angels of the seven churches**: and the **seven candlesticks which thou sawest are the seven churches**." - Revelation 1:19-20 KJV

John is commanded to write three things.

Timeframe	Source
"things which thou hast seen"	What John has just seen in Chapter 1.
"things which are"	Chapters 2 & 3 the Churches
"things which shall be hereafter"	Chapters 4-22 things that follow the Churches.

Revelation is the only book in the Bible that provides its own outline. Here we are given the primary sections into which the book is divided. That is important, as we will see.

The seven golden candlesticks represent the seven churches in Asia. The seven stars are the seven angels of the churches. The angels of the churches provide help and support to those that truly seek the Lord and His truth. They are Jewish believers in Christ under the law of Moses, and we will see this distinction as we examine the seven letters to the churches. Jesus is dictating these letters to the Apostle John. What we have are seven epistles from the Lord Jesus Christ.

The Church of Ephesus
Greeting:
*"Unto the angel of the **church of Ephesus** write; These things saith he that holdeth the **seven stars** in his right hand, who walketh in the midst of the **seven golden candlesticks**," - Revelation 2:1 KJV*

Jesus immediately identifies Himself as the one holding the "seven stars" and walking among the "seven golden candlesticks" from chapter one. He controls the seven churches determining whether they continue to exist or warrant destruction. If they do not live up to God's standard, they are in danger of obliteration.

Commendation
*"I know thy works, and thy **labor**, and thy **patience**, and how thou canst not bear them which are evil: and thou hast tried them which say they are apostles, and are not, and hast found them **liars**. And hast **borne**, and hast **patience**, and **for my name's sake hast labored, and hast not fainted**."*
- Revelation 2:2-3 KJV

Each letter Jesus states: "I know thy works." There is no mention of grace, only works. These churches are works-based assemblies of Jewish believers under the Law of Moses. No one in the seven churches has the assurance of salvation. They must continue doing the works of the law and endure until the coming of the Lord. These are tribulation churches, not the Body of Christ, Pauline churches.

Believers at Ephesus are commended for their hard work and patience in the Lord. They patiently keep the law and care for each other while waiting for the return of the Lord at the end of the Tribulation. But some that came to Ephesus were false apostles. The believers at Ephesus found them to be liars and booted them out of the church. Too bad we don't do that today. The believers at Ephesus became consumed with the works of the law rather than faith in Christ, their Messiah. That problem plagued the Pharisees of Jesus' day. They thought they could earn their righteousness apart from faith in God. However, the paradigm at Ephesus is faith plus works. As James states, faith without works is dead (only if you are a Jew under the Law of Moses, James 2:20).

Criticism
*"Nevertheless I have somewhat against thee, because thou hast **left thy first love**. Remember therefore from whence thou art fallen, and repent,*

and do the **first works**, or else I will come unto thee quickly, and will **remove thy candlestick** out of his place, except thou **repent**." - Revelation 2:4-5 KJV

Even though they were doing great things, Jesus criticized them for leaving their "first love." They had put the works of the law above their faith in their Messiah Jesus Christ. They were to seek the Lord, not just good works. Jesus commands the believers at Ephesus to do the "first works."

"But seek ye first the kingdom of God, and his righteousness; and all these things shall be added unto you." - Matthew 6:33 KJV

Their "first works" was the excitement and joy felt believing in their Messiah, Jesus Christ. Their original love for Jesus overflowed with praise and worship. That is where they need to return. Jesus will remove their candlestick if they do not return to their "first love." That means that He will destroy their church if they don't repent and seek Him. Today Ephesus is an archeological site. The following photo shows the entrance to the library.

By Stan Shebs, CC BY-SA 3.0, https://commons.wikimedia.org/w/index.php?curid=71125

Commendation cont'd.
"But this thou hast, that thou hatest the deeds of the Nicolaitans, which I also hate." - Revelation 2:6 KJV

The Lord adds another commendation about the Nicolaitans. The believers at Ephesus hate the Nicolaitans, those that want to impose a hierarchy of clergy over believers. Jesus hates that religious structure as it always leads to corruption and abuse of power as we see today in the Church of Rome.

Closing
*"He that hath an ear, let him hear what the Spirit saith unto the churches; To him that **overcometh** will I give to eat of the **tree of life**, which is in the midst of the paradise of God." - Revelation 2:7 KJV*

"He that hath an ear." What kind of ear is Jesus referring to—A spiritual ear that can hear spiritual truth. Those listen to what the Holy Spirit is saying to the church at Ephesus with their spiritual ears. Even though the letter to Ephesus is not written to the Body of Christ, we can still glean spiritual truth from it. We are to do all we can to ensure we do not leave our "first love." People can become so involved in church activities they have no time for Jesus or Bible study. We must overcome all distractions that seek to move us away from our first love, even church-related activities.

The overcomer passage relates to the Jewish believers under the law. Only the overcomers will be rewarded to "eat from the tree of life" and dwell in the "paradise of God." That is a salvation issue that those in the Tribulation must do. They must overcome the antichrist system to be rewarded with eternal life. Eating from the tree of life does not apply to us in the church. We already have eternal life, so eating from the tree of life for eternal life is unnecessary.

The Church at Smyrna

Greeting

"And unto the angel of the church in Smyrna write; These things saith the **first and the last**, *which was* **dead**, *and is* **alive**,*" - Revelation 2:8 KJV*

Jesus greets the believers at Smyrna with His eternal existence being the first and the last. He "was dead" (for three days) and "is alive" for ever more. The fact that His greeting mentions His death identifies Him with the martyred believers at Smyrna. They are known as the "Martyred Church," or "Tribulation martyrs."

Commendation

*"I know thy works, and **tribulation**, and **poverty**, (but thou art rich) and I know the **blasphemy** of them which say they are Jews, and are not, but are the **synagogue of Satan**." - Revelation 2:9 KJV*

Jesus knows their works. He knows their suffering, pain, and poverty because they stand for Him. Even though they lack material possessions, including food, clothing, and shelter, they are rich in spiritual food, the clothing of righteousness, and the filling of the Spirit of wisdom and peace. They will dwell in the house of the Lord forever. They endure blasphemy, ridicule, and insults from fake Jews—Jews that pretend to follow Moses but have sold out to the antichrist system. They are antichrist collaborators. Just as in WWII, there were Jews that collaborated with the Nazis. The same will happen in the 7-year Tribulation. They seek to protect their hide by ratting out their fellow Jews. These fake Jews are from the synagogue of Satan. In other words, they are doing Satan's will, not God's. Satan empowers the antichrist, his minions, and fake Jews.

Command and Reward

*"Fear none of those things which thou shalt suffer: behold, the devil shall cast some of you into **prison**, that ye may be tried; and ye shall have **tribulation ten days**: be thou **faithful unto death**, and I will give thee a **crown of life**." - Revelation 2:10 KJV*

Do not fear suffering and tribulation. The devil will put some of them in prison, and others will be martyred. Jesus tells them to be "faithful unto death," letting them know that He is with them and identifies with them in death. What is happening to the believers at Smyrna happened to Jesus Christ on the cross. For their faithfulness unto death, Jesus will reward them with a "crown of life," a unique crown given to those martyred for their faith.

Closing
*"He that hath an ear, let him hear what the Spirit saith unto the churches; He that **overcometh** shall not be hurt of the **second death**." - Revelation 2:11 KJV*

Those martyred for their faith during the 7-year Tribulation will escape the second death, the Great White Throne judgment, and the lake of fire. They overcame persecution, pain, and suffering. They did not give in by recanting their faith. They stayed strong in the faith, even unto death.

The Church at Pergamos

Greeting
"And to the angel of the church in Pergamos write; These things saith he which hath the sharp sword with two edges;" - Revelation 2:12 KJV

Jesus greets this church speaking of His Word, the "sharp sword with two edges." He will have some strong words to say to the believers at the church of Pergamos.

Commendation
*"I know thy works, and where thou dwellest, even where **Satan's seat** is: and thou **holdest fast my name**, and hast not denied my faith, even in those days wherein Antipas was my faithful martyr, who was slain among you, where **Satan dwelleth**." - Revelation 2:13 KJV*

Jesus again opens the commendation with the words "I know thy works." Jesus knows all, whether done in public or secret. Nothing gets past Him. Remember that. In each letter, we see that good works are essential for salvation. He notes that where they live is "Satan's seat." That could be a reference to the Altar of Zeus.

By Ingo Mehling - Own work, CC BY-SA 3.0,
https://commons.wikimedia.org/w/index.php?curid=18040000

Pergamos (Pergamon) had an Acropolis on the nearby hill where the Altar of Zeus once stood. The Germans dismantled it and the altar now resides at the Berlin Museum, as shown below.

By Gryffindor, This panoramic image was created with AutostitchapterStitched images may differ from reality. - Own

work, Public-Domain,
https://commons.wikimedia.org/w/index.php?curid=2975718

Here is the stage at the Democrat National Convention where Obama gave his acceptance speech in 2008. Notice any resemblance? I'll let you figure out the rest.

But the believers at Pergamos did not worship at Satan's seat. They held fast to the name of Jesus Christ, their Messiah, and remained faithful to Him. Even faced with martyrdom, as Antipas was slain for the faith, they stayed true and did not deny their Lord and Savior Jesus Christ. Jesus labels Pergamos as "where Satan dwells." It is hard to get one's head around the extent of the evil, both spiritual and secular, represented by these terms and the impact they still have today. Obama accepted the presidency on a replica of the Altar of Zeus, Satan's Seat. What does that say about him? It seems he still has a significant influence in the Presidency through President Biden.

Criticism
*"But I have a few things against thee, because thou hast there them that hold the **doctrine of Balaam**, who taught Balac to cast a **stumbling block** before the children of Israel, to eat things sacrificed unto idols, and to commit fornication." - Revelation 2:14 KJV*

The doctrine of Balaam in this instance pertains to sexual immorality and fornication. Balaam counseled Balak, king of Moab, to send the women of Moab to the camp of the Israelites so the women would intermarry and bring their pagan idols to the men of Israel. There were some women in Pergamos trying to corrupt believers through fornication and idol worship. That God hates, it is a "stumbling block" to following the Lord. Fornication appeals to the lusts of the flesh and leads to spiritual formication with idols.

*"So hast thou also them that hold the **doctrine of the Nicolaitans**, which thing I hate." - Revelation 2:15 KJV*

The church at Pergamos also had a problem with the Nicolaitans. However, they allowed them into the church even though the Lord hates that doctrine. It seems the Nicolaitans will make progress setting up unbiblical hierarchies and leaders over believers.

Command
*"**Repent**, or else I will come unto thee quickly, and will fight against them with the **sword of my mouth**." - Revelation 2:16 KJV*

They are commanded to repent, just like every other sinner. If those involved in fornication or an ungodly clerical hierarchy do not repent, the Lord will come against them with His Word. He will charge them with the spiritual crimes of which they are guilty. Unless they repent, their judgment is sure. That is a passage for the Tribulation because only at His second coming could Jesus fight against them with the "sword of my mouth," His words.

Closing
*"He that hath an ear, let him hear what the Spirit saith unto the churches; To him that **overcometh** will I give to **eat of the hidden manna**, and will*

give him a **white stone**, and in the stone a new name written, which no man knoweth saving he that receiveth it." - Revelation 2:17 KJV

Instead of eating "things sacrificed to idols," these believers were to follow their Messiah Jesus entirely, and He will give them "hidden manna," spiritual food from heaven. A new name on a white stone will be theirs, signifying innocence as their sins are washed away by the blood of Jesus Christ. Notice that only the overcomer makes it through the Tribulation to be rewarded. Again, that does not apply to us in the church, as we are all overcomers. None of us will suffer the Tribulation.

The Church in Thyatira
Greeting
"And unto the angel of the church in Thyatira write; These things saith the Son of God, who hath his eyes like unto a flame of fire, and his feet are like fine brass;" - Revelation 2:18 KJV

The Lord Jesus Christ greets these believers with the symbolism of "eyes like unto flames of fire" and "feet like fine brass." That means holiness and judgment. Jesus is ready to pronounce judgment upon this church, and it will not be pretty. That is another clue that this church is not part of the Body of Christ as we are not under any judgment or condemnation from the Lord. Paul writes in Romans chapter 8: "There is therefore now **no condemnation** to them which are in Christ Jesus, who walk not after the flesh, but after the Spirit." - Romans 8:1 KJV

Commendation
"*I know thy works, and **charity**, and **service**, and **faith**, and thy **patience**, and thy **works**; and the last to be **more than the first**.*" - *Revelation 2:19 KJV*

Jesus notes their faith, service, charity and general good works. Their last deeds are more fruitful than their first. They have a more organized, effective outreach to the community and are probably well respected. But there is another side to the coin.

Criticism
"*Notwithstanding I have a few things against thee, because thou sufferest that woman **Jezebel**, which calleth herself a **prophetess**, to teach and to seduce my servants to commit **fornication**, and to **eat things sacrificed unto idols**. And I gave her space to **repent** of her fornication; and she repented not. Behold, I will cast her into a **bed**, and them that commit adultery with her into **great tribulation**, except they repent of their deeds. And I will kill her **children** with death; and all the churches shall know that I am he which searcheth the reins and hearts: and I will give unto every one of you according to your works.*" - *Revelation 2:20-23 KJV*

Wow, Jesus is not happy with that bunch. It seems they have a lying, deceiving false prophetess in their midst seducing believers into fornication and eating things sacrificed to idols. We saw the same problem in the church of Pergamos. This prophetess is corrupting believers by appealing to their carnal desires and good food. That strategy still works very well today. If you want to fill your church, simply preach sermons that appeal to the flesh and serve food. There will be standing room only. I know; I have seen this in person.

Jesus gave the Jezebel prophetess much time to repent, but she did not. She likes her place of authority and her sin. Jezebel and her followers, children, will be cast into "great tribulation" if they do not repent. Interesting term, "great tribulation." Jesus used this term to refer to the last half of the 7-year Tribulation in Matthew 24:21. The ungodly believers at Thyatira and their prophetess were given the first half of the Tribulation to repent, but they did not. Now they will go through the great tribulation, the last half of the 7-year Tribulation. They will suffer and most likely die.

Commendation cont'd.
*"But unto you I say, and unto the rest in Thyatira, as many as **have not this doctrine**, and which have **not known the depths of Satan**, as they speak; I will put upon you none other burden. But that which ye have already **hold fast till I come**." - Revelation 2:24-25 KJV*

There were some true believers at Thyatira that did not follow this evil Jezebel. One would need to fall far into moral depravity and spiritual fornication to know the "depths of Satan." The depths of Satan can only be known during the last half of the Tribulation as that's when he is cast down to the earth, releasing his anger (Revelation 12). The genuine believer holds fast to the person of Jesus Christ and walks in His ways. Jesus would add no other burden on them. Having tolerated Jezebel and her ungodly followers was enough. Jesus encouraged them to "hold fast till I come." A command for those in the Tribulation as Jesus returns at the end of the seven years.

Closing
*"And he that **overcometh**, and keepeth my works unto the end, to him will I give **power over the nations**. And he shall rule them with a **rod of iron**, as the vessels of a potter shall they be broken to shivers: even as I received of my Father. And I will give him the **morning star**. He that hath an ear,*

let him hear what the Spirit saith unto the churches." - Revelation 2:26-29 KJV

The overcomer that remains faithful to the Lord Jesus Christ will be given the power to rule over the nations. He will have a "rod of iron" with which to judge. Wow, this is some severe authority being given to the overcoming Saints. Just as Jesus was given power over the nations and everything else, Jesus will pass control to the saints to rule with Him with a "rod of iron." Those will rule with Jesus in His earthly kingdom, which is for Israel, not the Body of Christ. Our inheritance is in heavenly places.

The term "morning star" is only used twice in Scripture. The other occurrence refers to Jesus himself as the "bright and morning star." We know the morning star is the planet Venus. It appears above the horizon before sunrise as a sign of hope for a new and better day. Jesus is that hope for all that believe, especially those enduring the Tribulation.

The Church at Sardis
Greeting
*"And unto the angel of the church in Sardis write; These things saith he that hath the seven Spirits of God, and the seven stars; I know thy works, that thou hast a name that thou livest, and art **dead**." - Revelation 3:1 KJV*

Do you think the folks at Sardis were a little unhappy when they read that greeting? I guess Jesus never took a course in How to Win Friends and Influence People. He just spoke the truth and let the chips fall where they may. We should do the same and ditch Political Correctness, but I digress. The "seven Spirits of God" are the seven angels of the churches as they are associated with the seven stars.

Jesus controls these angelic entities as He sees fit and for His good pleasure. He decides if the church at Sardis will stand or fall. It seems the church has a reputation for being alive. Believers were looking busy to the community. But Jesus said they are "dead". They are spiritually dead, so all the activity was in vain, being done in the flesh.

Command
*"Be watchful, and **strengthen the things which remain**, that are ready to die: for I have not found thy works **perfect before God.** Remember therefore how thou hast received and heard, and hold fast, and repent. If therefore thou shalt not watch, I will come on thee as a **thief**, and thou shalt not know what hour I will come upon thee." - Revelation 3:2-3 KJV*

There is some faint spark of life remaining. Jesus commands them to strengthen what little remains. Their works have not risen to God's standards, so they have their work cut out for them. Notice that their works are being evaluated for salvation, not their faith. They must return to the works of the law and faith in their Messiah, Jesus Christ, and repent. Otherwise, Jesus will come as a thief when you least expect Him. He is not coming for dinner, but in judgment on this dead church. That is another clue about a Tribulation church. Jesus will come as a thief to those that aren't watching. Jesus comes to us, the body of Christ, at the Rapture to take us home, not for judgment.

Commendation
*"Thou hast a **few names** even in Sardis which **have not defiled their garments**; and they shall walk with me in **white**: for they are **worthy**." - Revelation 3:4 KJV*

The true believers in Sardis battled trying to stay focused on Jesus in a dead church full of dead works. But they persisted with great love and patience. They have "not defiled their garments" with all the dead activities of the flesh. They have kept their garments white with the righteousness of Jesus Christ, and the Lord has declared them worthy. What a glorious declaration to be called "worthy" by the Lord Jesus Christ. They were a doer of the word, not a hearer only, as James commands. Notice the concentration on works with no mention of grace.

Closing
*"He that **overcometh**, the same shall be clothed in **white** raiment; and I will **not blot out his name out of the book of life**, but I will confess his name **before my Father**, and before his angels. He that hath an ear, let him hear what the Spirit saith unto the churches." - Revelation 3:5-6 KJV*

The overcomer will be clothed in white as he has remained faithful and true to the Lord Jesus Christ. Jesus will not "blot out his name out of the book of life." That might be what happens to the others that were declared "dead." That can only refer to Jews under the law. Our salvation in the body of Christ is sealed the moment we believe, not at the end of our life or the Rapture. As a true Christian, your name cannot be blotted out of the book of life.

The Church in Philadelphia
Greeting
*"And to the angel of the church in Philadelphia write; These things saith he that is holy, he that is true, he that hath the key of David, he that **openeth**, and no man **shutteth**; and **shutteth**, and no man **openeth**;" - Revelation 3:7 KJV*

This greeting is from He that is holy and true, having the key of David. What is the key of David? We read the prophecy in Isaiah.

"And the key of the house of David will I lay upon his shoulder; so he shall open, and none shall shut; and he shall shut, and none shall open." - Isaiah 22:22 KJV

Having the key of David puts you in charge of the kingdom and whatever you open stays open until you shut it. Whatever you close stays closed until you open it. Jesus has the key of David, so whatever He opens or shuts remains that way. He controls who enters the kingdom and who does not.

Commendation
*"I know thy works: behold, I have set before thee an **open door**, and no man can shut it: for thou hast a little strength, and hast **kept my word**, and hast not denied my name. Behold, I will make them of the synagogue of Satan, which say they are Jews, and are not, but do lie; behold, I will make them to come and worship before thy feet, and to know that I have loved thee." - Revelation 3:8-9 KJV*

Jesus has opened the door to the kingdom for this assembly of believers. Even though they have little strength, they have kept the faith and not denied or recanted their faith in the Lord Jesus Christ. It seems they are harassed by some Jewish collaborators working for the antichrist system. Someday these fake believers will worship the Lord Jesus Christ at the feet of the faithful followers of Messiah Jesus.

Promise
*"Because thou hast **kept** the word of my patience, I also will **keep thee from the hour of temptation**, which shall come upon **all the world**, to try them that dwell upon the earth." - Revelation 3:10 KJV*

That's a promise that during the 7-year Tribulation a remnant of Jews will be protected by the Lord during the last 3 ½ years

(Revelation 12:6). The believers at Philadelphia kept the Lord's Word, so in return, He will keep them from the "great tribulation," the last half of the Tribulation, which comes upon the whole world. The phrase "keep thee from" means "out of" and not "protected through." The "hour of temptation" that befalls the whole world is the "time of Jacob's trouble" or the "Great Tribulation," as Jesus called it, the last half of the 7-year Tribulation. So, the Lord has promised to keep faithful believers out of the great Tribulation. They are protected and kept separate by the Lord during that time. This is restated in Revelation chapter 12:

*"And to the woman were given two wings of a great eagle, that she might fly into the wilderness, into her place, where she is nourished for **a time, and times, and half a time**, from the face of the serpent."* – *Revelation 12:14 KJV*

The woman is the remnant of Israel. She is protected for 3 ½ years.

Command
*"Behold, **I come quickly**: hold that fast which thou hast, that no man take **thy crown**."* - *Revelation 3:11 KJV*

Jesus announces that He is coming quickly, meaning that the attendant events will happen quickly when He comes. There will be no time to prepare, so they must always be ready for His appearance. He also instructs believers to hold fast, hang in there and keep the faith. Protect their reward in heaven, stay on track with Jesus so they can't be deceived and cheated out of their crown.

Closing
"Him that overcometh will I make a pillar in the temple of my God, and he shall go no more out: and I will write upon him the name of my God, and

the name of the city of my God, which is new Jerusalem, which cometh down out of heaven from my God: and I will write upon him my new name. He that hath an ear, let him hear what the Spirit saith unto the churches." - Revelation 3:12-13 KJV

The overcomer will be a "pillar," a leader, a prominent person in the temple of the Lord during the Millennial Kingdom. Jesus said they would rule and reign with Him. They will have God's name written on them and their new home, the New Jerusalem.

The Church of the Laodiceans
Greeting
"And unto the angel of the church of the Laodiceans write; These things saith the Amen, the faithful and true witness, the beginning of the creation of God;" - Revelation 3:14 KJV

Notice that the previous six letters were to believers at a specific city. This letter is to the church of the Laodiceans, implying it was their assembly and not the Lords. These folks had fallen away from the Lord, as we will see. Here Jesus is a "faithful and true witness" against these people.

Criticism
"I know thy works, that thou art neither cold nor hot: I would thou wert cold or hot. So then because thou art lukewarm, and neither cold nor hot, I will spue thee out of my mouth." - Revelation 3:15-16 KJV

Not good! Jesus knows their works, and He is not pleased. They are lukewarm, neither hot nor cold. Hot water is useful for cooking and cleaning. Cold water is useful as a refreshing drink on a hot day. But lukewarm water is not useful for cooking or drinking. Jesus says that since the folks at Laodicea are lukewarm, they are of no use to Him. They make the Lord sick. So, He will vomit them out of His mouth. Wow, how bad could these people be? They are not bad by the world's standards, simply useless by God's standards.

"Because thou sayest, **I am rich**, *and increased with goods, and have need of nothing; and knowest not that thou art* **wretched, and miserable, and poor, and blind, and naked**.*" - Revelation 3:17 KJV*

These people think they are doing just great. They have money and stuff. They need nothing, or so they believe. The Lord Jesus has quite a different opinion. He is looking at their spiritual state of being and sees something bad. They are "wretched, and miserable, and poor, and blind, and naked" in His view. Their spiritual condition was precisely the opposite of what they thought. That's how deception works. Those deceived generally don't realize it until the Lord opens their eyes to their true state of deception.

Interesting that in this letter, people who thought they were doing just fine were doing very poorly. Contrast that with the letter to the church at Smyrna, who thought they were doing poorly, but Jesus said they were doing just fine and had no criticism or extra burden for them. We should keep this in mind when we start thinking we are doing ok. Stay in the word so you will have Jesus' perspective on your life.

"I counsel thee to buy of me **gold** *tried in the fire, that thou mayest be rich; and* **white raiment**, *that thou mayest be clothed, and that the shame of thy nakedness do not appear; and* **anoint thine eyes** *with eyesalve, that thou mayest see. As many as I love,* **I rebuke and chasten**: *be zealous therefore, and* **repent**.*" - Revelation 3:18-19 KJV*

Buy gold from the Lord. Gold is holiness. You buy it with your life and live it each day. With His gold, you are truly rich, rich in the things of the Lord, an eternal richness. White raiment speaks to righteousness. We are to be clothed in the righteousness of Christ that the nakedness of carnality and worldliness does not appear.

Eye salve was a product of Laodicea. They are to anoint their eyes with the word of God so they can see what they have become in God's sight. Remember, the Lord rebukes and chastens those he loves when they fall into sin, so repent early and save yourself a lot of grief.

"Behold, I stand at the door, and knock: if any man hear my voice, and open the door, I will come in to him, and will sup with him, and he with me." - Revelation 3:20 KJV

That is quite bizarre. Notice that Jesus is outside the church wanting to get in. They are so caught up in religion and worldly distractions they don't even realize Jesus has left the building. Don't let your life get in this shape. Don't be so busy that Jesus is left out. The most crucial aspect of your existence is your relationship with Jesus Christ.

Closing
*"To him that **overcometh** will I grant to sit with me in my throne, even as I also **overcame**, and am set down with my Father in his throne. He that hath an ear, let him hear what the Spirit saith unto the churches." - Revelation 3:21-22 KJV*

Only the overcomer in these letters will fare well at the second coming of Jesus Christ at the end of the Tribulation.

*"Wherefore gird up the loins of your mind, be sober, and **hope to the end** for the grace that is to be brought unto you **at the revelation of Jesus Christ**," - 1Pe 1:13 KJV*

Peter is instructing Jews during the Tribulation to "hope to the end." Grace comes to them at the "revelation of Jesus Christ," His second coming at the end of the Tribulation. We in the church, the body of Christ, receive grace the moment we believe.

The Church Age

Many believe that these seven churches represent the present Church Age. Nothing could be further from the truth. These seven churches, or assemblies, are Jewish believers during the Tribulation. They follow their Messiah Jesus and keep the commandments of the law. That's why the emphasis is on works and not grace. Some of the churches are under the condemnation of the Lord for their lack of good works. That cannot refer to us, the body of Christ, as Paul tells us:

*"There is therefore **now no condemnation** to them which are in Christ Jesus, who walk not after the flesh, but after the Spirit." - Rom 8:1 KJV*

CONFIDENTIAL

BRIEFING

Point of interest:

a) The seven churches are seven actual churches that existed at the time of John's writing.
b) The seven churches represent assemblies of Jewish believers following their Messiah Jesus and keeping the commandments of the Law of Moses hence the emphasis on works.
c) The only remaining application of the seven churches is to the 7-year Tribulation.

Come Up Hither

*"After this I looked, and, behold, a **door** was opened in heaven: and the first **voice** which I heard was as it were of a **trumpet** talking with me; which said, **Come up hither**, and I will shew thee things which must be **hereafter**." - Revelation 4:1 KJV*

John sees a "door opened in heaven," he hears a voice as a trumpet talking with him. Many equate this with the Rapture of the church. It sounds familiar, but there are several issues. The first is that the apostle John is an apostle to Israel, not the Church, the body of Christ. Paul is our apostle. That means that John would not be writing to the Body of Christ but Israel. Also, there is no resurrection of dead saints mentioned in the passage. For more information on how to rightly divide the book of Revelation, get my "Master Key to Understanding the Bible" book at:

https://www.amazon.com/dp/B0815V4JN6

*"For the Lord himself shall descend from heaven with a shout, with the **voice** of the archangel, and with the **trump** of God: and the dead in Christ shall rise first:" - 1 Thessalonians 4:16 KJV*

John hears a voice like a trumpet saying, "Come up hither." John is taken up to heaven to preview the events of the Day of the Lord and Jesus' second coming.

Jesus is the door. We can only enter through him. Jesus is the door in heaven through which John is entering.

*"Then said Jesus unto them again, Verily, verily, I say unto you, **I am the door** of the sheep. ... **I am the door.** by me if any man enter in, he shall be saved, and shall go in and out, and find pasture." - John 10:7, 9 KJV*
*"Jesus saith unto him, **I am the way, the truth, and the life**: no man cometh unto the Father, but by me." - John 14:6 KJV*

*"And **immediately** I was in the spirit: and, behold, a throne was set in heaven, and **one sat on the throne**. And he that sat was to look upon like a jasper and a sardine stone: and there was a rainbow round about the throne, in sight like unto an **emerald**." - Revelation 4:2-3 KJV*

Immediately John was taken in the Spirit. John sees one sitting on the throne. Previously, two were sitting on the throne, the Father and Jesus. Both are on the throne during the Dispensation of Grace.

Since Jesus is no longer on His Father's throne, something must have changed. Yes, indeed, the Church Age is over. The body of Christ has been Raptured. The saints are in heaven, and the 7-year Tribulation is about to start. Jesus is no longer at the Father's right hand interceding for the saints as we saints are no longer on earth dealing with the world, the flesh, and the devil. We are now in heaven.

The throne of God is beautiful beyond words. Full of diamonds (jasper), sardine stones (red), and green emeralds form a vibrant halo or rainbow around the throne.

*"And round about the throne were **four and twenty seats***: *and upon the seats I saw four and twenty elders sitting, clothed in **white raiment***, *and they had on their heads **crowns of gold***." - *Revelation 4:4 KJV*

That is a very remarkable verse that we will discuss in chapter five. Just note for now, there are "elders" sitting on thrones, clothed in white and having gold crowns. Since they are called elders, they represent a group from earth whose work is finished as they are seated and crowned.

"And out of the throne proceeded lightnings and thunderings and voices: and there were seven lamps of fire burning before the throne, which are the seven Spirits of God." - Revelation 4:5 KJV

There is a great deal of activity around the throne of God. The power and majesty of God cannot be restrained; it must burst forth. There are seven lamps of fire before the throne. These are the seven lampstands we read about in chapter one representing the seven churches. The seven spirits could be the seven angels to the churches.

Four Living Creatures

*"And before the throne there was a **sea of glass** like unto crystal: and in the midst of the throne, and round about the throne, were **four beasts** full of eyes before and behind." - Revelation 4:6 KJV*

There is a sea of glass before the throne. Transparent in nature and apparently empty. It being empty is important as we will read more about the "sea of glass" later. Near the throne, there are four beasts, living creatures, full of eyes front and back. They see everything that happens in the proximity of God's throne. They also lead the praise and worship by continually proclaiming the holiness of God. "Holy, Holy, Holy, Lord God Almighty, which was, and is, and is to come."

*"And the first beast was like a **lion**, and the second beast like a **calf**, and the third beast had a face as a **man**, and the fourth beast was like a flying **eagle**. And the four beasts had each of them six wings about him; and they were full of eyes within: and they rest not day and night, saying, Holy, holy, holy, Lord God Almighty, which was, and is, and is to come." - Revelation 4:7-8 KJV*

The four faces of the living creatures could represent the four gospels as each presents Jesus Christ in a different light, reflecting some aspect of His being and ministry.

Face	Gospel	Attribute	Audience
Lion	Matthew	Lion of the tribe of Judah, King of the Jews	The Jews
Calf	Mark	The Calf or Ox is for service and sacrifice. Jesus as the servant and sacrifice for sin	Simple gospel for the Romans
Man	Luke	The man Jesus Christ as a historical figure	Detailed gospel for the Greeks
Eagle	John	Emblem of Royalty soaring in the clouds above humanity	For all showing Jesus as God in the flesh

*"And when those **beasts** give glory and honour and thanks to him that sat on the throne, who liveth for ever and ever, The **four and twenty elders** fall down before him that sat on the throne, and **worship him** that liveth for ever and ever, and **cast their crowns before the throne**, saying, Thou art worthy, O Lord, to receive glory and honour and power: for **thou hast created all things**, and for thy pleasure they are and were **created**."* - *Revelation 4:9-11 KJV*

The four living creatures continue to give praise, glory, and honor to God Almighty, the Father, sitting on the throne. The twenty-four elders join in the chorus and worship God Almighty by casting their gold crowns before the throne. They worship the Lord God as Creator of all things. That is the basic level of understanding and worship as all humans can know God as the Creator even if they were never exposed to the gospel. The Apostle Paul makes this clear in the first chapter of his book to the Romans.

*"For the invisible things of him from the **creation of the world** are clearly seen, being understood by the **things that are made**, even his eternal power and Godhead; so that they are without excuse:"* - *Romans 1:20 KJV*

*"Who changed the truth of God into a lie and worshipped and served the **creature** more than the **Creator**, who is blessed forever. Amen."* - *Romans 1:25 KJV*

The knowledge of God as Creator is in every man, but some ignore and hate that knowledge moving away from God to false religions based on works and earth worship.

The Sealed Book

*"And I saw in the right hand of him that sat on the throne a **book written within and on the backside, sealed with seven seals**. And I saw a strong angel proclaiming with a loud voice, **Who is worthy to open the book, and to loose the seals thereof**?" - Revelation 5:1-2 KJV*

As "God the Father" sits on the throne, He holds a book in His right hand. This book has writing on the outside cover and is sealed with seven seals. Can you imagine the importance of this book? God Almighty is holding it. Of all the books in the universe, what could this be? What is its preeminence? This book could be a legal document. The writing on the cover states the legal requirements that must be met by the person desiring to open the book.

Many believe, as I do, that this book is the title deed to planet earth. God gave Adam a 6000-year lease on planet earth, granting him dominion over the world and all its creatures. When Adam sinned against the Lord God by obeying the serpent, Satan, Adam relinquished that lease to the devil. That's why Satan is called the "prince of this world" (John 14:30). Well, the 6000-year lease is up, and someone must be found legally qualified to take possession of the earth. He must be qualified to break the seals and open the book.

*"And **no man** in heaven, nor in earth, neither under the earth, was able to open the book, neither to look thereon. And I **wept much**, because **no man was found worthy** to open and to read the book, neither to look thereon." - Revelation 5:3-4 KJV*

John knows the nature of this book and the importance of finding someone to open it. But no one could be found on all the earth. They even looked under the earth and in heaven for a man to open the book, but no man was found worthy. John is distraught by this development. The translators of the KJB are very polite here as describing John as merely weeping. John is upset to the point of almost convulsing. He knows that all is lost to the forces of darkness unless someone can open the book and break the seals to take possession of the earth from Satan.

*"And one of the **elders** saith unto me, **Weep not** behold, the **Lion of the tribe of Juda, the Root of David**, hath prevailed to **open the book**, and to **loose the seven seals** thereof." - Revelation 5:5 KJV*

The situation seems desperate, almost hopeless. No man can be found to open the sealed book. Then one of the elders pipes up, "Weep not," stop crying. Notice that an "elder" talks with John, not an angel or one of the four living creatures. The elders are not weeping as they seem to know what the book is and who can open it. The elder proclaims there is one that is legally qualified to open the book and break the seals. Since the fall of humanity came through the man Adam, only another man could correct Adam's failure. Only a man could redeem the descendants of Adam and the world. The man, Jesus Christ.

The elder declares the "Lion of the tribe of Juda, the Root of David" can open the book. We instantly know this is the Lord Jesus Christ but notice the names. They are not Church type names. They are Jewish in nature, meaning that Jesus is dealing with the Jews, not the Church. The "Lion of the tribe of Juda" is entirely Jewish, having little meaning to Gentiles, which the church primarily consists of. The "Root of David" is also wholly Jewish as the promises to King David were for the Jews; Gentiles were excluded. So, the opening of the book and breaking the seals pertain to the Jews, to Israel, not the Church. That is another one of those little clues that help us discern what is happening and who's involved.

*"And I beheld, and, lo, in the **midst of the throne** and of the **four beasts**, and in the **midst of the elders**, stood a **Lamb** as it had been slain, having **seven horns** and **seven eyes**, which are the seven Spirits of God sent forth into all the earth. And he came and **took the book out of the right hand** of him that sat upon the throne."* - Revelation 5:6-7 KJV

Finally, right there among them is the one who can open the book. Right before the throne, among the living creatures and the elders. He is called the "Lamb" that appears to have been slain. He is Jesus Christ, the sacrificial Lamb of God who died on the cross for the world's sin. But why was Jesus' sacrificial death on the cross sufficient for Him to open the book, the title deed of the earth?

In the gospel of John, we read a very familiar verse.

*"For God so **loved the world**, that **he gave** his only begotten Son, that whosoever believeth in him should not perish, but have everlasting life. For God sent not his Son into the world to condemn the world; but that **the world through him might be saved**."* - John 3:16-17 KJV

God the Father did not send Jesus to only die for the sins of humankind. Jesus died for the "world." That includes not only humanity but the entire creation that fell under the curse after Adam sinned.

*"And unto Adam he said, Because thou hast hearkened unto the voice of thy wife, and hast eaten of the tree, of which I commanded thee, saying, Thou shalt not eat of it: **cursed is the ground for thy sake; in sorrow shalt thou eat of it all the days of thy life**,"* - Genesis 3:17 KJV

Both man and earth are under the curse of sin. That is why John's gospel declares that "God so loved the world." The "world," both humanity and planet earth, are his creation, and He will redeem them both through Jesus Christ. Therefore, Jesus has the legal right to open the book and break the seals. He is the redeemer of all God's creation, not just sinful men.

John depicts Jesus as having "seven horns" and "seven eyes." Horns are symbolic of power. Seven is the number of perfection. Jesus is the perfect, all-powerful Son of God, the second person of the Trinity. Seven eyes are symbolic of the omniscience of God, knowing and seeing everything. The "seven Spirits of God" could again reference the seven angels of the seven churches.

The 24 Elders

*"And when he had taken the book, the four beasts and **four and twenty elders fell down before the Lamb**, having every one of them harps, and golden vials full of odours, which are the prayers of saints. And **they sung a new song**, saying, Thou art worthy to take the book, and to open the seals thereof: for thou wast slain, and **hast redeemed us to God by thy blood out of every kindred, and tongue, and people, and nation**, And hast made us unto our God **kings and priests**: and we shall **reign on the earth**." - Revelation 5:8-10 KJV*

Again, we see the 24 elders worshipping the Lamb, the Lord Jesus Christ. They worship with music and the prayers of the saints. But they are singing a "new song." They praise the Lord that He has redeemed them by His blood from "every kindred, and tongue, and people, and nation." These are Jews delivered from the nations in which they were scattered.

The number 24 has no significance to the church, the body of Christ, but it does to the Jews. There were 12 Jewish apostles of the Lord

Jesus and 12 patriarchs of the 12 tribes of Israel. Also, there are 12 gates for the 12 tribes and 12 foundations for the 12 apostles in the New Jerusalem. That accounts for the 24 elders. They are the elders of Israel.

*"And I beheld, and I heard the voice of many angels round about the throne and the beasts and the elders: and the number of them was **ten thousand times ten thousand, and thousands of thousands**, Saying with a loud voice, Worthy is the Lamb that was slain to receive power, and riches, and wisdom, and strength, and honour, and glory, and blessing. - Revelation 5:11-12 KJV*

It seems like everybody is invited to this praise and worship service. The living creatures, the 24 elders, and a myriad of angels. 10,000 x 10,000 = 100,000,000 (one hundred million). Multiply that by "thousands of thousands"; perhaps billions of angels are there. The entire "heavenly host" is present to witness what comes next in chapter six.

"And every creature which is in heaven, and on the earth, and under the earth, and such as are in the sea, and all that are in them, heard I saying, Blessing, and honour, and glory, and power, be unto him that sitteth upon the throne, and unto the Lamb for ever and ever. And the four beasts said, Amen. And the four and twenty elders fell down and worshipped him that liveth for ever and ever." - Revelation 5:13-14 KJV

The First Six Seals
White Horse Rider
*"And I saw when the **Lamb opened one of the seals**, and I heard, as it were the noise of thunder, one of the four beasts saying, **Come and see**. And I saw, and behold a **white horse**: and he that sat on him had a **bow**,*

and a **crown** was given unto him: and he went forth **conquering, and to conquer.**" - Revelation 6:1-2 KJV

Jesus has possession of the book with seven seals, and here in chapter six, He breaks the first seal. One of the four living creatures tells John to "come and see." John sees a rider on a white horse going forth upon the earth. That rider is the first of the infamous Four Horsemen of the Apocalypse. The rider on the white horse has a bow but no arrows signifying that he is not a warrior but a military strategist. He is a clever, calculating tactician using any means to achieve his goal of conquering nations. That is what he will do and why he is sent forth "to conquer." The Antichrist comes on the world scene riding a white horse, symbolic of someone coming to save the day and solve a significant problem. In this case, he confirms a peace covenant as we read in Daniel chapter 9.

"And he shall **confirm the covenant with many for one week** and in the midst of the week he shall cause the sacrifice and the oblation to cease..." - Daniel 9:27 KJV

"And through his **policy** also he shall cause **craft to prosper** in his hand; and he shall magnify himself in his heart, and **by peace shall destroy many**: he shall also stand up against the Prince of princes; but he shall be broken without hand." - Daniel 8:25 KJV

The Antichrist will "confirm" a peace treaty with Israel and many other nations in the Middle East. Part of this treaty will be the re-establishment of the covenant of Moses. Through his "policy" of false peace, there will be a short economic boom in the Middle East. The Jews will build the 3rd Temple, re-institute the Priesthood and commence animal sacrifices. That has already begun showing the closeness of this covenant being signed. The artifacts for Temple worship are completed. The Priesthood and the High Priest have already been chosen and confirmed by the newly formed Sanhedrin. We are living in the last of the last days just prior to the start of the Tribulation.

To the Antichrist, peace is a weapon. How can peace be used as a weapon? First, you make a peace treaty with your adversary. Then you lull them to sleep with trade agreements and other economic or social cooperation. Then when they least expect it, you hit them with a surprise attack, catch them completely off guard and defeat them. That is a straightforward, simple strategy; it just takes a little time. That is what the Antichrist will do as he breaks the 7-year covenant with Israel in the "midst," 3 ½ years into the process. The white horse rider will ride through the entire 7-year Tribulation.

Red Horse Rider

*"And when he had opened the **second seal**, I heard the second beast say, Come and see. And there went out another horse that was **red**: and power was given to him that sat thereon **to take peace from the earth**, and that they should **kill one another**: and there was given unto him a **great sword**." - Revelation 6:3-4 KJV*

The second horseman rides to curse the earth with war. He has the power to "take peace from the earth." Notice that he does not start wars but removes peace. After removing peace from the entire earth, men will start wars. Military wars, civil wars, religious wars, and race wars will rage in the absence of peace. Throughout history, a plethora of wars of every type imaginable has plagued humanity. The curse of the red horse rider will accelerate and exacerbate man's hatred for his fellow man to the point of global chaos and calamity. The red horse rider will continue to take peace from the earth for the duration of the 7-year Tribulation. Whatever peace might come to the world during this time will be a false peace.

The Black Horse Rider

*"And when he had opened the **third seal**, I heard the third beast say, Come and see. And I beheld, and lo a **black horse**; and he that sat on him had a **pair of balances** in his hand. And I heard a voice in the midst of the four beasts say, A **measure of wheat for a penny**, and **three measures of barley for a penny**, and see thou **hurt not the oil and the wine**." - Revelation 6:5-6 KJV*

What follows war is scarcity, famine, and disease. This rider has a "pair of balances" to measure food as it is being rationed. A measure of food for one person will cost a day's wage. A family will get three measures of barley, barely enough to survive. Chaos will increase as people fight and kill for their next meal. Starving, ungodly people will do anything for food. Many will die, and diseases (pestilence) will be epidemic. Famine and disease will increase throughout the 7-year tribulation, especially for those who do not take the beast's mark, making them unable to buy and sell via normal channels. Oh, and don't forget to wear your mask.

The Pale Horse Rider

*"And when he had opened the **fourth seal**, I heard the voice of the fourth beast say, Come and see. And I looked, and behold a **pale horse**: and his name that sat on him was **Death**, and **Hell followed with him**. And power was given unto them over the **fourth part of the earth**, to kill with **sword**, and with **hunger**, and with **death**, and with the **beasts of the earth**." - Revelation 6:7-8 KJV*

What follows famine, starvation, and disease? Death. The "pale" horse is a "pale green" horse, a sickly-looking color. This rider has a name, Death. His companion Hell follows close behind him. Most that die during the 7-year Tribulation will enter hell.

These four horsemen have power over one-fourth of the people on earth. That's 2 billion people. They kill with the sword, a reference to the red horse rider. Hunger and starvation will kill a great many, a reference to the black horse rider. And Death, the rider of the pale horse, will kill through the "beasts of the earth" which are not only animals but biological weapons of bacteria and viruses. We have recently witnessed a dress rehearsal of using biological weapons globally with the recent pandemic. This level of death and destruction is unimaginable. Jesus said this would be the worst period to befall planet earth, and if he did not cut those days short, no one would survive. These are extinction-level events that culminate at the second coming of Jesus Christ.

Martyrs

*"And when he had opened the **fifth seal**, I saw under the altar the souls of them that were **slain for the word of God**, and for the testimony which they held: And they cried with a loud voice, saying, How long, O Lord, holy and true, dost thou not **judge and avenge our blood on them that dwell on the earth**? And white robes were given unto every one of them; and it was said unto them, that they should **rest yet for a little season**, until their fellow servants also and their brethren, that **should be killed as they** were, should be fulfilled."* - Revelation 6:9-11 KJV

The fifth seal speaks to martyrs of Jesus Christ, "slain for the word of God." They are seen under the altar, perhaps in the sea of glass mentioned earlier. Interesting that they cry out to the Lord for vengeance. When Stephen was martyred, he said, "forgive them for they know not what they do." These souls under the altar are looking for retribution, not grace and mercy. Another hint that the Church

186

Age is over. These "souls" have a spiritual body that can wear a white robe, but they will not receive their glorified bodies until after the second coming of Jesus Christ. They are not Christians, the body of Christ. They are Jews martyred during the Tribulation.

Jesus quiets them, saying they should rest for a while until the others who will be martyred join them. The martyrdom of believers will continue for the duration of the 7-year Tribulation.

Catastrophic Events
*"And I beheld when he had opened the **sixth seal**, and, lo, there was a **great earthquake**; and the **sun became black** as sackcloth of hair, and the **moon became as blood**; And the **stars of heaven fell** unto the earth, even as a fig tree casteth her untimely figs, when she is shaken of a mighty wind. And the **heaven departed** as a scroll when it is rolled together; and **every mountain and island were moved out of their places**."* - Revelation 6:12-14 KJV

The events that proceed from the sixth seal are beyond our imagination as we have nothing which to compare. We've all seen footage of the tsunami, volcanos, and hurricanes, but nothing on the scale of this sixth seal. It is difficult to imagine these cosmic events involving the sun, moon, stars, and a "great earthquake." A great earthquake could open huge cracks in the earth's surface releasing vast amounts of steam, ash, and debris into the atmosphere. That might account for the sun and moon being darkened, but what about the stars falling from heaven? A solar eclipse could block the sun, or a lunar eclipse could turn the moon blood-red but not simultaneously. There must be a third object in the heavens that blocks the sun turning it black and illuminates a blood-red moon from refracted sun light.

Enter Planet 7X (Planet X, Nibiru, binary star, brown dwarf, etc.). Gill Broussard has done incredible work on Planet 7X, and you can download his charts at www.planet7x.net. He relates the previous passings of Planet 7X to Bible events that mere earthly phenomena cannot explain. Get Gill's work; it is both fascinating and well researched.

Luke 21:26

Men's hearts failing them for fear, and for looking after those things which are coming on the earth: for the powers of heaven shall be shaken.

Gill Broussard, Planet 7X Charts, May 2015

A larger-than-earth planetary object passing near earth would have devastating consequences. The effect of its gravity, electromagnetic force, and plasma debris trail could easily cause all the results detailed in the passage of scripture. The sun could be blocked, blackened as the object approaches earth while turning the moon blood-red from refracted sunlight. A blackened sun would not be seen against black space. We would have total darkness on earth just as when Jesus was crucified. At the same time, the moon would be blood red. At the crucifixion, there were three hours of darkness. That cannot be an eclipse as they last only 7-10 minutes.

The extreme forces exerted upon the earth could easily cause a "great earthquake" globally. The "stars of heaven fell unto the earth" could be a massive meteor shower from the debris trail of Planet 7X, or it could appear as the stars falling if the earth's axis is altered or also if the rotation speed is increased. Mountains collapsing and islands moving could be from the great earthquake and the extreme forces of Planet 7X as it passes near to earth.

I am not trying to explain away the Power of God with natural phenomena. But natural forces are just some of God's weapons He uses to bring the people of earth to repentance. Planet 7X is just one of God's many weapons of judgment.

This passage in Revelation is from the book of Joel.

"And I will shew wonders in the heavens and in the earth, blood, and fire, and pillars of smoke. The sun shall be turned into darkness, and the moon into blood, before the great and the terrible day of the LORD come." - Joel 2:30-31 KJV

Notice these events precede the "great and the terrible day of the Lord." That is a reference to the last half of the 7-year Tribulation, which Jesus referred to as the "great tribulation." So, these events occur during the first half of the 7-year Tribulation. The Apostle Peter also quotes Joel in Acts chapter 2.

*"And the kings of the earth, and the great men, and the rich men, and the chief captains, and the mighty men, and every bondman, and every free man, **hid themselves in the dens and in the rocks of the mountains;** And said to the mountains and rocks, Fall on us, and hide us from the face of him that sitteth on the throne, and from the **wrath of the Lamb: For the***

great day of his wrath is come, and who shall be able to stand?" - Revelation 6:15-17 KJV

When this devastation arrives, everyone will be looking for a place to hide. The elites have been building underground bunkers for decades, preparing for such an occurrence. The government has enormous underground facilities across the country stocked with food and water for years. Isaiah the Prophet spoke of this also.

"And they shall go into the **holes of the rocks**, and into the **caves of the earth**, for **fear of the LORD**, and for the glory of his majesty, when he ariseth to **shake terribly the earth**. ... To go into the clefts of the rocks, and into the tops of the ragged rocks, for fear of the LORD, and for the glory of his majesty, when he ariseth to **shake terribly the earth**." - Isaiah 2:19, 21 KJV

That is precisely what will happen when Planet 7X passes; the earth will "shake terribly." The ungodly will go underground for "fear of the LORD," thinking they can somehow escape the shaking and not gaze upon "the glory of His majesty" that exposes and illuminates their sin.

They say, "hide us from the face of him that sitteth on the throne, and from the wrath of the Lamb: For the great day of his wrath is come; and who shall be able to stand." The ungodly know what is happening. They are hiding from the "wrath of the Lamb," the wrath of the Lord Jesus Christ as He is opening the seals. They know they are ungodly. They know His wrath has come upon them. They know deep in their hearts they cannot stand against Him. Notice that the "wrath of the Lamb" begins with the seven seals. Some think the wrath starts later in the book with the seven bowls or vials of wrath, but that is wrong. Chapter six of Revelation begins the "wrath of the Lamb." Yet another clue that the Church age is over. The Church has already been Raptured as we are not destined for wrath, especially the wrath of the Lamb as we are the Body of Christ.

"Much more then, being now justified by his blood, we shall be saved from wrath through him." - Romans 5:9 KJV

"For God hath not appointed us to wrath, but to obtain salvation by our Lord Jesus Christ," - 1 Thessalonians 5:9 KJV

The fact that the wrath of the Lamb starts in chapter 6 is excellent proof of the pretribulation rapture. We, the church, are the body of Christ. Would Jesus subject His own body to His wrath? Self-inflicted pain is a mental disorder. The idea that Jesus would torture and kill members of His own body is ludicrous.

BRIEFING

Point of interest:
a) the seven seals judgments are opened in succession but persist to the end of the 7-year tribulation.
b) martyrs for Jesus Christ are multitude in the last 3-½ years of the tribulation.
c) earthquakes, cosmic anomalies, huge storms, great hail, volcanic activity, intense meteor activity also frequent during the 7-year tribulation.
d) the 24 elders are symbolic of Israel.

Person of interest:

a) The white horse rider, aka the Antichrist, comes on the world scene via a peace agreement with Israel.

Discussion:

Chapter 6 marks the beginning of the 7-year Tribulation. The scene is heaven and a sealed scroll that no one is qualified to open. John is distraught that none can open the scroll. But the Lamb, Jesus Christ, can open the scroll as He paid the price with His blood. Interesting that one of the elders knew what was happening and was not at all upset. He understands that Jesus died on the cross not just for believers but for the entire cursed world. That was probably one of the 12 disciples. After Jesus takes the scroll from the Father, He begins breaking the seals on the scroll. Each seal brings a judgment to the earth. The white horse rider is the Antichrist bringing a false peace. The red horse rider brings takes peace from the earth. The black horse rider brings famine and disease. The pale horse rider, Death, brings death, and his sidekick Hell takes their souls. The four horsemen of the Apocalypse, strange cosmological events, and martyrs mark the beginning. Things are about to get much worse.

The 144,000 Witnesses

*"And after these things I saw four angels standing on the four corners of the earth, holding the **four winds of the earth**, that the wind should not blow on the earth, nor on the sea, nor on any tree. And I saw another angel ascending from the east, having the **seal of the living God**: and he cried with a loud voice to the four angels, to whom it was given to **hurt the earth and the sea**, Saying, **Hurt not** the earth, neither the sea, nor the trees, till we have **sealed the servants of our God in their foreheads**." - Revelation 7:1-3 KJV*

"After these things" simply refers to what John sees next. It does not mean that the previous six seals have run their course. The six seals persist throughout the 7-year Tribulation. "Four angels" are at the four cardinal points of a compass regarding Israel. One each to the north, south, east, and west. They are holding back the "four winds of the earth" and sea. The four winds of chaos, calamity, and judgment are about to blow on the earth and sea.

Another angel appears with the "seal of the living God." He instructs the first four angels not to release their destructive winds until he has "sealed the servants of our God in their foreheads." Once the "servants" or messengers of God are "sealed", then the four winds can blow. These servants are sealed in their "foreheads" with an externally visible seal. What this seal looks like, we cannot know, but those that see the seal at that time will know what it represents, witnesses for the Lord Jesus Christ.

In Ezekiel chapter 9 there was a similar situation where a remnant was sealed.

"And the LORD said unto him, Go through the midst of the city, through the midst of Jerusalem, and set a mark upon the foreheads of the men that sigh and that cry for all the abominations that be done in the midst thereof." Ezekiel 9:4 KJV

In Jerusalem, there were people appalled and sorrowed by the corruption and abominations that plagued the nation. Sound familiar? Many in America are saddened by the unprecedented apostasy in the church and the corruption and abuse of power in government and media. The Jewish remnant wept and groaned over the destruction and desolation that was coming upon them. Ezekiel sends six men through the city of Jerusalem, marking the foreheads of that remnant weeping over the city. God placed His seal upon the faithful remnant in Ezekiel's day just as He will place His seal upon a remnant in the last days.

Even today in the body of Christ, we are sealed by the Holy Spirit.

*"Who hath also **sealed** us, and given the earnest of the Spirit in our hearts."*
- 2 Corinthians 1:22 KJV

*"In whom ye also trusted, after that ye heard the word of truth, the gospel of your salvation: in whom also after that ye believed, ye were **sealed** with that holy Spirit of promise," - Ephesians 1:13 KJV*

*"And grieve not the holy Spirit of God, whereby ye are **sealed** unto the day of redemption." - Ephesians 4:30 KJV*

We are "sealed" unto the "day of redemption," that being the Rapture of the Church when our bodies are finally changed into glorified bodies completing the three stages of our redemption: soul, spirit, and body.

After God's servants are sealed, then the judgments of the 7-year Tribulation will continue. 144,000 witnesses, 12,000 from each tribe.

"And I heard the number of them which were sealed: and there were sealed an hundred and forty and four thousand of all the tribes of the children of Israel.
Of the tribe of Juda were sealed twelve thousand.
Of the tribe of Reuben were sealed twelve thousand.
Of the tribe of Gad were sealed twelve thousand.
Of the tribe of Aser were sealed twelve thousand.
Of the tribe of Nepthalim were sealed twelve thousand.

Of the tribe of Manasses were sealed twelve thousand.
Of the tribe of Simeon were sealed twelve thousand.
Of the tribe of Levi were sealed twelve thousand.
Of the tribe of Issachar were sealed twelve thousand.
Of the tribe of Zabulon were sealed twelve thousand.
Of the tribe of Joseph were sealed twelve thousand.
Of the tribe of Benjamin were sealed twelve thousand." - Revelation 7:4-8
KJV

Now that the 144,000 are sealed on earth, the four winds of heaven held back by the four angels can blow, and the judgments continue. The scene moves back to heaven with another large group of believers.

The Tribulation Saints

"After this I beheld, and, lo, a great multitude, which no man could number, of all nations, and kindreds, and people, and tongues, stood before the throne, and before the Lamb, clothed with white robes, and palms in their hands; And cried with a loud voice, saying, Salvation to our God which sitteth upon the throne, and unto the Lamb." - Revelation 7:9-10 KJV

This "great multitude" of believers come from all "nations," "kindreds," "people," and "tongues" (languages). They are mostly Jews with a small number of Gentiles. That is a preview of those martyred for Jesus Christ during the 7-year Tribulation, as we will see.

"And all the angels stood round about the throne, and about the elders and the four beasts, and fell before the throne on their faces, and worshipped God, Saying, Amen: Blessing, and glory, and wisdom, and thanksgiving, and

honour, and power, and might, be unto our God for ever and ever. Amen."
- Revelation 7:11-12 KJV

Another praise and worship service ignites with the myriad of believers, and angelic hosts gathered around the throne of God. Notice that the "elders" are mentioned as a separate group from the "great multitude" of the previous verse. They are not the same.

"And one of the elders answered, saying unto me, What are these which are arrayed in white robes? and whence came they? And I said unto him, Sir, thou knowest. And he said to me, These are they which came out of great tribulation, and have washed their robes, and made them white in the blood of the Lamb." - Revelation 7:13-14 KJV

Here again, the elder has the answer. He asks John, who is this "great multitude" arrayed in white robes from verse 9, and where did they originate? John does not know. The elder answers his question. "These are they which came out of great tribulation." These are martyred saints from the 7-year Tribulation, specifically the last half. A preview is given to John of things to come as this group will not be complete until the end of the seven years. Do not confuse these "Tribulation Saints" with the Church Saints as they are two distinct groups of believers. Church saints were all raptured before the 7-year Tribulation. Tribulation saints are those martyred during the 7-year Tribulation.

"Therefore are they before the throne of God, and serve him day and night in his temple: and he that sitteth on the throne shall dwell among them. They shall hunger no more, neither thirst any more; neither shall the sun light on them, nor any heat. For the Lamb which is in the midst of the throne shall feed them, and shall lead them unto living fountains of waters: and God shall wipe away all tears from their eyes." - Revelation 7:15-17 KJV

Their trials and afflictions on earth are through. They are with the Lord Jesus Christ in heaven. No more hunger or thirst. No more scorching sunlight or heat. These are specific characteristics of the 7-year Tribulation. There is a great heat that comes upon the earth in chapter 16 that will affect everyone. These saints no longer endure such torment. They are now with Jesus Christ, and He will give them fountains of living water which was a scarcity on earth. Jesus will wipe away their tears flowing from their suffering and seeing others die without Christ slipping into the hands of the Pale Horse Rider.

THE MANY MARTYRS SEEN IN HEAVEN CAME OUT OF 'GREAT TRIBULATION,' THESE ARE NOT THE CHURCH SAINTS, THEY ARE THE MARTYRS FROM THE 7-YEAR TRIBULATION.

The Seventh Seal

"And when he had opened the seventh seal, there was silence in heaven about the space of half an hour. And I saw the seven angels which stood before God; and to them were given seven trumpets." - Revelation 8:1-2 KJV

When the Lord Jesus Christ opened the seventh seal, there was silence in heaven for half an hour. Quite a contrast to what we have seen with the singing, praise, and worship. We can't say for sure, but it seems to me that the angelic host, the elders, and the living creatures are overwhelmed by what they see coming. They could have thought the seven seals would be the totality of the judgments, the wrath of the Lamb. But now, they are greeted with another set of seven judgments worse than the seals. Seven angels come forth, and they are given seven trumpets of judgment. That is not good as a trumpet sounds the alarm and warning that something terrible will happen. Such is the case with these seven.

"And another angel came and stood at the altar, having a golden censer; and there was given unto him much incense, that he should offer it with the prayers of all saints upon the golden altar which was before the throne. And the smoke of the incense, which came with the prayers of the saints, ascended up before God out of the angel's hand. And the angel took the censer, and filled it with fire of the altar, and cast it into the earth: and there were voices, and thunderings, and lightnings, and an earthquake." - Revelation 8:3-5 KJV

Before the trumpets begin to blow, another angel appears with a golden censer. The Temple Institute in Jerusalem has re-created many of the vessels and instruments used in Temple ceremonies. They will be put to use when the third temple is constructed. All the vessels of the earthly temple are mere replicas of the originals in heaven.

The angel presents to God the incense and the "prayers of all saints," those believers in the 7-year Tribulation. Then the angel fills the censer with fire from the alter of incense before God and casts it down to the earth. Another judgment of fire revealing God's wrath towards ungodly men. That was accompanied by voices, and thunderings, and lightning, and another earthquake. We know the earthquake will be great; otherwise, there would be no need to mention it. There are several great earthquakes during the 7-year Tribulation causing massive destruction on an unparalleled scale.

The Seven Trumpets

"And the seven angels which had the seven trumpets prepared themselves to sound. The first angel sounded, and there followed hail and fire mingled with blood, and they were cast upon the earth: and the third part of trees was burnt up, and all green grass was burnt up." - Revelation 8:6-7 KJV

The sounding of the first trumpet brings "hail and fire mingled with blood." That is reminiscent of Moses in Egypt before the Exodus.

"And Moses stretched forth his rod toward heaven: and the LORD sent thunder and hail, and the fire ran along upon the ground; and the LORD rained hail upon the land of Egypt." - Exodus 9:23 KJV

Hail and fire are mentioned several times in the Old Testament.

"The LORD also thundered in the heavens, and the Highest gave his voice; hail stones and coals of fire." - Psalm 18:13 KJV

"He gave them hail for rain, and flaming fire in their land." - Psalm 105:32 KJV

"Fire, and hail; snow, and vapour; stormy wind fulfilling his word:" - Psalm 148:8 KJV

But in Revelation, the hail and fire are mingled with blood, the blood of ungodly people. Usual pea-sized hail is not large enough to injure people to the point of bleeding or even death. This hail severely pummels people causing their blood to flow in the streets. Because of the fire, a third of the trees are burned up, and all the grass is burned. That is very interesting and begs the question, how are only a third of the trees consumed by fire. I will give a possible scenario later in the trumpet discussion.

"And the second angel sounded, and as it were a great mountain burning with fire was cast into the sea: and the third part of the sea became blood; And the third part of the creatures which were in the sea, and had life, died; and the third part of the ships were destroyed." - Revelation 8:8-9 KJV

A mountain in scripture generally means an actual physical mountain or a kingdom based on the context. Here it seems like a real physical mountain is intended. This mountain is burning with fire which is a volcano erupting. This volcanic eruption is so violent that a massive portion of the volcano is "cast into the sea." The Mediterranean Sea is the probable victim of this disaster, most likely the eastern third. There are many volcanoes in and around the Mediterranean Sea. Mt. Etna on Sicily could be a likely suspect as it is currently active. There are 24 large volcanoes under the waters of the Mediterranean Sea. Many are rumbling with signs of activity. The Super Volcano Campi Flegrei near Naples shows signs of awakening after being dormant for nearly 500 years. Campi Flegrei is credited as the largest eruption in recorded history, with an active eruption lasting eight days.

This coming massive volcanic eruption turns a third of the sea to blood with ash and debris. This toxic pollution kills one-third of the sea life and destroys a third of the ships in the area. In our modern era, we have never seen this level of volcanic destruction. That will dwarf Mt. St. Helens.

*"And the **third angel sounded**, and there fell a **great star** from heaven, **burning** as it were a lamp, and it fell upon the **third part of the rivers**, and upon the fountains of waters; And the name of the star is called Wormwood: and the third part of the waters became wormwood; and many men died of the waters, because they were made bitter." - Revelation 8:10-11 KJV*

A "great star from heaven" falls to the earth. A giant meteor hits the earth and pollutes a third of the rivers. That event pollutes the fresh water supply in the same region as the volcanic eruption polluting the salt water. A likely suspect might be the headwaters of the Tigris and Euphrates rivers in Turkey. This meteor is named "Wormwood," meaning bitter or poison. Those drinking the water will die. Regardless of where this meteor falls, a third of the fresh water is poisoned. Even now, clean fresh water is a vanishing commodity in much of the world. Imagine if this fell on the Great Lakes. What a devastating blow to America.

*"And the **fourth angel sounded**, and the **third part of the sun** was smitten, and the third part of the moon, and the third part of the stars; so as the third part of them was darkened, and the day shone not for a third part of it, and the night likewise." – Revelation 8:12 KJV*

The fourth angel sounds, and a third part of the sun, moon, and stars do not shine. They are darkened, the sun in the daytime and the moon and stars at night. The previous trumpet calamities shaded them. The fire and brimstone, the volcano (burning mountain), the meteor falling from heaven all pushed a tremendous amount of smoke, dust, and fine particulates into the atmosphere clouding the sun, moon, and stars. Since we are talking thirds here, this darkness is most likely regional and not global.

*"And I beheld, and heard an angel flying through the midst of heaven, saying with a loud voice, **Woe, woe, woe, to the inhabiters of the earth** by reason of the other voices of the trumpet of the three angels, which are yet to sound!" – Revelation 8:13 KJV*

There is a pause in the action as an angelic announcement issues from heaven. The following three trumpet judgments are not of the severity of the first four; they are much worse. The angel calls each a "woe," a condition of great suffering, affliction or grief, ruinous trouble, or calamity. Things on earth have just gone from bad to worse for the "inhabiters of the earth." These people are the "earth dwellers," those that love the earth and call it home as differentiated from believers whose citizenship is in God's kingdom.

THE FIRST FOUR TRUMPET JUDGMENTS FALL UPON THE PHYSICAL EARTH AND ATMOSPHERE AFFECTING VEGETATION, THE SEA, FRESH WATER SUPPLIES AND THE AIR BUT ONLY BY A THIRD. THESE ARE REGIONAL JUDGMENTS BUT COULD EASILY HAVE FAR-REACHING EFFECTS.

The First Woe

*"And the **fifth angel sounded**, and I saw a **star fall from heaven unto the earth**: and to him was given the **key of the bottomless pit**. And he opened the bottomless pit; and there arose a **smoke** out of the pit, as the smoke of a **great furnace**; and the **sun** and the **air** were **darkened** by reason of the **smoke of the pit**." - Revelation 9:1-2 KJV*

The first woe begins with an angel (star) coming quickly from heaven as if it were falling. The angel arrives on earth at the entrance to the "bottomless pit" with the key. When he opens the pit, great smoke billows out as from a "great furnace," a blast furnace heated by the fires of hell itself. That could be a massive split in the earth's crust opening a deep crevasse exposing super-hot magma from which issue vast amounts of smoke, ash, and toxic fumes, further polluting the atmosphere, and obscuring the sun. Where is the entrance to the "bottomless pit" located? We can't say for sure, but I would bet somewhere in the Middle East near the Euphrates River.

*"And there came out of the smoke **locusts** upon the earth: and unto them was given power, as the **scorpions** of the earth have power. And it was commanded them that they should **not hurt the grass** of the earth,*

*neither any green thing, neither any tree; but **only those men which have not the seal of God** in their foreheads." - Revelation 9:3-4 KJV*

Out of the smoke from the great furnace of the bottomless pit come locusts. These locust creatures have the stinging power of scorpions. They are not to eat the grass, crops, and tree leaves as ordinary locusts would, but they are to sting people that God has not sealed. The only ones on earth with the seal of God are the 144,000 that were sealed back in chapter 7. Everyone else is fair game, especially those that follow the Antichrist. These locusts don't eat green vegetation. They are commanded to torment people with a near-lethal sting.

*"And to them it was given that **they should not kill them**, but that they should be **tormented five months**: and their torment was as the torment of a **scorpion**, when he striketh a man. And in those days shall men seek death, and shall not find it; and shall desire to die, and death shall flee from them." - Revelation 9:5-6 KJV*

None will die from the sting of these demonic locusts. For five months, they are tormented with excruciating pain. Pain so severe they will seek death, but death alludes them. Indeed, a strange scenario that people cannot commit suicide to escape the pain. Even modern pain killers are of no avail. Death, the pale green horse rider from chapter six, can't take these tormented souls to hell. The grace of God works in mysterious ways. Perhaps after the tormenting pain has passed, some repent and turn to God. Had they been able to die, their fate in hell would have been sure.

*"And the shapes of the locusts were like unto **horses prepared unto battle**; and on their heads were as it were **crowns like gold**, and their faces were as the **faces of men**. And they had hair as the **hair of women**, and their teeth were as the teeth of **lions**." - Revelation 9:7-8 KJV*

Now things get a bit strange. I can easily picture a locust that can sting as locusts and scorpions are similar in size. These locusts that arise from the bottomless pit are not terrestrial locusts but some form of demonic locust or some evil hybrid locust-scorpion concocted by Satan and his minions. John likens them to battle horses having something like crowns of gold on their heads. If that is not enough, they have the faces of men, hair as a woman, and teeth like a lion. So, are they big like a horse? If they were small like an ordinary locust, why would so much detail be included in their description? There is something else going on here. Let's continue with the report.

*"And they had breastplates, as it were **breastplates of iron**, and the sound of their wings was as the **sound of chariots** of many horses running to battle. And they had tails like unto scorpions, and there were **stings in their tails**: and their power was to **hurt men five months**." - Revelation 9:9-10 KJV*

These locusts have armor that looks like iron breastplates. Their wings make a loud noise like charging chariots, not the buzz of little insects. Again, John mentions the sting of their tails that it hurts men for five months but does not kill them.

Some liken this to military equipment like Apache helicopters. Some details seem to match, but Apache helicopters and other such military equipment don't simply sting; they kill. The earth-dwellers must wait and see what these creatures look like.

*"And they had a **king over them**, which is the **angel of the bottomless pit**, whose name in the Hebrew tongue is **Abaddon**, but in the Greek tongue hath his name **Apollyon**. One woe is past; and, behold, there come two woes more hereafter." - Revelation 9:11-12 KJV*

Another strike against these locusts being military equipment is they have a king. That means they are living entities, part of the underworld kingdom. The king's name is Apollyon/Abaddon, which means "the Destroyer." Interesting that one of Allah's 99 names is al-Mumit, "the bringer of death, the destroyer." This king of the bottomless pit is called an "angel." A fallen angel from the pit and one of Satan's most powerful as he leads a horde of demonic creatures to plague humankind. Could this "angel of the bottomless pit" be posing as Allah or the Mahdi? The Mahdi is the soon coming Muslim savior according to their teachings. He is the Biblical Antichrist. He already has a horde of demon-possessed followers perpetrating Islamic terrorism across the planet. Or perhaps this angel is the Antichrist as he also "ascends from the bottomless pit." The first woe of stinging demonic locusts is passed. God help those believers that must endure the second.

As strange as these flying demonic locust/scorpion creatures seem, there is a previous occurrence of such in the days of the Exodus from Egypt some four thousand years ago.

*"And the LORD sent **fiery serpents** among the people, and they bit the people; and **much people of Israel died**. Therefore the people came to Moses, and said, We have sinned, for we have spoken against the LORD, and against thee; pray unto the LORD, that he take away the serpents from us. And Moses prayed for the people. And the LORD said unto Moses, Make thee a **fiery serpent**, and set it upon a pole: and it shall come to pass, **that every one that is bitten, when he looketh upon it, shall live**. And Moses made a serpent of brass, and put it upon a pole, and it came to pass, **that if a serpent had bitten any man, when he beheld the serpent of brass, he lived**." - Numbers 21:6-9 KJV*

The fiery serpents of Moses day were deadly. God had sent them as punishment for Israel talking against God and Moses. The locust/scorpion serpent of the 7-year Tribulation does not have the power of death but torments people for five months with a nasty sting. Both are judgments from God to drive people to repentance.

These demonic creatures ascend from a crevasse in the earth's surface, an unknown species of stinging locust-like entities: could be a militarized hybrid species, miniature drones released by the millions to disable entire populations or devilish creatures from the pit of hell.

The Second Woe

*"And the **sixth angel sounded**, and I heard a voice from the four horns of the golden altar which is before God, Saying to the sixth angel which had the trumpet, Loose the **four angels** which are bound in the **great river Euphrates**. And the four angels were loosed, which were prepared **for an hour, and a day, and a month, and a year, for to slay the third part of men**."* - Revelation 9:13-15 KJV

The sixth angel sounds his trumpet of woe accompanied by a shouting voice from the altar "loose the four angels which are bound in the great river Euphrates." These four angels have been bound for who knows how long waiting for the precise hour, day, month, and year. Bound at the headwaters of the Euphrates River, the hour of their release has come. The Euphrates begins in Turkey then flows through Syria and Iraq, ancient Babylon, all players in God's end-times scenario. These four angels have but one purpose, to prepare for the slaughter of 1/3 of humanity. Whether this refers to 1/3 of the population in the region of the Euphrates River, the Middle East, or the entire planet is not clear. But this will be a mass slaughter, the likes of which the world has never seen.

The phrase "an hour, and a day, and a month, and a year" proves the precision of God's prophetic timeclock. That is not simply an assortment of events unfolding in some random or loosely organized fashion. The precise flow of events set in motion by God does not require man's help or consensus. Regardless of the plans and schemes conjured by world leaders, the prophetic plan of God takes center stage and unfolds by His might and power.

*"And the number of the army of the horsemen were **two hundred thousand thousand**: and I heard the number of them. And thus I saw the horses in the vision, and them that sat on them, having breastplates of **fire, and of jacinth, and brimstone**: and the heads of the horses were as the **heads of lions**; and out of their mouths issued **fire and smoke and brimstone**." - Revelation 9:16-17 KJV*

The Apostle John is amazed by the number 200 million. He states clearly that he "heard the number of them" in case there be any doubt. What follows is another bizarre set of details that baffle the imagination—an army of horsemen, 200 million strong. Horse riders having breastplates of fire, jacinth, a dark red color, and brimstone, a yellow sulfur color. They have heads like lions, and out of their mouth comes fire, smoke, and brimstone. Interesting that the flag of China is red and yellow and they boast of a two hundred million man army.

Could those entities be an armored light infantry vehicle or some other vehicle with a cannon? Fire would come out of the mouth, the barrel of the gun. Heads like lions could refer to the helmet with all the gear it carries. Whatever these 200 million, they will be hard to miss and even more challenging to contend with. Many will die in their wake. The pale horse rider will be quite busy.

*"By these three was the **third part of men killed**, by the fire, and by the smoke, and by the brimstone, which issued out of their mouths. For their power is in their mouth, and in their tails: for their tails were like unto serpents, and had heads, and with them they do hurt." - Revelation 9:18-19 KJV*

John is making a valiant attempt at describing 21ˢᵗ century military weaponry with 1ˢᵗ century lingo—a near impossible task.

That massive army kills a third of humanity with fire, smoke, and brimstone. Nuclear blasts certainly would produce vast amounts of fire, smoke, and brimstone. We read of a similar scenario in Ezekiel chapter 39 where HAZMAT teams searched for radioactive body parts.

The power of these entities is in their mouth. Rockets, missiles, and artillery shells come out the front, which would seem like the mouth. Bombs would fall from the bottom of a plane to seem like the tail due to the airspeed. But what comes out of their mouth and tails does much "hurt."

*"And the rest of the men which were not killed by these plagues yet **repented not** of the works of their hands, that they should **not worship devils**, and idols of gold, and silver, and brass, and stone, and of wood: which neither can see, nor hear, nor walk: Neither repented they of their murders, nor of their sorceries, nor of their fornication, nor of their thefts." - Revelation 9:20-21 KJV*

God's desired effect of the plagues unleashed upon humankind is repentance. But people harden their hearts against God. Angered by the devastation, their hatred for God grows worse and worse. They cling to their idols of gold, silver, brass, stone, and wood, thinking that their idols will somehow save them. But they are simply materials of the earth, showing that these people love the world and the things in it much more than their Creator. They are citizens of this world, locked into the world systems run by the Antichrist. They are not citizens of heaven, nor do they want to be. They are "earth dwellers."

The earth dwellers would not repent of their murders, sorceries, fornication, nor their thefts. They love their sin and refuse to give it up for the chance to be saved. They have sealed their fate in the lake of fire.

Time No Longer

Chapter 10 is a short interlude for an announcement. A great angel appears to have some spectacular characteristics like the Lord Jesus Christ.

*"And I saw **another mighty angel** come down from heaven, clothed with a cloud: and a **rainbow** was upon his head, and his face was as it were the sun, and his feet as pillars of fire: And he had in his hand a **little book** open: and he set his right foot upon the sea, and his left foot on the earth," - Revelation 10:1-2 KJV*

This angel descends from heaven to earth, clothed with clouds, a rainbow over his head and his face shining as the sun. His feet are as pillars of fire symbolic of judgment. That sounds like Jesus, but Jesus does not come back to earth until chapter 19, when He returns on a white horse with His holy angels to save Israel. This angel has a little book in his hand. He stands with one foot on the land and one on the sea, meaning that his pronouncements are for the earth.

*"And cried with a loud voice, as when a lion roareth: and when he had cried, seven thunders uttered their voices. And when the seven thunders had uttered their voices, I was about to write: and I heard a voice from heaven saying unto me, **Seal up those things which the seven thunders uttered, and write them not.**" - Revelation 10:3-4 KJV*

The angel cries out with a loud voice like a lion. At the same time, seven thunders utter their voices as well. Just as John was about to write, he is commanded not to record what was said. That means that John understood the thunderous words but was forbidden to write them down. They were probably too horrific.

*"And the angel which I saw stand upon the sea and upon the earth lifted up his hand to heaven, And sware by him that liveth for ever and ever, who created heaven, and the things that therein are, and the earth, and the things that therein are, and the sea, and the things which are therein, that **there should be time no longer.**" - Revelation 10:5-6 KJV*

The mighty angel prepares to make another pronouncement. He lifts his hands and praises the Lord God Almighty, Jesus Christ. He praises Him as Creator of heaven and earth who lives forever and ever. Next, he makes a strange statement "that there should be time no longer." Time in this context refers to the passing of time or a period of time. In other words, there will be no more delay. The end of God's prophetic plan is near, and everything will now pass quickly.

*"But in the days of the voice of the seventh angel, when he shall begin to sound, the **mystery of God should be finished**, as he hath declared to his servants the prophets."* - Revelation 10:7 KJV

As the seventh angel sounds his trumpet, the mystery of God will be finished. So, what is the "mystery of God?" Wisdom and understanding of spiritual matters given to the righteous, the godly that seek and obey the Lord down through the ages. The wicked do not seek God, so they do not have divine wisdom and understanding about the things of God, His creation, and His purpose for humankind. They only have the worldly wisdom of men. The mystery of God would also include God's plan of salvation for those that believe and His plan of judgment for the ungodly.

That could also mean that everyone that comes to the Lord during the 7-year Tribulation has already done so. There are no more candidates for salvation left on the earth; thus, the end is very near. There will be no further delay in executing God's wrath. The scriptures say that God is longsuffering, not wanting that any should perish. Well, now that longsuffering is over, and without delay, the end will come.

*"And the voice which I heard from heaven spake unto me again, and said, Go and **take the little book** which is open in the hand of the angel which standeth upon the sea and upon the earth. And I went unto the angel, and said unto him, Give me the little book. And he said unto me, Take it, and **eat it up**, and it **shall make thy belly bitter**, but it shall be **in thy mouth sweet as honey**."* - Revelation 10:8-9 KJV

The same voice that told John not to write what the voice of the thunders spoke now tells him to take the little book from the mighty angel. In this context, the little book is the word of God. The angel commands John to take it and "eat it up," meaning to consume it, not just for personal edification but to proclaim the content to others.

After eating the book, it's bitter in John's belly but sweet in his mouth. The word of God is Truth. Truth is always sweet to those desiring to hear the truth as John was. But truth can be a burden when called upon to proclaim it to a lost and dying world. It becomes bitter on one's belly as most will not receive it and even persecute you for speaking it. Exactly what's happening today. Truth is the new hate speech.

People that speak the truth are ridiculed, laughed at, denigrated, slandered, and marginalized. Even in the church, most Christians don't want the truth as it challenges and convicts lukewarm superficial pew warmers just playing church. They want their ears tickled, desiring to be flattered, complemented, praised, and told how honored we are just by their presence. What nonsense, they should be admonished to repent. But pastors won't do that as they don't want to offend anyone nor take a hit in the offering plate. The true gospel is an offense, so get over it. Change your cowardly, politically correct mindset. Speak the truth and let the chips fall where they may. You are not responsible for the reactions of others.

*"And I took the little book out of the angel's hand, and **ate it up**, and it was in my mouth sweet as honey: and as soon as I had eaten it, my belly was bitter. And he said unto me, **Thou must prophesy again** before many peoples, and nations, and tongues, and kings." - Revelation 10:10-11 KJV*

John eats the little book. Sure enough, it was sweet in his mouth but bitter in his stomach. The voice announces to John that he would prophesy the words of the little book before "many peoples, and nations, and tongues, and kings." Through the Book of Revelation,

John has prophesied before an innumerable host of people, both small and great, paupers and kings. He is testifying to us now as we study. The book of Revelation will be the number one underground best seller during the 7-year Tribulation, second only to the whole Bible.

Tribulation Temple

*"And there was given me a reed like unto a rod: and the angel stood, saying, Rise, and measure the temple of God, and the altar, and them that worship therein. But the **court which is without the temple leave out**, and measure it not; for it is **given unto the Gentiles**: and the **holy city shall they tread under foot forty and two months**." - Revelation 11:1-2 KJV*

The scene changes. John is given a measuring rod and instructed to measure the temple of God in preparation for its construction. The third Temple will be built during the early days of the 7-year tribulation. John measures the Temple and the altar. Recently, construction of the Temple altar was completed in Jerusalem. Everything is ready for the construction of the Tribulation Temple. Once the 7-year Tribulation begins, the temple will be constructed quickly. Visit www.templeinstitute.org for more info.

Next, John is commanded not to measure the outer court because that area is given to the Gentiles. If the tribulation temple is built on the Temple Mount, then it's conceivable that the site of the outer court might now contain one of the Muslim mosques. We know this passage refers to the Tribulation temple. John is told that the holy city of Jerusalem will be occupied by a foreign army for 42 months, 3 ½ years, the last half of the 7-year tribulation.

*"And I will give power unto **my two witnesses**, and they shall prophesy a **thousand two hundred and threescore days**, clothed in sackcloth. These are the **two olive trees**, and the **two candlesticks** standing before the God of the earth." - Revelation 11:3-4 KJV*

After completing the tribulation Temple, two men of God will appear and prophesy to Israel for 1260 days or 3 ½ years. They will prophesy of the coming judgment and call the nation to repentance. Sackcloth, or burlap, is not the most fashionable attire but fitting for their message. Most reject the message of pending destruction and the call for repentance. The Antichrist and his minions will attempt to marginalize these two witnesses, but that won't be possible. God calls these His two olive trees, His two candlesticks that do His will and speak His word in the earth. Olive trees yield oil to light the candlesticks that shine the living word of God to the world. The word of God is alive; it is spirit and truth.

*"It is the spirit that quickeneth; the flesh profiteth nothing: the words that I speak unto you, they are **spirit**, and they are **life**." - John 6:63 KJV*

*"And if any man will hurt them, **fire proceedeth out of their mouth**, and devoureth their enemies: and if any man will hurt them, he must in this manner be killed. These have power to shut heaven, that it **rain not in the days of their prophecy**: and have power over waters to **turn them to blood**, and to **smite the earth with all plagues**, as often as they will." - Revelation 11:5-6 KJV*

The two witnesses are quite unique. If someone tries to kill them, fire from the mouth of the two witnesses will consume them. They have the power to stop the rain causing drought and famine. They turn water to blood and bring various plagues upon the earth. That sounds very similar to what Moses did in Egypt just before the Exodus. Of course it does, as Moses is one of the two witnesses.

Some say that Enoch is one of the witnesses because he never died, and scripture states that it is appointed unto man once to die and then the judgment. Interesting that the context of Hebrews 9:27 is specifically that Jesus Christ died once for all as a sacrifice for sin. Then He sits in judgment for all. Let's look at the verse for Enoch's translation.

*"By faith Enoch was translated that **he should not see death**; and was not found, because God had translated him: for before his translation he had this testimony, that he pleased God." - Hebrews 11:5 KJV*

The passage states that God took Enoch so that "he would not see death." God did not take Enoch so he could return to earth at a later time and die. The two witnesses are Moses and Elijah. The same two appeared with Jesus on the Mount of Transfiguration (Matthew Ch. 17).

"And when they shall have finished their testimony, the beast that ascendeth out of the bottomless pit shall make war against them, and shall overcome them, and kill them. And their dead bodies shall lie in the street of the great city, which spiritually is called Sodom and Egypt, where also our Lord was crucified." - Revelation 11:7-8 KJV

After testifying for 3 ½ years, Moses and Elijah are suddenly killed by the Antichrist, the "beast that ascends out of the bottomless pit." This phrase refers back to the king of the locusts that ascend from the bottomless pit, proving that the Antichrist is no mere man. He is a fallen angel taking the form of a man and empowered by Satan. He could be posing as a super-intelligent powerful alien savior who comes to save the world. Keep an open mind as he will be unlike anything previously seen on earth.

He, the Antichrist, is given authority to kill the two witnesses. Their dead bodies lie in the street in Jerusalem, showing the immense level of contempt held for God's two witnesses by those in power. The Antichrist and his follower's hatred for these two is boundless. Darkness always hates the Light. We know the city in question is Jerusalem, as that is where Jesus was crucified. During the 7-year Tribulation and even now, it is like "Sodom and Egypt." Did you see the latest gay pride parade in Jerusalem? At least 25,000 showed up to promote perversion and promiscuity. Egypt is a type of the corrupt criminal world system in which Jerusalem is very much entrenched. This corruption will be exponential when they make a covenant with the devil for a few short years of peace.

*"And they of the people and kindreds and tongues and nations shall **see their dead bodies three days and an half,** and shall not suffer their dead bodies to be put in graves. And **they that dwell upon the earth shall rejoice over them, and make merry, and shall send gifts one to another; because these two prophets tormented them that dwelt on the earth.**" - Revelation 11:9-10 KJV*

Those around the world following the Antichrist will see the dead bodies of the two witnesses lying in the street in Jerusalem. With the truth squelched, let the party begin. The earth dwellers enjoy looking at the two dead bodies. As a symbol of victory over God, they do not want them laid to rest in graves. They revel as the light no longer shines on their dark hearts, for they love their sin. The celebration party continues for three days with gifts exchanged, applauding the death of God's two witnesses—Moses and Elijah no longer speak tormenting truth. Party on you sinners. Their seeming victory over

Moses and Elijah encourages them to believe they can defeat Jesus Christ.

*"And after three days and an half the **Spirit of life from God entered into them, and they stood upon their feet**, and great fear fell upon them which saw them. And they heard a great voice from heaven saying unto them, **Come up hither**. And they **ascended up to heaven in a cloud**, and their enemies beheld them." - Revelation 11:11-12 KJV*

Now, you know, God always has the last word, right? You know the old saying, "he who laughs last laughs best." Just when the party is raging, and the depraved have been raising the rooftops for 3 ½ days, the Spirit of God shows up to crash the party. Suddenly, Moses and Elijah stand to their feet; they're alive by the Spirit of God. Can you imagine the shock and awe in the faces of the proud, arrogant revelers at that moment? "Great fear" befalls the hearts of the partiers. Not only do they see the two witnesses come back to life, but they hear a voice from heaven calling them home, "Come up Hither." Not sure if God will use King James English or not, but the heathen will understand. Overcome, they gaze, frozen in fear, as the two witnesses ascent up to heaven, disappearing into the clouds. The party is over! Judgment is on the way.

*"And the same hour was there a **great earthquake**, and the **tenth part** of the city fell, and in the earthquake were slain of men **seven thousand**: and the remnant were affrighted, and gave glory to the God of heaven. The second woe is past; and, behold, the third woe cometh quickly." - Revelation 11:13-14 KJV*

A great earthquake completes the second woe. The epicenter is Jerusalem, and a tenth part of the city falls in ruin. The devastation kills seven thousand men. Fear grips even the remnant of God, but they still praise God and give Him glory. The second woe is past, and the third is coming quickly.

CONFIDENTIAL

BRIEFING

Point of interest:

a) The third temple is built in Jerusalem early in the 7-year Tribulation.

b) 144,000 Jews sealed by God as witnesses.

c) the two witnesses appear at the temple prophesying for 3 ½ years, then they are killed by Antichrist.

d) the two witnesses come back to life and ascend to heaven. People are in great fear.

e) Destruction from Volcanoes and meteors pollutes much of the fresh and salt water on the earth.

f) Destruction comes by a third which could be the Americas.

g) Horrific creatures released from the earth to torment mankind for five months.

Persons of interest:

a) Two witnesses: Moses and Elijah

Discussion:

Survival on earth is increasingly more difficult as food and fresh water are in short supply. The atmosphere is highly polluted, affecting light from the sun and moon. Get out of the big cities and find some believers in rural areas. People in big cities are the first to be overcome by the Antichrist and his oppressive regime.

The Third Woe

*"And the seventh angel sounded; and there were great voices in heaven, saying, **THE KINGDOMS OF THIS WORLD ARE BECOME THE KINGDOMS OF OUR LORD, AND OF HIS CHRIST; AND HE SHALL REIGN FOR EVER AND EVER**. And the four and twenty elders, which sat before God on their seats, fell upon their faces, and worshipped God, Saying, We give thee thanks, O Lord God Almighty, which art, and wast, and art to come; because thou hast taken to thee thy great power, and hast reigned."*
- Revelation 11:15-17 KJV emphasis mine

The third woe, the seventh trumpet judgment, is the most severe of all. But before it unfolds, there's a coronation service that takes place in heaven. A pronouncement comes, **"THE KINGDOMS OF THIS WORLD ARE BECOME THE KINGDOMS OF OUR LORD AND OF HIS CHRIST, AND HE SHALL REIGN FOR EVER AND EVER."** Coronated King Jesus Christ is given the kingdoms of this world. Jesus is coronated in heaven first, giving Him the right to come to earth and claim His possession from the control of the Antichrist and Satan. Jesus Christ will rule this earth until the New Earth replaces it, and then He will reign there. His reign is for ever and ever.

The twenty-four elders fall before the Lord and worship Him. The time is drawing near when Israel will rule and reign with Jesus Christ in the Millennial Kingdom. The time has come, the Lord has taken His rightful place of power and authority. He will reign forever as King of Kings and Lord of Lords.

*"**And the nations were angry,** and thy wrath is come, and the time of the dead, that they should be judged, and that thou shouldest give reward unto thy servants the prophets, and to the saints, and them that fear thy name, small and great; and shouldest destroy them which destroy the earth. And*

the temple of God was opened in heaven, and there was seen in his temple the ark of his testament: and there were lightnings, and voices, and thunderings, and an earthquake, and great hail." - Revelation 11:18-19 KJV

The nations are angry as they do not want to live under the righteous rule of Jesus Christ. They know His wrath is upon them because of their continuous sin and corruption. As the end of the 7-year tribulation nears, evil men will be judged and sent to hell to await the final judgment at the Great White Throne. But the righteous are rewarded for their faithful service. The Lord will put a stop to all the destruction of the earth caused by evil men.

Back at the temple in heaven, the actual arc of the covenant appears accompanied by lightning, thunder, and voices followed by another earthquake and great hail. God's favorite weapons are naturally simple yet highly effective.

Great Wonder in Heaven

*"And there appeared a **great wonder in heaven**, a **woman clothed with the sun, and the moon under her feet**, and upon her head a **crown of twelve stars**: And she being with child cried, **travailing in birth**, and pained to be delivered." - Revelation 12:1-2 KJV*

This great wonder appears in the heavens, not on the earth. A woman in heaven clothed with the sun and the moon at her feet could only be a star cluster or constellation. In this case, it is the constellation Virgo. But the question is, when is Virgo clothed with the sun with the moon at her feet? What is her crown of twelve stars? Is there a time when this configuration is present in the heavens? This pattern was seen in Virgo on September 23, 2017 and again on September 23, 2023 as shown below. Both events came and went without any prophetic happenings. However, the Hamas attack on Israel soon followed on October 7, 2023.

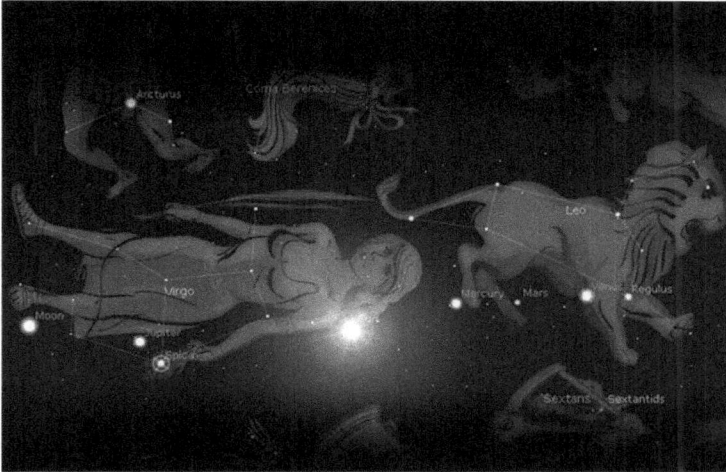

From the above image, Virgo is clothed with the light of the sun, so this would be a daytime image using software as it will not be visible with the naked eye. The moon is at her feet. A crown of 12 stars is at her head with the constellation Leo. Leo typically has only nine stars, but three planets, Mercury, Venus, and Mars, align with the constellation. So, this alignment fits the requirements of the scripture passage.

The passage also states that the woman is pregnant and about to give birth. Notice that the Planet Jupiter is in Virgo around the area of the womb. That was a hot topic up until September 23, when nothing happened. Most likely it will appear again during the 7-year Tribulation.

*"And there appeared another wonder in heaven; and behold a **great red dragon**, having seven heads and ten horns, and seven crowns upon his heads. And his tail drew the third part of the stars of heaven, and did cast*

them to the earth: and the dragon stood before the woman which was ready to be delivered, for **to devour her child as soon as it was born**." - Revelation 12:3-4 KJV

As the woman is nearing her delivery, the great red dragon appears in heaven also. The dragon is Satan as he has seven heads, ten horns, and seven crowns. He wants to devour her child a soon as it is born.

"And she brought forth a **man child**, who was to rule all nations with a **rod of iron**: and her child was caught up unto God, and to his throne." - Revelation 12:5 KJV

What does all this mean? The traditional interpretation is that the woman is Israel, and the man child is Jesus. When he was born, Herod, the dragon, tried to kill him. After Jesus' resurrection, he was taken to heaven, up to the throne of God. I tend to agree with the traditional understanding for a change.

"And the woman fled into the wilderness, where she hath a place prepared of God, that they should feed her there a **thousand two hundred and threescore days**." - Revelation 12:6 KJV

Persecution from the Antichrist forces the woman, Israel, to flee into the wilderness. That happens at the midpoint of the 7-year Tribulation when the Antichrist perpetrates the abomination of desolation. Jesus tells the Jews in the Olivet Discourse:

"When ye therefore shall see the **abomination of desolation**, spoken of by Daniel the prophet, stand in the holy place, (whoso readeth, let him understand:) Then let them which be in Judaea **flee into the mountains**: Let him which is on the housetop not come down to take any thing out of his house: Neither let him which is in the field return back to take his *clothes. And woe unto them that are with child, and to them that give suck in those days! But pray ye that your flight be not in the winter, neither on the sabbath day:* **For then shall be great tribulation,** *such as was not since the beginning of the world to this time, no, nor ever shall be." - Matthew 24:15-21 KJV*

At the midpoint of the 7-year Tribulation, Jesus instructs the Jews to "flee to the mountains." Don't come home to pack your clothes, just run. Pray you don't have little children as they will slow you down. Pray it is not the Sabbath as there are travel rules to obey. That is a Jewish scenario; the church is not involved as we have been previously raptured. Israel is still on earth enduring the Tribulation, and they flee to the mountains and wilderness.

Satan Cast Out of Heaven

"And there was war in heaven: **Michael and his angels fought against the dragon,** *and the dragon fought and his angels, And prevailed not; neither was their place found any more in heaven. And the* **great dragon was cast out, that old serpent, called the Devil, and Satan, which deceiveth the whole world:** *he was cast out into the earth, and his angels were cast out with him." - Revelation 12:7-9 KJV*

Satan has had continual access to heaven as he comes before God as the accuser of the brethren. Satan is not our accuser as we already have eternal life in Jesus Christ, and we have been in heaven for 3 ½ years. Satan accuses those in the Tribulation, especially Jews, as their salvation is not secure until the second coming of Jesus Christ or their martyrdom.

But the time has come for Satan to be kicked out of heaven. Michael has the task to remove the devil, so the war is on. One can only imagine what a war between angels could be like.

The devil is outnumbered as Michael has 2/3 of the host of heaven. Satan is routed, and there is no place left for him to hide in heaven. He is cast down to the earth and his angels with him. That is not a good thing if you missed the Rapture. Now you must deal directly with Satan and his horde of fallen angels as they are here on earth. They will manifest and be seen. After all, what do they have to lose now? Either way, it's bad news for humanity.

"And I heard a loud voice saying in heaven, Now is come salvation, and strength, and the kingdom of our God, and the power of his Christ: for the **accuser of our brethren is cast down,** *which accused them before our God day and night.* **And they overcame him by the blood of the Lamb, and by the word of their testimony; and they loved not their lives unto the death.***" - Revelation 12:10-11 KJV*

Heaven is finally cleansed of the devil and his angels. The kingdom, power, strength, and salvation are soon to come to earth at the second coming of Jesus Christ. The overcomers on earth are those that have resisted the Antichrist and his mark. That has cost many their lives, but they are eternally secure in Christ. They overcame the Antichrist and Satan by "the blood of the Lamb and by the word of their testimony." They kept the faith at all costs. They loved Jesus more than their own lives as "they loved not their lives unto death." Their testimony for Christ was more valuable than their own life. Praise God.

"Therefore **rejoice, ye heavens,** *and ye that dwell in them.* **Woe to the inhabiters of the earth** *and of the sea! for the devil is come down unto*

you, having great wrath, because he knoweth that **he hath but a short time**." - *Revelation 12:12 KJV*

Those in heaven are rejoicing and celebrating the removal of Satan. But those on earth will experience another layer of wrath as if things weren't already bad enough—another woe for the earth dwellers. The devil is mad as he knows that his time is short. In a few short years, he will be locked in the bottomless pit for one thousand years. He is going to wreak as much death and destruction as he can while he has time.

*"And when the dragon saw that he was **cast unto the earth**, he **persecuted the woman** which brought forth the man child. And to the woman were given **two wings of a great eagle**, that she might fly into the wilderness, into her place, where she is nourished for **a time, and times, and half a time**, from the face of the serpent." - Revelation 12:13-14 KJV*

After Satan is cast to the earth, he persecutes Israel, the woman. Someone comes to Israel's aid with a massive airlift to a facility in the wilderness where they are sustained for "a time, and times, and half a time"; 3 ½ years. The remnant of Israel is protected from the face of the serpent. Exactly how this will play out is not known from the text, but God protects His people.

*"And the serpent cast **out of his mouth water** as a flood after the woman, that he might cause her to be carried away of the flood. And the **earth helped the woman**, and the earth opened her mouth, and **swallowed up the flood** which the dragon cast out of his mouth. And the dragon was wroth with the woman, and went to **make war with the remnant of her seed**, which keep the commandments of God, and have the testimony of Jesus Christ." - Revelation 12:15-17 KJV*

Water is symbolic of many people. The serpent sends many people as in an army after the remnant of Israel that they might be carried away, destroyed. But the earth helped the woman by opening and swallowing the pursuing army or at least a significant portion of it. Another earthquake could cause that fissure in the earth. That infuriates the devil even more as his every effort seems to be thwarted by God. He then sends another army to make war with the remnant of believers in Israel.

The Beast

*"And I stood upon the sand of the sea, and saw **a beast rise up out of the sea, having seven heads and ten horns**, and upon his horns **ten crowns**, and upon his heads the **name of blasphemy**. And the beast which I saw was like unto a **leopard**, and his feet were as the feet of a **bear**, and his mouth as the mouth of a **lion**: and the **dragon gave him his power, and his seat, and great authority.**" - Revelation 13:1-2 KJV*

The "sands of the sea" refer to the sea of humanity in the Middle East, not the shore of the Mediterranean. Out of this sea of humanity comes a "beast" with seven heads, blasphemous names, and ten crowns. The seven heads are seven major kingdoms controlled by the devil. Five of them are historical being Egypt, Assyria, Babylon, Media-Persia, and Greece. The ten crowns are the ten kings that control the final Satanic kingdom. We will read more about these heads and kings in Revelation Chapter 17.

The beast system is the final world kingdom, the New World Order, the Global Government, the seventh head. It has a leopard body, meaning that its armies are swift to make war and conquer. With feet like a bear and a mouth like a lion, it crushes and devours everything in its path. This "beast" also refers to the Antichrist that controls the final Satanic kingdom seeking world dominance. The real power behind the Antichrist and his empire is the dragon, Satan, as he gives the beast his "power, and his seat, and great authority." The beast kingdom is the feet of iron and clay of Daniel chapter two, the fourth beast of Daniel chapter seven, the little horn of Daniel chapters seven and eight.

*"And I saw **one of his heads as it were wounded to death**, and his deadly wound was healed: and all the world **wondered after the beast**. And they worshipped the dragon which gave power unto the beast: and they worshipped the beast, saying, **Who is like unto the beast? who is able to make war with him?**" - Revelation 13:3-4 KJV*

One of the beast's heads receives a mortal wound, but the deadly wound is healed. That could refer to the Antichrist receiving a mortal head wound and returning to life imitating the resurrection of Jesus Christ. Those left behind after the Rapture will see how this plays out. Everyone will be amazed at the power of the beast. They will worship him, not understanding they are honoring the power behind him, Satan, the dragon. The Antichrist will seem virtually unstoppable. People will ask, "Who is like unto the beast? who is able to make war with him?" No one at that time, but one is coming soon that will make short work of him.

*"And there was given unto him a **mouth speaking great things and blasphemies**, and power was given unto him to continue **forty and two months**. And he opened his mouth in blasphemy against God, to blaspheme his name, and his tabernacle, and them that dwell in heaven." - Revelation 13:5-6 KJV*

One of the hallmarks of the Antichrist is his big mouth. He speaks great blasphemous words against God, Jesus Christ, and His saints.

The Antichrist rules this final New World Order for 42 months or 3 ½ years, the last half of the 7-year Tribulation. That puts the Antichrist takeover of the final kingdom at the midpoint of the 7-year Tribulation.

*"And it was given unto him to **make war with the saints**, and to overcome them: and power was given him over all kindreds, and tongues, and nations. And all that dwell upon the earth shall worship him, whose names are not written in the book of life of the Lamb slain from the foundation of the world." - Revelation 13:7-8 KJV*

The Antichrist is given power over the saints. These are the tribulation saints, those saved during the 7-year Tribulation. These are not the Church saints because we were previously raptured.

The Antichrist comes from the "gates of hell," the bottomless pit. An angel was sent to unlock the gates so he could ascend with the locusts. The Antichrist is given power over the Tribulation saints. Why is the Antichrist given dominion over the Tribulation saints? They must be tried, and their faith tested. They are in a world entirely controlled by the Antichrist, for the restraining power of the Holy Spirit has been removed (2 Thessalonians Chapter 2). Also, many of the Tribulation saints could have been saved before the Rapture, but they kept putting it off, seeking their desires instead of the Lord.

The Antichrist has absolute power "over all kindreds, and tongues, and nations." He rules the New World Order in the Middle East and the world. The people of the earth whose names are not written in the "book of life of the Lamb" worship the beast, the Antichrist, and his kingdom.

*"**If any man have an ear, let him hear**. He that leadeth into captivity shall go into captivity: he that killeth with the sword must be killed with the sword. Here is the patience and the faith of the saints." - Revelation 13:9-10 KJV*

He that has a "spiritual ear" let him hear the spiritual truth of the passage. If you follow the Antichrist, your fate in hell is sealed. The Antichrist will lead many into spiritual captivity damning their souls to perdition. He and his minions kill many by the sword, as beheading is the preferred method of execution during the Tribulation and the least expensive. But he will also be slain with the sword, the sword of the Spirit, the Word of God.

When Jesus returns, He has a sharp sword protruding from His mouth, the word of God. The patience of the saints is to wait on the Lord as He will deal quickly and finally with the Antichrist at His second coming. The Tribulation saints must continue to the end of the Tribulation to be saved. They must patiently wait for the Lord's return enduring whatever may come their way, including martyrdom.

I have often used the name "Antichrist," but interestingly enough, the Apostle John does not use that name in the Book of Revelation. He does use that name in his two epistles.

*"Little children, **it is the last time**: and as ye have heard that **antichrist shall come**, even now are there **many antichrists**; whereby we know that it is the last time. ... Who is a liar but he that denieth that Jesus is the Christ? **He is antichrist, that denieth the Father and the Son**." - 1 John 2:18, 22 KJV*

*"And every spirit that confesseth not that Jesus Christ is come in the flesh is not of God: and **this is that spirit of antichrist**, whereof ye have heard that it should come; and **even now already is it in the world**."* - 1 John 4:3 KJV

*"For many deceivers are entered into the world, who confess not that Jesus Christ is come in the flesh. **This is a deceiver and an antichrist.**"* - 2 John 1:7 KJV

There are many noteworthy items in these verses as follows.

- "it is the last time" –John wrote that phrase 2000 years ago. The kingdom program for Israel was postponed because Israel completely rejected their king and his kingdom. Instead, God implemented the dispensation of grace to save Gentiles. After the Rapture, God will resume Israel's kingdom program beginning with the 7-year Tribulation culminating with the second coming of the Lord Jesus Christ.
- "antichrist shall come" – There is a specific individual named the Antichrist that will come and fulfill the prophecies of an evil end times ruler.
- "many antichrists" – Many have an antichrist spirit in their speech and behavior. They have a spirit of antichrist but are not the Antichrist.
- "denieth that Jesus is the Christ" – Anyone that denies that Jesus of Nazareth is the Messiah that has come to die on the cross for the sin of mankind is a liar and has a spirit of antichrist.
- "Father and the Son" – denying the Father and Son as part of the Trinity is a spirit of Antichrist.
- Anyone denying that the Son, Jesus Christ, is the eternal Son of God second member of the godhead, has a spirit of antichrist.

- "Jesus Christ has come in the flesh" – denying that Jesus was God in the flesh is a spirit of antichrist. Stating that Jesus Christ was a created being or just a man is the spirit of antichrist.
- The spirit of antichrist has been on the earth since the birth of Jesus.
- Anyone that states that Jesus Christ, the only begotten Son of God, second person of the Trinity has not come in the flesh has a spirit of antichrist.
- Islam denies that Jesus is the Son of God. Islam denies that Jesus was crucified. Islam denies the Trinity. Islam is the spirit of antichrist.

The False Prophet

*"And I beheld **another beast coming up out of the earth**, and he had **two horns like a lamb**, and he **spake as a dragon**. And he exerciseth all the power of the first beast before him, and causeth the earth and them which dwell therein to **worship the first beast**, whose deadly wound was healed." – Revelation 13:11-12 KJV*

A second beast arises "out of the earth." Many think this to be a religious leader like the Pope who tries to unite the world's religions into one global pagan system. That system could resemble ancient Rome, wherein you could practice any religion you desired as long as you acknowledged Caesar as King or the Pope as the supreme religious leader. This beast comes from the earth (land) as opposed to the sea as the first beast. The land could refer to Israel. This beast could be a man posing as a prophet like Elijah; hence he is given the title "false prophet." He has all the power of the Antichrist and causes the people to worship him "whose deadly wound was healed" by a fake resurrection. This false prophet poses as a great religious leader but speaks like the dragon, Satan. He is of his father, the devil.

*"And he doeth great wonders, so that he **maketh fire come down from heaven** on the earth in the sight of men, And **deceiveth** them that dwell on the earth by the means of those miracles which he had power to do in the sight of the beast; saying to them that dwell on the earth, that they should make an image to the beast, which had the wound by a sword, and did live."* - *Revelation 13:13-14 KJV*

The false prophet performs "great wonders," even calling fire down from heaven. He mimics the miracle of Elijah with the prophets of Baal found in 1 Kings 18:21-40. The false prophet deceives many by his miracles. They worship the beast making an image of the beast, the Antichrist, who was wounded by the sword and lived. Another verse supporting the fake resurrection of the Antichrist mimicking the resurrection of Jesus Christ. Look at pictures of the World War II era. Giant images of Hitler, Stalin, and Mussolini littered the landscape. Statues in cities and squares honoring these evil men. Not much has changed.

*"And he had power to **give life unto the image of the beast**, that the image of the beast should both speak, and cause that **as many as would not worship the image of the beast should be killed**. And he causeth all, both small and great, rich and poor, free and bond, to **receive a mark in their right hand, or in their foreheads**."* - *Revelation 13:15-16 KJV*

The false prophet has some unique abilities. He gives life to the image of the Antichrist that it speaks. Is that a Hollywood special effects stunt? Perhaps some Artificial Intelligence-powered robot. Maybe a 3D hologram. However, accomplished, it's straight from Satan himself. The speaking image tells all to worship the Antichrist and his image on the pain of death. Those that refuse will be hunted down and killed.

At this point, everyone will be required to receive a "mark in their right hand or their foreheads." That could be an RFID chip implant in those countries that have the technology available. Notice that the mark goes "in" the right hand or forehead, not "on" the right hand or forehead as a stamp or tattoo might be placed. That gives credence that a microchip could fulfill these prophetic passages.

*"And that no man might buy or sell, save he that had **the mark, or the name of the beast, or the number of his name**. Here is wisdom. Let him that hath understanding count the number of the beast: for it is the number of a man; and his number is **Six hundred threescore and six**." - Revelation 13:17-18 KJV*

But there is more to this than just a microchip implant in the skin. There are three alternatives for restricting commerce. The "mark" or the "name of the beast" or the "number of his name." If someone has but one of these three, they can "buy and sell." The mark, the name, or the number will put you in good standing with the Antichrist kingdom. That covers everyone from the most technologically advanced countries to the most primitive. People from every country and way of life can show their allegiance to the Antichrist via one of these three methods: the mark, name, or number. There is much discussion about the number of the beast, "666". But that is only one of the three alternatives to identifying oneself with the Antichrist. Muslims wear a bandana on their forehead identifying themselves with groups like Hamas and Hezbollah.

BRIEFING

Point of interest:

a) The Antichrist comes to full power at the midpoint of the 7-year tribulation.

b) The false prophet causes all to worship the beast on pain of death. He forces people to receive a 'mark' in their hand or forehead, possibly a microchip, before they can buy or sell.

c) food is rationed – the only means of buying food at government-controlled centers is by having the 'mark' – food is the coercion to receive the 'mark'.

d) large chain retail stores like Walmart, Home Depot and Lowes will be converted to government distribution center so everything can be controlled.

Persons of interest:

a) Antichrist aka the beast, leader of the New World Order.

b) False Prophet, leader of a global religious system

Discussion:

The Antichrist system uses food and water to coerce people into accepting the mark of the beast. People will do just about anything when they get hungry, even sell their souls. Beware of this scenario as you will be required to take the mark of the beast to buy food. Refuse to take the mark and save your soul. If you take the mark, you will burn forever in the lake of fire. Better to starve or be martyred than to take the mark.

The 144,000 Return

*"And I looked, and, lo, a Lamb stood on the mount Sion, and with him an **hundred forty and four thousand**, having his Father's name written in their foreheads. And I heard a voice from heaven, as the voice of many waters, and as the voice of a great thunder: and I heard the voice of harpers harping with their harps:" - Revelation 14:1-2 KJV*

The 144,000 witnesses sealed by God back in Revelation chapter seven are now with the Lamb, the Lord Jesus Christ. Is their ministry finished on earth? Have they been martyred for their message? Not sure, but a great praise and worship service is about to begin. Voices, loud as thunder, break forth, as music from a host of harpers fills the heavens.

*"And **they sung as it were a new song before the throne**, and before the four beasts, and the elders: and no man could learn that song but **the hundred and forty and four thousand**, which were redeemed from the earth. These are they which were not defiled with women; for they are virgins. These are they which follow the Lamb whithersoever he goeth. These were redeemed from among men, being the firstfruits unto God and to the Lamb. And in their mouth was found no guile: for they are without fault before the throne of God." - Revelation 14:3-5 KJV*

In the previous passage, the 144,000 were with the Lamb on Mount Sion. That is in Jerusalem. Now they appear before the throne in heaven. The text states they are "redeemed from the earth." They are also declared the "firstfruits unto God and to the Lamb." They are the first fruits of those saved during the 7-year Tribulation—tribulation saints. Also, they are Jesus' brethren, Jews, a particular group of men redeemed by God for His special purpose.

The Everlasting Gospel

*"And I saw another angel fly in the midst of heaven, having the **everlasting gospel** to preach unto them that dwell on the earth, and to every nation, and kindred, and tongue, and people, Saying with a loud voice, **Fear God, and give glory to him; for the hour of his judgment is come: and worship him that made heaven, and earth, and the sea, and the fountains of waters**." - Revelation 14:6-7 KJV*

Another angel flies through the heavens preaching the "everlasting gospel" to those on the earth. Everyone will hear this gospel, "every nation, and kindred, and tongue, and people." This everlasting gospel is not quite what we might expect as it makes no direct mention of Jesus Christ, grace, nor faith. It says, *"Fear God, and give glory to him; for the hour of his judgment is come: and worship him that made heaven, and earth, and the sea, and the fountains of waters."* It harkens all to fear God as Creator, like Romans chapter 1. Even if someone has never heard about Jesus Christ, they can still see and know God as Creator by observing His creation, the earth, sun, moon, and stars. The heavens declare the glory of God. Throughout the entire history of humanity, God could always be seen and understood as the Creator of all.

Babylon and the Beast

*"And there followed another angel, saying, **Babylon is fallen, is fallen**, that great city, because she made all nations drink of the wine of the wrath of her fornication." - Revelation 14:8 KJV*

Another angel proclaims that "Babylon is fallen, is fallen..." Ancient Babylon exists no more. Over the centuries, it simply fell into disrepair and ceased to exist. Today it is just an archeological site having a few of its structures restored by Saddam Hussein. The new

Babylon will be the center for the pagan religion of the Middle East. We will discuss this later when we review Revelation Chapter 17-18.

*"And the third angel followed them, saying with a loud voice, **If any man worship the beast** and his image, and receive his mark in his forehead, or in his hand, The same shall **drink of the wine of the wrath of God**, which is poured out without mixture into the cup of his indignation; and he shall be **tormented with fire and brimstone** in the presence of the holy angels, and in the presence of the Lamb:" - Revelation 14:9-10 KJV*

Yet another angel appears with an announcement for the followers of the Antichrist. For all those that worship the Antichrist by receiving his mark, they will drink from the cup of God's wrath. It will be served without mixture, not watered down, but the pure wrath of God. The worshippers of Antichrist will be tormented by fire and brimstone seen by the holy angels and the Lord Jesus Christ. They will always know what they could have obtained had they followed Jesus Christ instead of the Antichrist.

*"And the **smoke of their torment ascendeth up for ever and ever** and they have **no rest day nor night**, who worship the beast and his image, and whosoever receiveth the mark of his name. Here is the **patience of the saints**: here are they that keep the commandments of God, and the faith of Jesus." - Revelation 14:11-12 KJV*

The followers of Antichrist are tormented forever and ever in the fire and brimstone, the lake of fire. They have no rest, no relief, no hope of rescue. They are doomed to torment for all eternity. That is the horrific reward for following the Antichrist and taking his mark. The patience of the saints is to keep the faith of Jesus Christ and endure whatever comes their way during the 7-year Tribulation.

*"And I heard a voice from heaven saying unto me, Write, **Blessed are the dead which die in the Lord from henceforth**: Yea, saith the Spirit, that they may rest from their labours; and their works do follow them."* - Revelation 14:13 KJV

A voice from heaven declares something that sounds a bit strange to the normal flow of life. But remember, this is for the tribulation saints that are having a very rough go of it. "Blessed are the dead which die in the Lord from henceforth." In other words, things are so bad that death is a blessing. Jesus said this period would be the worst of all human history. Even the saints are barely able to survive.

Also, the Antichrist has been given power over the saints, so they are being martyred at a phenomenal rate. For many, death will be a welcome relief. I know that is difficult to understand, but we have never lived in those horrific conditions. Someone who survived the Nazi death camps may relate to this level of suffering, but most cannot, especially in America. After their martyr's death, they rest from their labor in heaven. Their works follow them, meaning that they will be rewarded for their obedience to Jesus Christ. They will have a Crown of Life for giving their life for their testimony in Christ Jesus.

Harvest of the Wicked

*"And I looked, and behold a white cloud, and upon the cloud one sat like unto the Son of man, having on his head a golden crown, and **in his hand a sharp sickle**. And another angel came out of the temple, crying with a loud voice to him that sat on the cloud, **Thrust in thy sickle, and reap**: for the time is come for thee to reap; for the harvest of the earth is ripe. And he that sat on the cloud thrust in his sickle on the earth; and **the earth was reaped**."* - Revelation 14:14-16 KJV

A mighty angel sits on a cloud with a sharp sickle in his hand. At first, this sounds like it might be Jesus, but it is not as this angel takes orders from another angel. Jesus doesn't take orders; He gives them. The command is given to "thrust in thy sickle and reap: for the time is come for thee to reap; for the harvest of the earth is ripe." The instruction is to thrust your sickle into the earth and reap. What is being reaped? Well, it is not the saints and indeed not grapes. The wicked followers of Antichrist are what is reaped.

The unrighteous, rebellious sinners that mocked God and Christ are now getting some well-deserved payback. They are being reaped, cut down, and removed. I love it when the wicked get what they deserve. They have been given many chances to repent and follow Jesus Christ but have scoffed at Jesus each time. God will only endure so much. His patience has run out.

*"And another angel came out of the temple which is in heaven, **he also having a sharp sickle**. And another angel came out from the altar, which had power over fire; and cried with a loud cry to him that had the sharp sickle, saying, **Thrust in thy sharp sickle, and gather the clusters of the vine of the earth; for her grapes are fully ripe**. And the angel thrust in his sickle into the earth, and gathered the vine of the earth, and cast it into the **great winepress of the wrath of God**. And the winepress was trodden without the city, and **blood came out of the winepress**, even unto the horse bridles, by the space of a thousand and six hundred furlongs." - Revelation 14:17-20 KJV*

There's a spectacular abundance of wicked followers of Antichrist. So much so that another angel is needed to complete the job of reaping the earth. This second angel is commanded to "Thrust in thy sharp sickle." Now the wicked are referred to as "grapes." These evil "grapes" are gathered and cast into the "great winepress of the wrath of God." This reaping occurs outside the city of Jerusalem. What flows from the winepress is not grape juice but blood. The wicked are in the winepress, and their blood flows for a "thousand and six hundred furlongs" precisely 200 miles. That is quite a distance for the tiny country of Israel. A river of blood 200 miles long and four feet deep. Unimaginable! A prediction of the blood bath that occurs at the Battle of Armageddon at the end of the 7-year Tribulation.

Seven Bowls of Wrath

"And I saw another sign in heaven, great and marvellous, seven angels having the seven last plagues; for in them is filled up the wrath of God. And I saw as it were a sea of glass mingled with fire: and them that had gotten the victory over the beast, and over his image, and over his mark, and over the number of his name, stand on the sea of glass, having the harps of God."
- Revelation 15:1-2 KJV

The scene is back in heaven with seven splendid angels, each with a bowl filled with the "wrath of God." These "seven last plagues" are destined to be poured out upon the earth and the kingdom of the Antichrist. But first, there appears a sea of glass and fire. Standing on that sea is a great multitude of saints martyred for their faith in Jesus. They did not take the mark of the beast, his name, or his number. They did not worship the beast or his image. They were victorious by maintaining their faith even to the point of death. That is the same "sea of glass" we read about in Revelation chapter four. Then it was empty; now it is filled with the martyrs of Jesus Christ.

*"And they sing the **song of Moses** the servant of God, and the **song of the Lamb**, saying, Great and marvellous are thy works, Lord God Almighty; just and true are thy ways, thou King of saints. Who shall not fear thee, O Lord,*

and glorify thy name? for thou only art holy: for all nations shall come and worship before thee; for thy judgments are made manifest." - Revelation 15:3-4 KJV

These martyred saints "sing the song of Moses" and the "song of the Lamb." That tells me that most, if not all, are Jews that came to a saving knowledge of Jesus Christ. They sing, "Great and marvelous are thy works, Lord God Almighty; just and true are thy ways, thou King of saints. Who shall not fear thee, O Lord, and glorify thy name? for thou only art holy: for all nations shall come and worship before thee; for thy judgments are made manifest."

*"And after that I looked, and, behold, the temple of the tabernacle of the testimony in heaven was opened: And **the seven angels** came out of the temple, having the **seven plagues**, clothed in pure and white linen, and having their breasts girded with golden girdles. And one of the four beasts gave unto the seven angels **seven golden vials full of the wrath of God**, who liveth for ever and ever. And the temple was filled with smoke from the glory of God, and from his power; and no man was able to enter into the temple, till the seven plagues of the seven angels were fulfilled." - Revelation 15:5-8 KJV*

Final preparations are made for the seven angels to receive the seven bowls of the wrath of God. The temple in heaven is opened, and one of the four living creatures that stood before God brings the seven bowls out of the temple. Smoke fills the temple, and no one can enter until the wrath of God is dispensed. The seven angels each have their bowl of wrath. Time has come for them to be poured out upon the earth.

*"And I heard a great voice out of the temple saying to the seven angels, Go your ways, and **pour out the vials of the wrath of God upon the earth**.*

*And the **first** went, and poured out his vial upon the earth; and there fell a **noisome and grievous sore** upon the men which had the **mark of the beast**, and upon them which **worshipped his image**." - Revelation 16:1-2 KJV*

The first angel pours his bowl upon the earth, specifically on those that received the mark of the beast. A "noisome and grievous sore" befalls them—noisome means disgusting, fetid, stinking, noxious large sore. We are not talking about a little pimple; these are injurious, almost debilitating nasty sores. Grievous sores might be a delayed reaction to receiving the microchip implant if that is what the mark of the beast turns out to be. Hundreds of millions of people will be infected with these putrid sores. It will be a pandemic, and they won't understand why. Governments and health service organizations will be helpless to relieve this global malady. Where is Anthony Fauci when you need him? Just kidding!

*"And the **second angel** poured out his vial upon **the sea**, and it became as the **blood of a dead man**: and every living soul **died** in the sea." - Revelation 16:3 KJV*

This angel pours his bowl of wrath on the sea, and it becomes like the blood of a dead man. The blood of a dead man is partially coagulated with a deep red color. From this plague, everything in the sea dies. That completes the second trumpet judgment that turned a third of the sea to blood. Turning the sea of Galilee to blood and everything in it dying would not be that spectacular on a global scale. Sure, it would be disastrous for those living nearby, but only for them. Turning the entire oceans of the planet would be fatal for all life on earth as our oxygen comes from the sea. That might be too spectacular. However, turning the Mediterranean Sea to blood might have the desired impact. I am only speculating at this point; those still alive must wait and see.

*"And the **third angel** poured out his vial upon the **rivers and fountains of waters**; and they became **blood**. And I heard the angel of the waters say, Thou art righteous, O Lord, which art, and wast, and shalt be, because thou hast judged thus. For **they have shed the blood of saints and prophets, and thou hast given them blood to drink**; for they are worthy. And I heard another out of the altar say, Even so, Lord God Almighty, true and righteous are thy judgments." - Revelation 16:4-7 KJV*

This bowl of wrath completes the third trumpet judgment by turning fresh water into blood. That could be local to the Middle East, particularly the Antichrist kingdom. The "angel of the waters" proclaimed that this judgment of God is righteous. The Antichrist's followers have shed the blood of many saints. Now God is giving them blood to drink. They like blood so much, let them drink it.

"And the fourth angel poured out his vial upon the sun; and power was given unto him to scorch men with fire. And men were scorched with great heat, and blasphemed the name of God, which hath power over these plagues: and they repented not to give him glory." - Revelation 16:8-9 KJV

This fourth bowl of wrath completes the fourth trumpet as the heat of the sun is dramatically increased. That could be a massive solar flare or coronal mass ejection hitting the earth, causing great fires and heat. The people of earth continue to curse God for these events instead of repenting. They know God is releasing these plagues upon the earth, but each one makes them more rebellious.

*"And the fifth angel poured out his vial upon the **seat of the beast; and his kingdom was full of darkness;** and they **gnawed their tongues for***

pain, And blasphemed the God of heaven because of their pains and their sores, and ***repented not of their deeds***." - *Revelation 16:10-11 KJV*

With this bowl of wrath, great darkness befalls the kingdom and seat of the Antichrist. As his seat is now Jerusalem, thick malevolent darkness engulfs the city. An evil, oppressive darkness that causes people to gnaw their tongues for pain, distracting their senses from the darkness. Hard to imaging such a thing, but it is coming. Now they have sores, fire, darkness, and pain, yet they continue to curse God. The kingdom of Antichrist is in bad shape as they have little or no fresh water to drink either. Food is scarce also, but they continue their blasphemy.

"And the sixth angel poured out his vial upon the great river Euphrates; and the water thereof was dried up, that the way of the kings of the east might be prepared." - Revelation 16:12 KJV

Preparations are finalized for the big one, the battle of Armageddon. With this bowl of wrath, the Euphrates River dries up so the armies from the east can come to the Near East. The Euphrates River is currently drying up as I write. The armies could include troops from Iran to China. They come not to battle each other but to fight the return of the white horse rider of chapter 19, the Lord Jesus Christ. The 7-year Tribulation is drawing to a close; just one main event left before the second coming of Jesus Christ.

*"And I saw **three unclean spirits like frogs** come out of the mouth of the dragon, and out of the mouth of the beast, and out of the mouth of the false prophet. For they are the **spirits of devils, working miracles, which go forth unto the kings of the earth and of the whole world, to gather them to the battle of that great day of God Almighty**." - Revelation 16:13-14 KJV*

Three demonic spirits emerge from the Antichrist, the False Prophet, and Satan. These three "spirits of devils" deceive nations with many false miracles. They go forth to gather the remaining armies of the world to "that great day of God Almighty." The battle to end all wars, not for land, wealth, or resources, but to prevent the return of the King, Jesus Christ—Satan's last-ditch effort to remain in control of planet earth, but he fails miserably.

*"**Behold, I come as a thief. Blessed is he that watcheth, and keepeth his garments**, lest he walk naked, and they see his shame. And he gathered them together into a place called in the Hebrew tongue Armageddon." - Revelation 16:15-16 KJV*

Verse 15 is interesting as the Lord says, "I come as a thief." Since the 7-year Tribulation is coming to an end, and the armies gather to prevent Jesus' second coming, how can the Lords return be as a thief? The fact is that those left behind after the Rapture do not know Bible prophecy. Most that took the time to learn about it decided to follow Jesus and were martyred. The saints still living are instructed to watch and be ready.

The bulk of those remaining are followers of the Antichrist, believing that his kingdom will last forever. However, that belief disintegrates quickly at the battle of Armageddon. The valley of Megiddo or the valley of Jezreel is in northern Israel, beginning at the Mediterranean Sea going southeastward to the Jordan River. That's the rally point for the armies as the battle will be centered around Jerusalem. Jesus returns to the Mount of Olives, precisely where He left this earth— ground zero for the mother of all battles, Armageddon.

*"And the seventh angel poured out his vial into the air; and there came a great voice out of the temple of heaven, from the throne, saying, **It is done**.*

And there were voices, and thunders, and lightnings; and there was a great earthquake, such as was not since men were upon the earth, so mighty an earthquake, and so great." - Revelation 16:17-18 KJV

The seventh bowl of God's wrath completes the divine judgments of the 7-year Tribulation. A great voice proclaims from the temple in heaven, "It is done," the fullness of God's wrath poured out upon sinful humanity. There is much activity in heaven with voices, thunders, and bolts of lightning. On earth, there is a massive earthquake, the worst the world has ever seen.

*"And the great city was divided into three parts, and **the cities of the nations fell**; and great Babylon came in remembrance before God, to give unto her the cup of the wine of the fierceness of his wrath. **And every island fled away, and the mountains were not found.**" - Revelation 16:19-20 KJV*

Jerusalem is split into three parts, and many cities around the world suffer catastrophic damaged or are destroyed. Remember, God never told humankind to build great cities. Nimrod was the first to create a great city on the plain of Shinar, ancient Babylon. God brought that project to a quick end by confusing their languages. God told mankind to spread across the earth, be fruitful and multiply. Big cities are an evil conspiracy to group people into large urban areas for easy control and surveillance.

Babylon the great comes to God's remembrance that she should drink from the cup of His wrath. The Antichrist kingdom, the New World Order, is the end times version of ancient Babylon. During the great earthquake, islands slip back into the sea, and mountains fall. The earth's surface will be reshaped by God in preparation for the Millennial Reign of Jesus Christ. Planet earth will appear quite different during the Lords Millennial Kingdom. Uninhabitable mountain ranges are reduced to rolling hills and plains suitable for living. Deserts blooming as Adam's curse is removed from the earth and sky.

*"And there fell upon men a **great hail out of heaven, every stone about the weight of a talent:** and men blasphemed God because of the plague of the hail; for the plague thereof was exceeding great." - Revelation 16:21 KJV*

The final judgment of the seventh bowl of wrath—great hailstones. Can you imagine being pummeled with hail weighing 70-100 pounds each? They will crush everything they hit. Yet another tool God uses to destroy things that will not be part of His kingdom. Hail is an excellent weapon. After it does its damage, it simply melts away—environmentally friendly weapons of mass destruction. Only God could achieve that.

The Great Whore of the Earth

*"And there came one of the seven angels which had the seven vials, and talked with me, saying unto me, Come hither; **I will shew unto thee the judgment of the great whore that sitteth upon many waters.** With whom the kings of the earth have committed fornication, and the inhabitants of the earth have been made **drunk with the wine of her fornication.**" - Revelation 17:1-2 KJV*

Here begins the end time passages about the false religious system. Islam is currently the predominant religion in the Middle East and has been since the 8th century. It is quickly gaining worldwide supremacy, especially in Europe, with millions of Muslim immigrants invading its shores. Currently (November 2023) we see demonstrations and riots worldwide in support of Hamas and the so-called Palestinians. Islamic control will increase dramatically after the Rapture when the restraining power of the Holy Spirit is removed.

Revelation chapters 17 and 18 backfill details of a corrupt religious system rising to complete totalitarian dominance during the Tribulation. Guided by an angel, the apostle John sees the coming judgment of this great idolatrous whore. This corrupt, pagan religious system sits upon "many waters." The many waters are peoples and nations under Islamic Sharia law. During the 7-year Tribulation, that will be a global conglomeration of pagan religions under the control of the Antichrist and the False Prophet. Perhaps even the Pope will convert to Islam.

Twenty-five percent of the world is Muslim. If the Antichrist is a Muslim, he will have one-fourth of the world's population following him as the Mahdi from day one. No need to spend years garnering a following. After the rapture, Muslim dominance will be even stronger.

If the Antichrist is Roman Catholic, he will have about 1.2 billion followers, many living in Latin America, Africa, and Europe, hardly any living in the Middle East. A Catholic, or Roman, Antichrist would have a near-impossible task of gaining control over a Muslim Middle East.

During the tribulation, this pagan religious system will drink from the cup of God's wrath as she has made others drink from the cup of her idolatrous fornication. Many people and groups have been working on a one-world religion for centuries. That will come together during the 7-year Tribulation, but it's nothing new. It's the continuation of the ancient Babylonian religion with modern terminology, technology, rituals, and garb. In the case of Islam, it's a throwback to the 7th century. Most do not know that the Muslim god Allah, the moon god, originated in ancient Babylon with Nimrod and Semiramis about 2400 B.C. Islam is a modern Babylonian religion.

"Fornication," in this context, is spiritual fornication, idol worship. The worship of anything other than God through the Lord Jesus Christ is idol worship, having a spiritual relationship with something other than Jesus Christ. The "wine of her fornication" could reference Middle East oil used to coerce nations into tolerance and acceptance of Islam.

*"So he carried me away in the spirit into the **wilderness**: and I saw a woman **sit upon a scarlet coloured beast**, full of names of blasphemy, having **seven heads and ten horns**. And the woman was arrayed in **purple and scarlet** colour, and decked with gold and precious stones and pearls, having a **golden cup** in her hand full of **abominations** and filthiness of her fornication:" - Revelation 17:3-4 KJV*

The Holy Spirit caries John away to the "wilderness" or desert. He is not taken to Rome, Tibet, Brooklyn, or Salt Lake City. Can you think of a supposed holy capital city located somewhere in the deserts of the Middle East? How about Mecca? Mecca is the epicenter of Islam and is in the Arabian desert close to the Red Sea. There John sees a woman sitting on a scarlet-colored beast. The woman represents the one world pagan religious system. The beast is the political-military system of the Antichrist.

The woman is riding the beast, meaning that the religious system has control over the political-military system, at least temporarily. That is precisely the structure of Islam as the religious leaders control every aspect of Muslim government and life. The beast kingdom of the Antichrist has names of blasphemy on the seven heads and ten horns. We have seen this beast several times here in Revelation and the Book of Daniel. It is the same old Global Satanic Conspiracy to rule the world and prevent the Messiah's return.

The woman is arrayed in purple and scarlet, which are colors of royalty as she governs the growing kingdom of the Antichrist. That is the situation during the first 3 ½ years of the Tribulation as the Antichrist rises to global power. The woman is holding a "golden cup" full of abominations of her idolatry. That relates back to Babylon as Jeremiah writes about the "wine of her fornication."

*"Babylon hath been a **golden cup** in the LORD'S hand, that made all the earth drunken: the nations have drunken of **her wine**, therefore the **nations are mad**." - Jeremiah 51:7 KJV*

*"And upon her forehead was a name written, **MYSTERY, BABYLON THE GREAT, THE MOTHER OF HARLOTS AND ABOMINATIONS OF THE EARTH**. And I saw the woman drunken with the **blood of the saints**, and with the **blood of the martyrs of Jesus**: and when I saw her, I wondered with great admiration." - Revelation 17:5-6 KJV*

The woman, symbolic of the end times global pagan religious system, has a name; "**MYSTERY, BABYLON THE GREAT, THE MOTHER OF HARLOTS AND ABOMINATIONS OF THE EARTH.**" Let's analyze the name.

- "MYSTERY" is a new entity not previously revealed or taught in Scripture.
- "BABYLON THE GREAT" is the ancient kingdom of Babylon. But this is the mystery or unrevealed end time manifestation of that

ancient kingdom. In other words, the 21st century version of a pagan Babylonian religion.

- "THE MOTHER OF HARLOTS AND ABOMINATIONS OF THE EARTH" Ancient Babylon was the origin of all false pagan religions which are abominations to God. So, this modern version is a harlot religion just like its mother. Its teachings are an abomination to the one true God.
- Conclusion: This end times pagan religious system that rules the Antichrist kingdom has its origins in ancient Babylon the Great. That begs the question, is Islam an ancient religion or did it start in the 7th century A.D. with the prophet Mohammad?

Let's look at some ancient artifacts that show how long pagans have been worshipping the moon god.

Stela of Nabonidus, (British Museum) #90837 Neo-Babylonian Dynasty (554BC-539BC) Acquired 1825 from the Middle East

"Basalt stela of Nabonidus in traditional dress with religious objects in his hands; in front of him are divine symbols (the star of Ishtar-Venus, the winged disc of the sun god Shamash and the crescent of the moon god Sin); the latter is the first and largest, showing supremacy." British Museum.

This basalt relief shows Nabonidus, the son of Nebuchadnezzar, King of Babylon. Nabonidus reigned only for a short time and turned the kingdom over to his son Belshazzar. Daniel the prophet was governor of Babylon while Nabonidus ruled. The exciting aspect is the emblem of the moon god Sin being first in line showing his supremacy over the other gods. This artifact predates Islam by 1000 years.

Cylinder-seal of Khashkhamer, patesi of Ishkun-Sin (in North Babylonia), and vassal of Ur-Engur, king of Ur (c. 2400 BC) (British Museum).

The only symbol of a god in this artifact is the crescent moon. This seal shows the worship of the moon god almost 3000 years before Muhammad, the founder of Islam. Ur is in the ancient kingdom of Babylon. There are hundreds of these ancient artifacts in the British Museum, the Louvre, and many other fine museums worldwide.

Islam is the worship of Allah, the moon god. The crescent moon is their symbol and is on every mosque. But the worship of the moon god can easily be traced back to ancient Babylon. The conclusion is that Islam is an ancient Babylonian pagan religion simply repackaged by Muhammad for desert Bedouins.

In the book of Judges, chapter eight, we read that Arab kings from Midian worshipped the moon god back in the days of Gideon. The story picks up after Gideon captures two kings of Midian, Zebah, and Zalmunna after they attacked Israel.

*"So Zebah and Zalmunna said, "Rise yourself, and kill us; for as a man is, so is his strength." So Gideon arose and killed Zebah and Zalmunna, and took **the crescent ornaments that were on their camels' necks**. ... Now the weight of the gold earrings that he requested was one thousand seven hundred shekels of gold, besides the **crescent ornaments**, pendants, and purple robes which were **on the kings of Midian**, and besides the chains that were around their camels' necks." - Judges 8:21, 26 NKJV*

The kings of Midian had crescent moon ornaments on their camels and around their necks showing their complete devotion to the moon god. Islam is nothing more than an ancient pagan moon god religion brought into the 21st century by Bible-hating waring minions of Satan. Someone once said that Islam is Satan's Masterpiece. I could not agree more.

*"And the angel said unto me, Wherefore didst thou marvel? I will tell thee the **mystery of the woman**, and of the beast that carrieth her, which hath the seven heads and ten horns. The beast that thou sawest **was, and is not; and shall ascend out of the bottomless pit**, and go into perdition: and they that dwell on the earth shall **wonder**, whose names were **not written in the book of life** from the foundation of the world, when they behold the beast that **was, and is not, and yet is**." - Revelation 17:7-8 KJV*

Here again, we see the word "mystery" associated with the woman, the end times pagan religious system. A mystery in scripture is something previously not revealed. The woman's identity has not been previously disclosed in scripture, so she is not ancient Babylon revived. She is a new form of an ancient Babylonian religion; she is Islam.

Remember the setting here. John sees events that transpire during the 7-year Tribulation. The woman, the global pagan religious system, is riding the beast, the political system, that comes to complete power at the midpoint of the Tribulation. The angel tells John that the beast *"was, and is not; and shall ascend out of the bottomless pit."*

There was a time before the Tribulation when the beast existed. Then went away to the bottomless pit for a while. But during the Tribulation, it ascends out of the bottomless pit to reign once again. Only to return to perdition, in this case, the lake of fire. So, was there a governing political system that existed in the Middle East before the Tribulation and then ceased to exist only to be revived during the Tribulation to be ruled by the Antichrist for a short time? Yes, there was.

The Ottoman Empire (1299 – 1922) ruled the Middle East region, including parts of Southern Europe, Western Asia, North Africa, and the Caucuses. The height of the Empire was the reign of Suleiman the Magnificent, who rebuilt the walls in Jerusalem and restored the Dome of the Rock Mosque. The Ottoman Empire was defeated at the end of World War I by British and French forces, and the land was partitioned into the countries we have today. At the same time, a Turkish revolt ended with creating a Turkish state that exists today. As the empire was collapsing, the Ottoman Turks killed several million Christians in Armenia and Smyrna. Bad habits are hard to break as the revived Ottoman Empire will do the same only many more will die.

The Ottoman Empire does not exist as of this writing, but many, including Turkey's President Erdogan, who views himself as the Caliph, desire to restore the Empire to its glory days. It will return during the Tribulation and be the seat of the Antichrist who ascends from the bottomless pit.

The revived Ottoman Empire will form after the Rapture. Those left on earth "whose names were not written in the book of life" will be in awe and wonderment of the newly revived Empire and its leader, the Antichrist. They come to the forefront in the Middle East on a peace platform that the world shall welcome. He that brings peace to the Middle East has the world on a silver platter, at least for a while, then all hell breaks loose.

*"And here is the mind which hath wisdom. The seven heads are **seven mountains**, on which the woman sitteth. And there are **seven kings**: five are fallen, and one is, and the other is not yet come; and when he cometh, he must continue a short space." - Revelation 17:9-10 KJV*

An aspect of God's "wisdom" is the use of symbolism. The passage states that the "seven heads are seven mountains." In prophetic passages, "mountains" are kingdoms. The angel is saying that the seven heads of the beast represent seven kingdoms. It also states, "there are seven kings" that control the seven kingdoms. Five of these seven kingdoms have fallen. That means they were historical at the time of John's writing. Those five kingdoms are clear from other prophetic Scriptures. They are Egypt, Assyria, Babylon, Media–Persia, and Greece. These five fallen kingdoms had hegemony over the Levant at some point in history. Since they no longer exist, they predate the Rapture.

But what about the kingdom that "is"? Is when? At the time of John? That would be the Roman Empire. But John sees events that occur in the Tribulation. The empire that "is" would be the one during the first half of the 7-year Tribulation. The sixth kingdom would be the revived Caliphate under the rule of the ten kings. That precedes the reign of the Antichrist during the last half of the Tribulation. The "other" kingdom then comes and "must continue a short space," meaning the consolidated Kingdom of the Antichrist during the last half of the Tribulation.

"And the beast that was, and is not, even he is the eighth, and is of the seven, and goeth into perdition." - Revelation 17:11 KJV

The Antichrist himself is the eighth as he is the head of the final world empire, the seventh head, for the last half of the Tribulation. He is not a different head but the head of the seventh kingdom, the revived Ottoman Empire. When he is destroyed, he will go back to the pit where he came from.

*"And the **ten horns** which thou sawest are **ten kings**, which have received no kingdom as yet; but **receive power as kings one hour with the beast**. These have one mind, and shall give their power and strength unto the beast." - Revelation 17:12-13 KJV*

The beast upon which the woman rides have ten horns. The ten horns are ten kings. These ten kings have countries or nations; else they would not be kings. But they have no Empire to exert control over the Middle East. They give their allegiance to the Antichrist, becoming part of his kingdom to rule with him, thereby establishing control over the region. Like the European Union model, countries give their allegiance to EU governance while maintaining their borders, language, and culture.

"These shall make war with the Lamb, and the Lamb shall overcome them: for he is Lord of lords, and King of kings: and they that are with him are called, and chosen, and faithful." - Revelation 17:14 KJV

At the end of the Tribulation, the revived Ottoman Empire will make war with the Lamb, Jesus Christ. They will do everything they can to prevent His return to earth to establish His kingdom. Jesus Christ is King of kings and Lord of lords coming to claim what is rightfully His. The saints that return with Him are the "called, and chosen, and faithful". They are the Old Testament and martyred saints that will enter the Millennial Kingdom.

"And he saith unto me, The waters which thou sawest, where the whore sitteth, are peoples, and multitudes, and nations, and tongues. And the ten horns which thou sawest upon the beast, these shall hate the whore, and shall make her desolate and naked, and shall eat her flesh, and burn her with fire." - Revelation 17:15-16 KJV

The angel then tells John that the waters upon which the woman sits are Gentile nations. That is in keeping with the Middle East as it is all Gentile except Israel. The ten horns or kings of the Antichrist empire will hate the woman and destroy her with fire. The political and military system will eliminate the religious system by destroying the Kaaba in Mecca, the center of Islam. The ten kings will burn Mecca with fire, perhaps a nuclear weapon. The Antichrist wants to be worshipped as god, so he destroys any religious system that directs worship to another, like Allah. He does not honor any god but proclaims himself god at the midpoint of the Tribulation.

*"For **God hath put in their hearts to fulfil his will,** and to agree, and give their kingdom unto the beast, until the words of God shall be fulfilled. And the woman which thou sawest is that **great city,** which reigneth over the kings of the earth."* - Revelation 17:17-18 KJV

God is directing the activities on earth from the throne room of heaven. God works through the ten kings to align with the Antichrist so God's judgments can be fulfilled. God wants the pagan new world religion destroyed and uses the ten kings to do it. Lastly, the woman is that "great city, which reigneth over the kings of the earth," Mecca. There is no other city in the Middle East that reigns over many countries, Jerusalem certainly doesn't. Every year several million Muslims take the pilgrimage, the hajj, to Mecca to walk around the Kaaba seven times. Westerners do not understand the importance of this event to Muslims. Below is the tent city of Mina that can accommodate 3-4 million Muslims for the hajj. Also, two pictures of the Grand Mosque and the Kaaba. Yes, those little dots are people. When the Antichrist/al-Mahdi takes the world stage, he will instantly have a Billion followers.

"And after these things I saw another angel come down from heaven, having great power; and the earth was lightened with his glory. And he cried mightily with a strong voice, saying, **Babylon the great is fallen, is fallen**, and is become the habitation of **devils**, and the hold of every **foul spirit**, and a cage of every **unclean and hateful bird**. For all nations have *drunk of the wine of the wrath of her fornication, and the kings of the earth have committed fornication with her, and the merchants of the earth are waxed rich through the abundance of her delicacies." - Revelation 18:1-3 KJV*

After the angel explains to John the woman riding the beast, another angel comes, having great power and glory. This angel cries, "Babylon the great is fallen, is fallen..." we read a similar passage in Isaiah.

*"The burden of the desert of the sea. As whirlwinds in the south pass through; so it cometh from the desert, from a terrible land. ... And, behold, here cometh a chariot of men, with a couple of horsemen. And he answered and said, **Babylon is fallen, is fallen**; and all the graven images of her gods he hath broken unto the ground." - Isaiah 21:1, 9 KJV* .

Some equate these two passages because they have a similar reference to Babylon. But the above passage in Isaiah refers to the fall of ancient Babylon in the 6th century BC. In Revelation above, we have the fall of end times Babylon the Great. That is a reference to the fall of the final great Babylonian pagan religion, Islam. Islam will fall on a spectacular scale unseen in the fall of ancient Babylon. God will pour out His wrath on this pagan false religion in an unprecedented fashion.

The nations have drunk the "wine of her fornication." Could that "wine" be Saudi oil? We have politicians that call Islam the religion of peace to preserve our oil interests in Saudi Arabia. I am thinking of presidents W and BO. They have drunk the wine. With billions of dollars to spend, Saudi Arabia has purchased an abundance of the world's delicacies. The Saudis have everything imaginable, even slaves. Islam is the only major religion that approves of and actively promotes slavery.

*"And I heard another voice from heaven, saying, **Come out of her, my people**, that ye be not partakers of her sins, and that ye receive not of her plagues. For her sins have reached unto heaven, and God hath remembered her iniquities." - Revelation 18:4-5 KJV*

Another angel calls out to believers living under the oppressive regime of the Antichrist. "Come out of her." During the 7-year tribulation, believers will be trapped within the physical boundaries of the Antichrist kingdom. The angel calls for them to flee before the wrath of God falls. Even though we are in chapter 18 of Revelation, this false religion system spans the entire Tribulation, not just the closing events. Tribulation saints are called to leave and not to be caught up in the plagues coming upon the Antichrist kingdom and false religious system. This call goes out before the Lord begins pouring His wrath directly upon the Antichrist and his followers. Probably sometime around the middle of the Tribulation.

*"Reward her even as she rewarded you, and **double unto her double according to her works**: in the cup which she hath filled fill to her double. How much she hath glorified herself, and lived deliciously, so much torment and sorrow give her: for she saith in her heart, **I sit a queen, and am no widow, and shall see no sorrow**. Therefore shall her plagues come **in one day**, death, and mourning, and famine; and she shall be utterly **burned with fire**: for strong is the Lord God who judgeth her." - Revelation 18:6-8 KJV*

The Lord will reward her (that great city, Mecca) double according to her works, her evil abominations. The cup of the wrath of God for the woman will be filled twice. The prophet Isaiah wrote of this in chapter 47 of his book.

*"Come down, and sit in the dust, O virgin **daughter of Babylon**, sit on the ground: there is no throne, O daughter of the Chaldeans: for thou shalt no more be called tender and delicate. ... Therefore hear now this, thou that art given to pleasures, that dwellest carelessly, that sayest in thine heart, I am, and none else beside me; **I shall not sit as a widow**, neither shall I know the loss of children: But these two things **shall come to thee in a moment in one day**, the loss of children, and widowhood: they shall come upon thee in their perfection for the multitude of thy sorceries, and for the great abundance of thine enchantments."* - Isaiah 47:1, 8-9 KJV

Revelation chapter 18 echoes Isaiah chapter 47. The "daughter of Babylon" is a daughter Babylonian religion, Islam. She proclaims never to be a widow without followers to worship her. But the Lord states that her destruction comes in "one day." In one day, she, Mecca, will be destroyed.

*"And the kings of the earth, who have committed fornication and lived deliciously with her, shall bewail her, and lament for her, when they shall see the **smoke of her burning, Standing afar off** for the fear of her torment, saying, Alas, alas, that great city Babylon, that mighty city! for in **one hour is thy judgment come**."* - Revelation 18:9-10 KJV

Those Sunni Muslim nations aligned with Saudi Arabia will lament and mourn the destruction of Mecca and the Kaaba. Her destruction will be so great that even from afar, they will see the "smoke of her burning." They are "standing afar off" in fear as a nuclear blast has destroyed Mecca. In "one hour," her destruction has come.

*"And the **merchants of the earth shall weep and mourn over her**, for no man buyeth their merchandise any more: The merchandise of gold, and silver, and precious stones, and of pearls, and fine linen, and purple, and silk, and scarlet, and all thyine wood, and all manner vessels of ivory, and all manner vessels of most precious wood, and of brass, and iron, and marble, And cinnamon, and odours, and ointments, and frankincense, and wine, and oil, and fine flour, and wheat, and beasts, and sheep, and horses, and chariots, and **slaves**, and **souls of men**." - Revelation 18:11-13 KJV*

The merchants of the earth shall mourn as Arabia will no longer be buying their merchandise due to the destruction of Mecca. Saudi Arabia currently purchases everything in the above list from gold to the souls of men. The Saudis import slaves from the Philippines and other developing countries for work and sex. They destroy the "souls of men" through their false religion Islam. Islam is also the leading sponsor of terrorism and the promotion of terrorism throughout the west. Don't forget that the 911 terrorists were from Saudi Arabia, not Iran. But Hamas and Hezbollah are Iranian proxies.

*"And the fruits that thy soul lusted after are **departed from thee**, and all things which were dainty and goodly are **departed from thee**, and thou shalt find them no more at all. The merchants of these things, which were made rich by her, **shall stand afar off** for the fear of her torment, weeping and wailing, And saying, Alas, alas, that great city, that was clothed in fine linen, and purple, and scarlet, and decked with gold, and precious stones, and pearls! - Revelation 18:14-16 KJV*

The lament continues over the destruction of Mecca, Saudi Arabia. The delicacies and fine foods are gone. Again, the merchants who were made rich from her oil money stand afar off, amazed at her destruction. No one wants to venture in towards ground zero. It's all gone, and they are dumbfounded.

"For in **one hour so great riches is come to nought**. And every **shipmaster**, and all the **company in ships**, and **sailors**, and as many as **trade by sea, stood afar off**, And cried when they saw the smoke of her burning, saying, What city is like unto this great city!" - Revelation 18:17-18 KJV

The port of Jeddah is on the Red Sea and is the primary port supplying Mecca and Medina, Islam's two most holy cities. The Jeddah Islamic Port is on the main international shipping route between the east and west. It is the largest shipping port in the Middle East and North Africa.

The distance from the port of Jeddah to Mecca is 41 miles as the crow flies. If Mecca were hit with a tactical nuclear weapon, it could easily be seen from Jeddah. And since the port of Jeddah supplies Mecca with a host of goods, the "shipmasters" and "sailors" that "trade by sea" would certainly lament her destruction as their livelihood would then be gone.

*"And they **cast dust on their heads**, and cried, weeping and wailing, saying, Alas, alas, that great city, wherein were made rich all that had **ships in the sea** by reason of her costliness! for **in one hour is she made desolate**." - Revelation 18:19 KJV*

What people in the 21st century still cast "dust on their heads" as a sign of great mourning? That's right, Muslims living in the Middle East. Sunni Muslims will mourn and wail over the destruction of Mecca. Again, mention is made to the "ships of the sea," which refers to the port of Jeddah near Mecca. The suddenness of Mecca's destruction is reiterated as "in one hour." The Holy Spirit frequently repeats important concepts so we will eventually get the truth of the matter.

"Rejoice over her, thou heaven, and ye holy apostles and prophets; for God hath avenged you on her. And a mighty angel took up a stone like a great millstone, and cast it into the sea, saying, Thus with violence shall that great city Babylon be thrown down, and shall be found no more at all." - Revelation 18:20-21 KJV

The host of heaven, including the prophets and the apostles, rejoice over the final destruction of Mecca, the center of the final pagan Babylonian religion, Islam. An angel casts a great stone into the sea. In this context, this would be the Red Sea. That could be the destruction of the port of Jeddah as it is on the Red Sea. The violent destruction of Mecca is with a nuclear weapon as she "shall be found no more at all."

Jeremiah has a prophecy concerning Arabia. The land from Edom to Teman will be destroyed, and those in the Red Sea (the port of Jeddah) will morn. Edom is east of the Dead Sea, and Teman is the southeast quarter of Arabia. In other words, the southern coast of Saudi Arabia adjacent to the Red Sea.

*"As in the **overthrow of Sodom and Gomorrah** and the neighbour cities thereof, saith the LORD, no man shall abide there, neither shall a son of man dwell in it. ... Therefore hear the counsel of the LORD, that he hath taken against **Edom**, and his purposes, that he hath purposed against the inhabitants of **Teman**: Surely the least of the flock shall draw them out: surely he shall make their habitations desolate with them. The earth is moved at the noise of their fall, at the **cry the noise thereof was heard in the Red sea**."* - Jeremiah 49:18, 20-21 KJV

Mecca will be destroyed in one hour as "Sodom and Gomorrah." Lot, the nephew of Abraham, was the only one to escape the destruction of Sodom. God destroyed Sodom once Lot and his family were clear of the city. Previously in verse 4, we read that God calls His people out of the beast kingdom before the destruction of Mecca and Arabia. Jeremiah predicts the noise of Mecca's destruction, and the mourners will be heard in the Red Sea. How much clearer can this be? Revelation chapter 18 is echoing Jeremiah 49. The destruction of Mecca, Arabia, and Islam comes suddenly. The false Babylonian religion of the Tribulation is gone in one hour. Payback time is coming!

One more thing. I do not hate Muslims. They are brainwashed as children to follow a Satanic system of servitude. They are a tremendous mission field, and many thousands are coming to Jesus Christ. I hate Satan with his multiple false religions that enslave millions to a terrible life and a destiny in the lake of fire. May God have mercy on their souls bringing many to salvation. But it is all coming to a dramatic finale with the second coming of Jesus Christ, Maranatha, come quickly, Lord Jesus!

*"And the voice of harpers, and musicians, and of pipers, and trumpeters, shall be **heard no more** at all in thee; and no craftsman, of whatsoever craft he be, shall be found any more in thee; and the sound of a millstone shall be **heard no more** at all in thee; And the light of a candle shall shine no more at all in thee and the voice of the bridegroom and of the bride shall be heard no more at all in thee: for thy merchants were the great men of the earth; for by thy sorceries were all nations deceived. And in her was found the blood of prophets, and of saints, and of all that were slain upon the earth."*
- Revelation 18:22-24 KJV

The time of recompense has come, some long-overdue payback is in order. There is no more music, no more luxuries, no more fine foods, no more electricity, no more marriage parties, and no more material abundance. All that is gone from the false religious system of the Tribulation. What remains is the blood of those slain in her path to domination. The blood of the saints is a reminder of the righteous judgment of the Lord God bringing destruction on her; Mystery, Babylon the Great, Mother of all Harlots and Abominations in the Earth.

Prepare for the King

"And after these things I heard a great voice of much people in heaven, saying, Alleluia; Salvation, and glory, and honour, and power, unto the Lord our God: For true and righteous are his judgments: for he hath judged the great whore, which did corrupt the earth with her fornication, and hath avenged the blood of his servants at her hand. - Revelation 19:1-2 KJV

A praise and worship service breaks out in heaven as a great multitude begin praising the Lord, saying, "Alleluia; Salvation, and glory, and honor, and power, unto the Lord our God: For true and righteous are his judgments: for he hath judged the great whore, which did corrupt the earth with her fornication, and hath avenged the blood of his servants at her hand." The righteous in heaven are praising the Lord for His judgments against the "great whore" that corrupted the earth with her false pagan idol-worshipping religion, Islam. That is the woman that rides the beast previously discussed, Mystery, Babylon the Great. God has finally released His vengeance upon her to avenge the "blood of his servants."

"And again they said, Alleluia. And her smoke rose up for ever and ever. And the four and twenty elders and the four beasts fell down and worshipped God that sat on the throne, saying, Amen; Alleluia. And a voice came out of the throne, saying, Praise our God, all ye his servants, and ye that fear him, both small and great." - Revelation 19:3-5 KJV

The praise and worship continue regarding the smoke of her burning rising forever and ever. An interesting passage in Isaiah relates to the same matter.

*"For it is the **day of the LORD'S vengeance**, and the year of **recompences for the controversy of Zion**. And the streams thereof shall be **turned into pitch**, and the dust thereof into **brimstone**, and the land thereof shall become **burning pitchapter** It shall **not be quenched** night nor day; the **smoke thereof shall go up for ever**. from generation to generation it shall lie waste; none shall pass through it for ever and ever." - Isaiah 34:8-10 KJV*

Note the similarities with the passages in Revelation previously mentioned.
- It is the day of the Lord's vengeance and wrath—the Tribulation.
- Over the controversy of Zion, the homeland for the Jews— controversy between Jews and Muslims.

- Streams turned to pitch. Streams are underground streams, as in oil wells and fields. Pitch is that black tar-like glob that remains after the volatile hydrocarbons have evaporated from crude oil.
- As this pitch burns, sulfur is released as crude oil contains much sulfur.
- The oil fields of Arabia will become burning pitch.
- The fire will not be quenched, and the smoke will ascend forever and ever.
- That is the future for Arabia. The motherland of the end times false religion and terrorism—Islam.

Next, the elders, which represent Israel, join in the worship. A voice from the throne declares, "Praise our God, all ye his servants, and ye that fear him, both small and great." Those that serve Satan and the Antichrist have no fear of God. Anyone having a fear of God will seek out His salvation.

"And I heard as it were the voice of a great multitude, and as the voice of many waters, and as the voice of mighty thunderings, saying, Alleluia: for the Lord God omnipotent reigneth. Let us be glad and rejoice, and give honour to him: **for the marriage of the Lamb is come, and his wife hath made herself ready**. *And to her was granted that she should be arrayed in fine linen, clean and white: for the* **fine linen is the righteousness of saints**. *- Revelation 19:6-8 KJV*

A great multitude praises the Lord and announces that the "marriage of the Lamb is come, and his wife hath made herself ready." That is the marriage of the Lord Jesus Christ to His previously divorced wife, Israel. This re-marriage has been in the making for over two thousand five hundred years. God gave Israel a bill of divorce around the time of the Babylonian captivity, as Jeremiah writes.

*"And I saw, when for all the causes whereby backsliding **Israel committed adultery** I had put her away, and **given her a bill of divorce**, yet her treacherous sister Judah feared not, but went and played the harlot also." -* Jeremiah 3:8 KJV

You cannot give a bill of divorce to someone unless you are married to them. So, was God ever the husband to Israel? What does the scripture say?

*"**For thy Maker is thine husband; the LORD of hosts is his name**, and thy Redeemer the Holy One of Israel; The God of the whole earth shall he be called." - Isaiah 54:5 KJV*

*"Surely as a **wife treacherously departeth from her husband**, so have ye dealt treacherously with me, O house of Israel, saith the LORD." -* Jeremiah 3:20 KJV

*"Not according to the covenant that I made with their fathers in the day that I took them by the hand to bring them out of the land of Egypt; which my covenant they brake, **although I was an husband unto them, saith the LORD**." - Jeremiah 31:32 KJV*

The Lord was the husband to Israel (and Judah). But because of idolatry, the Lord gave Israel a bill of divorce. At the second coming, the Lord remarries Israel. Notice that the passage states that *"his wife hath made herself ready."* The Lord's wife is Israel, not the church. We are the "body of Christ." You cannot be the bride and the body of Christ simultaneously. The Lord is not marrying himself.

We have been taught that the church was betrothed to Jesus Christ at Pentecost in 33 AD. We became part of that betrothal when we were saved. The marriage in heaven is to us, the church. But all that is mere bogus church tradition, not founded upon scripture.

*"And he saith unto me, Write, Blessed are they which are **called unto the marriage supper of the Lamb**. And he saith unto me, These are the true sayings of God. And I fell at his feet to worship him. And he said unto me, See thou do it not: I am thy fellowservant, and of thy brethren that have the testimony of Jesus: worship God: **for the testimony of Jesus is the spirit of prophecy**." - Revelation 19:9-10 KJV*

The "called unto the marriage supper of the Lamb" are the remnant of Israel saved and protected by God during the Tribulation. John is overcome because Israel is taking their rightful place with the Lord and he falls at the angel's feet to worship him. The angel stops him, stating that he too is a fellow servant of the Lord having the testimony of Jesus Christ. Jesus is the "spirit of prophecy." Especially here in the book of Revelation, the words of Jesus are prophetic, thereby referring to Israel.

The King of Kings

*"And I saw heaven opened, and behold a **white horse**, and he that sat upon him was called **Faithful and True**, and in righteousness he doth **judge and make war**. His eyes were as a **flame of fire**, and on his head were **many crowns**; and he had a name written, that no man knew, but he himself. And he was clothed with a **vesture dipped in blood**: and his name is called The Word of God." - Revelation 19:11-13 KJV*

The climax of the 7-year Tribulation has come. The King of Kings and Lord of Lords is gloriously returning to take possession of the earth and establish His Millennial Kingdom. He rides a dazzling white horse and is called "Faithful and True." He is faithful to His word prophesying His return. However, this time He is not coming as a meek and compassionate servant of the Father's will to die on the cross. He comes as a mighty warrior, God Almighty, to "judge and make war." The long-overdue payback for the Antichrist, his kingdom, and followers is about to be extracted. Previously all the plagues perpetrated upon the earth originated from heaven. Now the Lord Jesus Christ is returning to deal with the wicked personally. He is going to judge and make war on earth, not from heaven.

Jesus' eyes are like "flames of fire" as He casts judgment upon the wicked and unrighteousness of the earth. On His head are "many crowns." These are diadems of Royalty as He is King of Kings and Lord of Lords. He has a name that no one knows but Himself. The names given to Jesus in scripture are more descriptive than proper names. Names like shepherd, master, teacher, Redeemer, Savior, Prince of Peace etc., describe Jesus' character. This new name that no one knows describes another aspect of Jesus' character heretofore unknown. Perhaps that name describes Jesus as a man of war returning to "judge and make war."

Jesus' vesture dipped in blood is a reference to Isaiah chapter 63.

*"Who is this that cometh from **Edom**, with dyed garments from **Bozrah**? this that is glorious in his apparel, travelling in the greatness of his strength? I that speak in righteousness, mighty to save. **Wherefore art thou red in thine apparel**, and thy garments like him that treadeth in the winefat? **I have trodden the winepress alone**, and of the people there was none with me: **for I will tread them in mine anger, and trample them in my fury**, and **their blood shall be sprinkled upon my garments, and I will stain all my raiment**. For the **day of vengeance is in mine heart, and the year of my redeemed is come**." - Isaiah 63:1-4 KJV*

Wow! What a powerful passage about the second coming of Jesus Christ. In this text, Jesus is coming from Jordan (Edom and Bozrah). He is glorious, righteous, mighty to save, and great in His strength. He is asked why His garments are red as having tread a winepress. Jesus replies that he has trodden the winepress alone. But the winepress does not contain grapes but His enemies. He has tread His enemies in His anger and fury. It is their blood that has stained red Jesus' garments. Jesus proclaims that the day of Vengeance is in His heart. He has returned in anger to extract God's vengeance upon the ungodly. It is also the "year of my redeemed," meaning He has come to save Israel.

When Jesus started His earthly ministry in the Synagogue at Nazareth, He quoted from Isaiah chapter 61.

"The Spirit of the Lord GOD is upon me; because the LORD hath anointed me to preach good tidings unto the meek; he hath sent me to bind up the brokenhearted, to proclaim liberty to the captives, and the opening of the prison to them that are bound; To proclaim the acceptable year of the LORD, and the day of vengeance of our God; to comfort all that mourn;" - Isaiah 61:1-2 KJV

Here is Jesus' quote from the gospel of Luke chapter 4.

*"The Spirit of the Lord is upon me, because he hath anointed me to preach the gospel to the poor; he hath sent me to heal the brokenhearted, to preach deliverance to the captives, and recovering of sight to the blind, to set at liberty them that are bruised, **To preach the acceptable year of the Lord**. And he **closed the book**, and he gave it again to the minister, and sat down. And the eyes of all them that were in the synagogue were fastened on him." - Luke 4:18-20 KJV*

Notice that Jesus stopped with the phrase "To preach the acceptable year of the Lord." He then closed the book, gave it to the priest, and sat down. But that is not the end of the passage found in Isaiah chapter 61. It continues with the phrase "and the day of vengeance of our God." That refers to Jesus second coming when he deals with humankind with wrath and vengeance. He returns to judge and make war with the Antichrist and all those that hate Israel.

*"And the armies which were in heaven followed him upon **white horses, clothed in fine linen, white and clean**. And out of his mouth goeth a **sharp sword**, that with it he should **smite the nations**: and he shall rule them with a **rod of iron**: and he treadeth the **winepress of the fierceness and wrath of Almighty God**. And he hath on his vesture and on his thigh a name written, **KING OF KINGS, AND LORD OF LORDS.**"* - Revelation 19:14-16 KJV

The armies of heaven that ride with Jesus are the holy angels. They ride on white horses and are clothed with fine linen, white and clean, which is the righteousness of Christ's holy angels. Out of Jesus' mouth goes a sharp sword which is His Word, the Word of God. With it, He will judge and make war with the nations that have aligned with the Antichrist. Jesus shall rule them with a rod of iron, and Israel shall also rule with Jesus with a rod of iron (Revelation 2:27). Jesus treads the winepress of the wrath of God filed with God's enemies, not grapes. Jesus has the name "Kings OF KINGS, AND LORD OF LORDS" written on His thigh to easily be read while sitting on His horse.

All your Christian life, you were told that the church saints were returning with Jesus to rule and reign with Him in the Kingdom. But that's just another bogus church tradition? Again, what does the Bible say?

*"When the Son of man shall come in his glory, and **all the holy angels with him**, then shall he sit upon the throne of his glory:" - Matthew 25:31 KJV*

*"Whosoever therefore shall be ashamed of me and of my words in this adulterous and sinful generation; of him also shall the Son of man be ashamed, **when he cometh in the glory of his Father with the holy angels**." - Mark 8:38 KJV*

*"For whosoever shall be ashamed of me and of my words, of him shall the Son of man be ashamed, **when he shall come in his own glory, and in his Father's, and of the holy angels**." - Luke 9:26 KJV*

*"The same shall drink of the wine of the wrath of God, which is poured out without mixture into the cup of his indignation; and he shall be tormented with fire and brimstone in the presence of **the holy angels**, and in the **presence of the Lamb**." - Revelation 14:10 KJV*

Those coming with Jesus are His Holy Angels, not church saints. Those present with the Lamb at judgment are Holy Angels, not church saints. Sorry to burst anyone's bubble, but you need to understand the truth. You need to study the Bible.

*"And I saw an angel standing in the sun; and he cried with a loud voice, saying to all the **fowls that fly in the midst of heaven**, Come and gather yourselves together unto the **supper of the great God**; That ye may eat the flesh of kings, and the flesh of captains, and the flesh of mighty men, and the flesh of horses, and of them that sit on them, and the flesh of all men, both free and bond, both small and great." - Revelation 19:17-18 KJV*

The destruction of the ungodly at Jesus' return makes for a great supper for the "fowls that fly in the midst of heaven." There is much for the creatures of earth to feast upon, from the small to the great. Ezekiel tells a similar account of a great supper at the Lord's return.

*"And, thou son of man, thus saith the Lord GOD; Speak **unto every feathered fowl, and to every beast of the field**, Assemble yourselves, and come; gather yourselves on every side **to my sacrifice that I do sacrifice for you**, even a **great sacrifice upon the mountains of Israel**, that ye may **eat flesh**, and **drink blood**. Ye shall eat the flesh of the mighty, and drink the blood of the princes of the earth, of rams, of lambs, and of goats, of bullocks, all of them fatlings of Bashan. And ye shall eat fat till ye be full, and drink blood till ye be drunken, of **my sacrifice which I have sacrificed for you**. Thus ye shall be filled at my table with horses and chariots, with mighty men, and with all men of war, saith the Lord GOD." -* Ezekiel 39:17–20 KJV

The account in Revelation 19 and Ezekiel 39 pertain to the battle of Armageddon.

*"And I saw the **beast**, and the **kings of the earth, and their armies**, gathered together **to make war against him that sat on the horse, and against his army**. And the beast was taken, and with him the false prophet that wrought miracles before him, with which he deceived them that had received the mark of the beast, and them that worshipped his image. **These both were cast alive into a lake of fire burning with brimstone.** And the **remnant were slain with the sword of him that sat upon the horse**, which sword proceeded out of his mouth: and all the fowls were filled with their flesh." -* Revelation 19:19-21 KJV

Here we see the true reason for this last great battle at the return of Jesus Christ. The Antichrist, national leaders, and their armies gather around Jerusalem to "make war against him that sat on the horse, and against his army." We previously read in Revelation chapter 16 that the staging area for this final battle is called Armageddon, the valley of Jezreel in northern Israel. The goal of the Antichrist and those aligned with him is to PREVENT the second coming of Jesus Christ. They want to rule the world for a thousand years.

Adolf Hitler's goal with the Third Reich was to rule the world for a thousand years. The First Reich was the Holy Roman Empire under Charlemagne. The Second Reich was the pre-world war 1 German Empire under Kaiser Wilhelm. Hitler's Germany was to be the Third and final Reich. Interesting that the kingdom of the Antichrist is the fourth beast in Daniel chapter 7 and the fourth metal in Daniel chapter 2—the Fourth Reich. It will not be German, but Muslim.

But we know the Antichrist's dreams are pure folly as he and the false prophet are quickly taken: "both were cast alive into a lake of fire burning with brimstone." Jesus then slays the followers of the Antichrist with the sword of His word. Fresh meat is back on the menu for the fowls of heaven and the beasts of the earth. This last great battle will be a bloody carnage as blood flows for 200 miles at a depth of 4 feet.

Jesus returns to earth – the second coming of Jesus Christ – to judge and make war with the Antichrist and his armies. They are quickly defeated. The Antichrist and false prophet are cast alive into the lake of fire.

Thousand-Year Reign

*"And I saw an **angel** come down from heaven, having the **key of the bottomless pit** and a **great chain** in his hand. And he laid hold on the **dragon**, that old **serpent**, which is the **Devil**, and **Satan**, and bound him a thousand years, And cast him into the bottomless pit, and shut him up, and*

set a seal upon him, that he should deceive the nations no more, till the thousand years should be fulfilled: and after that he must be loosed a little season." - Revelation 20:1-3 KJV

An angel descends from heaven with the key to the bottomless pit and a great chain. He grabs Satan, binds him with the chain, and casts him into the bottomless pit. There Satan is bound and imprisoned for a thousand years. A seal of God is set upon him, and there he will remain till the thousand years are completed. After the thousand-year reign of Jesus Christ, Satan is loosed for a short time to deceive those born during the thousand years. They were born during a time when nothing could tempt them into rebellion against God. Now they must endure Satan's temptation, as have all other peoples that have ever lived. An interesting verse here clears up any ambiguity amongst the names of the devil. The dragon, the old serpent from the garden of Eden, the Devil, and Satan are one in the same person.

*"And I saw thrones, and they sat upon them, and **judgment was given unto them**: and I saw the souls of them that were **beheaded for the witness of Jesus**, and for the word of God, and which had not worshipped the beast, neither his image, neither had received his mark upon their foreheads, or in their hands; and they **lived and reigned with Christ a thousand years**." - Revelation 20:4 KJV*

John sees several thrones in heaven, and judgment was given to those sitting on them. These could be the twenty-four elders that sit on thrones as judgment will be given to them over Israel. Also, there are the "souls" of those that were beheaded for their witness of Jesus. Is there a false pagan religious system in the Middle East whose favorite form of execution is beheading? Yes, of course, Islam. These beheaded souls did not worship the beast, nor his image, and did not take the mark of the beast. They will live and reign with Jesus Christ for a thousand years. Notice that they are only "souls" as they have not received their glorified bodies yet. That will come very soon.

*"But the rest of the dead lived not again until the thousand years were finished. This is the **first resurrection**. Blessed and holy is he that hath part in the first resurrection: on such the **second death** hath no power, but they shall be priests of God and of Christ, and shall reign with him a thousand years." - Revelation 20:5-6 KJV*

The phrase "rest of the dead" refers to the lost dead for all the ages past and all the ungodly slain during the Tribulation. They will not "live again" until after the thousand-year reign of Jesus Christ. Then they will be resurrected just before the Great White Throne Judgment, which I will discuss shortly.

There is much confusion as to the "first resurrection." There are only two prophesied resurrections; the resurrection of the just (righteous) and the resurrection of the unjust (unrighteous) as we read below.

*"And shall come forth; they that have done good, unto the **resurrection of life**; and they that have done evil, unto the **resurrection of damnation**." - John 5:29 KJV*

*"And have hope toward God, which they themselves also allow, that there shall be a **resurrection of the dead, both of the just and unjust**." - Acts 24:15 KJV*

There are two prophesied resurrections. If not, then there could never be a "first resurrection." The first resurrection is the resurrection of the righteous. This resurrection began with the resurrection of Jesus Christ as he is the firstfruits of many brethren.

Jesus is the "firstfruits" of the first resurrection, the resurrection of the just.

*"But now is **Christ risen from the dead, and become the firstfruits** of them that slept. ... But every man in his own order: **Christ the firstfruits**, afterward they that are Christ's at his coming." - 1 Corinthians 15:20, 23 KJV*

Just before Jesus died on the cross He told the thief "today you shall be with me in Paradise." Paradise is the place all Old Testament saints went when they died to await the coming of the Messiah. Jesus went to Paradise and preached to those captives. Since they are righteous (just) saints they will be part of the first resurrection at Jesus' second coming. Read the story of Lazarus and the rich man for clarification on Paradise in Luke chapter 16.

But what about the Rapture? Isn't that a resurrection? Yes, it is. But it is a mystery resurrection as Paul declares in 1st Corinthians chapter 15.

"Behold, **I shew you a mystery**; We shall not all sleep, but we shall all be changed, In a moment, in the twinkling of an eye, at the last trump: for the trumpet shall sound, and the dead shall be raised incorruptible, and we shall be changed." - 1 Corinthians 15:51–52 KJV

The rapture resurrection was a mystery until revealed by the apostle Paul. Therefore, it is not part of the prophesied first resurrection, the resurrection of the just. The entire dispensation of grace with all its doctrines was a mystery. Therefore, it is not part of prophecy.

The fulfillment of the first resurrection is the resurrection of the Old Testament saints and the Tribulation saints at the second coming of

Jesus Christ at the end of the Tribulation. There are three aspects of the "first resurrection."

- The resurrection of the Old Testament saints at the second coming of Jesus Christ at the end of the Tribulation.
- The resurrection of the Tribulation saints at the second coming of Jesus Christ.
- The First resurrection primarily concerns the ancients and the Jews.

The first resurrection includes all the righteous of the Old Testament and those martyred during the 7-year Tribulation. The church saints, primarily Gentiles, were resurrected/raptured before the 7-year Tribulation in the mystery resurrection. In other words, all the righteous from Adam through the second coming of Jesus Christ at the end of the Tribulation tool part in the first resurrection or the rapture. Those that participate in the "first resurrection" are called blessed as the "second death" has no power over them. The "second death" happens to the lost after their resurrection for the Great White Throne judgment. All the lost, unrighteous dead will live again in resurrected bodies but will experience a "second death" as they are cast into in lake of fire for all eternity.

*"And when the thousand years are expired, **Satan shall be loosed out of his prison**, And shall go out to **deceive the nations** which are in the four quarters of the earth, Gog and Magog, to gather them together to battle: the number of whom is as the **sand of the sea**." - Revelation 20:7-8 KJV*

After the thousand-year reign of Jesus Christ, Satan will be loosed from his captivity in the bottomless pit. He will go throughout the earth, deceiving the nations and leading a final rebellion against God. It is interesting that no matter how good life is, there are always those with a rebellious heart. I am sure we all know people like that.

The number of people deceived into rebelling against God is massive, "as the sand of the sea."

*"And they went up on the breadth of the earth, and compassed the camp of the saints about, and the beloved city: and **fire came down from God out of heaven, and devoured them**. And the **devil that deceived them was cast into the lake of fire and brimstone**, where the beast and the false prophet are, and shall be tormented day and night for ever and ever." - Revelation 20:9-10 KJV*

This final rebellion is short-lived. As soon as the rebels gather to take Jerusalem, "the beloved city," God rains down fire from heaven and consumes them. The fire of God once again cleanses the earth of evil. Those participating in the final rebellion wait in hell for the Great White Throne judgment. Satan is then captured and cast into the lake of fire for all eternity. The Antichrist and the false prophet are already in the lake of fire. They were sent there at the second coming of Jesus Christ at the end of the 7-year Tribulation. The Satanic trinity, Satan, the Antichrist, and the false prophet are all in the lake of fire. Enjoy your eternal swim.

The Great White Throne

*"And I saw a **great white throne**, and him that sat on it, from whose face the earth and the heaven fled away; and there was found no place for them. And I saw the **dead, small and great, stand before God**, and the **books were opened**: and another book was opened, which is the book of life: and the **dead were judged out of those things which were written in the books, according to their works**." - Revelation 20:11-12 KJV*

At the Great White Throne Judgment (GWTJ), all the lost dead stand before the Lord. They will be judged according to their works. The present heaven and earth fled away as they have been redeemed. There are no ungodly remaining in heaven nor on earth. The GWTJ is for all the ungodly that have ever lived. All the lost dead are resurrected, given new bodies, to stand before God in judgment. Their works, good and evil, judge them. If their names are not in the book of life, they are cast into the lake of fire. It is a terrible thing to fall into the hands of a righteous God. As no one's works can measure up to God's standards, all that stand here in judgment are doomed. The only person whose name might be found in the book of life would be a righteous believer that died during the Millennial Kingdom. That person will be sent to the Kingdom upon the new earth which will soon be finished.

*"And the sea gave up the dead which were in it; and **death and hell delivered up the dead which were in them**: and they were judged every man according to their works. And **death and hell were cast into the lake of fire**. This is the **second death. And whosoever was not found written in the book of life was cast into the lake of fire**." - Revelation 20:13-15 KJV*

The sea gives up her dead. Death and hell, the pale horse rider, gives up the dead in them. After the judgment of the wicked lost, death and hell are cast into the lake of fire. The lost, standing before God in new bodies, must die once again and be cast into the lake of fire. That is the "second death." How sad it will be to be resurrected and receive a new body just to die again and be thrown into the lake of fire.

All Things are Made New

*"And I saw **a new heaven and a new earth**: for the first heaven and the first earth were passed away; and **there was no more sea**. And I John saw*

*the holy city, **new Jerusalem, coming down from God out of heaven**, prepared as a bride adorned for her husband." - Revelation 21:1-2 KJV*

All the lost dead have been sent to their eternal destiny, the lake of fire. The first and second resurrections, the just and the unjust, are complete. Now comes a new heaven and new earth. The old heaven and earth that we have today have either been replaced or entirely renovated by fire. Either way, they are now pristine and perfect. Interesting that there is no more sea. A sea is a body of saltwater. Saltwater is a mixture of fresh water and salt. God hates mixtures. Everything in the new heaven and earth will be pure. All rivers and lakes will be of pure fresh water. The new earth will be spectacularly beautiful and pristine.

The New Jerusalem comes down to earth from the third heaven to rest on or just above the earth's surface. The New Jerusalem is called a "bride adorned for her husband." We think it strange that a city could be spoken of as the bride. The Psalmist writes:

"For the LORD hath chosen Zion; he hath desired [it] for his habitation. This [is] my rest for ever: here will I dwell; for I have desired it." - Psalm 132:13–14 KJV

"Great [is] the LORD, and greatly to be praised in the city of our God, [in] the mountain of his holiness." - Psalm 48:1 KJV

*"Awake, awake; put on thy strength, O Zion; put on thy beautiful garments, **O Jerusalem, the holy city**: for henceforth there shall no more come into thee the uncircumcised and the unclean." - Isaiah 52:1 KJV*

Holy means set apart for God. Jerusalem is set apart for God.

Jerusalem is the city in which God chose to dwell. The New Jerusalem is the future dwelling of God and for all the righteous.

*"And I heard a great voice out of heaven saying, Behold, the **tabernacle of God is with men**, and he will dwell with them, and they shall be his people, and God himself shall be with them, and be their God. And **God shall wipe away all tears from their eyes**; and there shall be **no more death**, neither **sorrow**, nor **crying**, neither shall there be any more **pain**: for the **former things are passed away**. - Revelation 21:3-4 KJV*

God once again dwells with His creation. The restoration of fellowship between God and man is complete. Israel shall be God's people on earth, and He will be their God. Remember, we, the body of Christ are eternal in the heavens (2 Cor 5:1). He will wipe away all tears as we and they will no longer have any remembrance of the lost dead. There is no more death, sorrow, crying, or pain because all the former things are passed away. There will be no memories of the former things to make us sorrowful. We all know people that won't make it into the kingdom. For whatever reason, they simply would not believe and surrender to the Lord. We will have no memory of them to make us sad that they are in the lake of fire.

*"And he that sat upon the throne said, **Behold, I make all things new**. And he said unto me, Write: for these words are true and faithful. And he said unto me, **It is done**. I am Alpha and Omega, the beginning and the end. I will give unto him that is athirst of the fountain of the water of life freely." - Revelation 21:5-6 KJV*

The Lord states, "I make all things new." There is no semblance of anything from this fallen, sinful world. Everything is new, pristine, and perfect. We are entering the Perfect Age for all eternity. The Lord says, "It is done." God's plan of redemption for the world is now complete. Everything has been judged, restored, or recreated. The righteous have their glorious eternal reward in God's kingdom. We have a magnificent new heaven, and Israel a beautiful new earth. And the dazzling new Jerusalem where the Lord dwells with all. Words cannot describe it. The water of life will flow freely for all to drink. Just imagine how that pure water will taste.

*"**He that overcometh shall inherit all things**, and I will be his God, and he shall be my son. But the fearful, and unbelieving, and the abominable, and murderers, and whoremongers, and sorcerers, and idolaters, and all liars, shall have their part in the lake which burneth with fire and brimstone: which is the **second death**." - Revelation 21:7-8 KJV*

No matter when or where a person lives, there are things to overcome. There are continual challenges from the world, the flesh, and the devil we must overcome to have a victorious life on this earth and eternal life with Jesus Christ. But sadly, most Christians live with one foot in the world and the other in the church. Their worldly desires and passions neutralize them. The overcomers, those Tribulation saints mentioned in Revelation chapters two and three, will see a special reward from God.

The "fearful, and unbelieving, and the abominable, and murders, and whoremongers, and sorcerers, and idolaters, and all liars will have their part in the lake of fire, the second death." The "fearful" are the cowardly and faithless, unable to exercise faith even as a grain of mustard seed so they could be saved. The others are self-explanatory. All those will experience the "second death." They die a second time and then join the other lost in the lake of fire for all eternity.

*"And there came unto me one of the seven angels which had the seven vials full of the seven last plagues, and talked with me, saying, Come hither, I will shew thee the bride, the Lamb's wife. And he carried me away in the spirit to a great and high mountain, and shewed me that **great city, the holy Jerusalem, descending out of heaven from God**,"* - Revelation 21:9-10 KJV

An angel describes the New Jerusalem, the future home for the bride of Christ, Israel, and the Tribulation saints. The Old Testament saints will dwell on earth in the land grant made to Abraham and King David. The "great city, the holy Jerusalem," descends to earth from heaven to reside near Israel.

*"**Having the glory of God**: and her light was like unto a stone most precious, even like a jasper stone, clear as crystal; **And had a wall great and high, and had twelve gates**, and at the gates twelve angels, and names written thereon, which are the names of the twelve tribes of the children of Israel: On the east three gates; on the north three gates; on the south three gates; and on the west three gates."* - Revelation 21:11-13 KJV

The light of the New Jerusalem is the light of the Lord. The light of God illuminates the entire city as the streets are transparent gold. The construction materials are precious stones like diamonds that illuminate everything, even the interiors of dwellings. The wall around the city is massive, thick, and high. There are twelve gates in the city wall, three on each side for the names of the twelve tribes of Israel.

*"And the **wall of the city had twelve foundations**, and in them the names of the twelve apostles of the Lamb. And he that talked with me had a golden reed to measure the city, and the gates thereof, and the wall thereof. And **the city lieth foursquare**, and the length is as large as the*

breadth: and he measured the city with the reed, **twelve thousand furlongs**. The length and the breadth and the height of it are equal." - Revelation 21:14-16 KJV

The New Jerusalem has twelve foundations named after the twelve apostles of Jesus Christ. Everything Jewish for Israel's New Jerusalem. John is instructed to measure the city, the gates, and the wall. The city is four square, meaning that the base is a square with four equal sides. Each side of the city is 12,000 furlongs or 1,500 miles. The New Jerusalem is 1,500 miles on each side. That is about half the size of the United States.

"And he measured the wall thereof, **an hundred and forty and four cubits**, according to the measure of a man, that is, of the angel. And the building of the wall of it was of jasper: and the city was **pure gold, like unto clear glass**." - Revelation 21:17-18 KJV

The wall of the city is one hundred forty-four cubits high. That could be for the 144,000 thousand Jews sealed by God during the 7-year Tribulation. That works out to a wall 216 feet tall. The wall is transparent, clear as glass, so the light of God illuminates the entire wall and city.

"And the foundations of the wall of the city were garnished with **all manner of precious stones**. The first foundation was jasper; the second, sapphire; the third, a chalcedony; the fourth, an emerald; The fifth, sardonyx; the sixth, sardius; the seventh, chrysolite; the eighth, beryl; the ninth, a topaz; the tenth, a chrysoprasus; the eleventh, a jacinth; the twelfth, an amethyst. And the **twelve gates were twelve pearls**; every several gate was of one pearl: and the **street of the city was pure gold**, as it were **transparent glass**. - Revelation 21:19-21 KJV

The foundations of the wall are constructed of precious gems as listed. Interesting that things we hold dear here on earth, gold and precious gems, are mere construction materials for the New Jerusalem, like steel, lumber, and sheetrock. The wall has twelve gates, each a single colossal pearl. The street is of pure transparent gold. Everything has a translucent quality; nothing is entirely opaque. The transparent building materials allow the light of God to flow throughout the city. Everything is illuminated with the glory of God. Spectacular beyond our imagination!

"And I saw no temple therein: for the Lord God Almighty and the Lamb are the temple of it. And the city had no need of the sun, neither of the moon, to shine in it: for the glory of God did lighten it, and the Lamb is the light thereof." - Revelation 21:22-23 KJV

The New Jerusalem has no temple. None is needed since the Father, and the Son will reside there with the righteous saints. There is no need for external light, so the sun and the moon will be unnecessary. The light of the glory of God will shine for all eternity in the New Jerusalem. Jesus truly is the "light of the world."

*"And the nations of them which are saved shall walk in the light of it: and the kings of the earth do bring their glory and honour into it. And the gates of it shall not be shut at all by day: for **there shall be no night there**. And they shall bring the glory and honour of the nations into it. And there shall in no wise enter into it any thing that defileth, neither whatsoever worketh abomination, or maketh a lie: but they which are written in the Lamb's book of life." - Revelation 21:24-27 KJV*

The New Jerusalem will light the nations of the earth. The leaders of the countries will come to the New Jerusalem to honor the Lord God. The city's gates will always be open as there is no night there; the light of God shines forever. Nothing ungodly will enter the city as those whose names are not written in the Lamb's book of life are all in the lake of fire. Evil has been eradicated.

"And he shewed me a pure river of water of life, clear as crystal, proceeding out of the throne of God and of the Lamb. In the midst of the street of it, and on either side of the river, was there the tree of life, which bare twelve manner of fruits, and yielded her fruit every month: and the leaves of the tree were for the healing of the nations." - Revelation 22:1-2 KJV

The throne of God and the Lamb will be at the peak of the city. From the throne flows a "pure river of water of life." On the sides of the river is the tree of life. As Adam and Eve needed only one tree, the New Jerusalem could have several stands of the tree of life for all to use. Each side of the river of life will have many trees of life. They give twelve types of fruit, one each month. Fruit will be in abundance. There will be no lack in the new city. The leaves are for the "healing of the nations." There is no more war, sickness, or plagues as the curse that was upon the old earth is gone.

"And there shall be no more curse: but the throne of God and of the Lamb shall be in it; and his servants shall serve him: And they shall see his face; and his name shall be in their foreheads." - Revelation 22:3-4 KJV

The curse is gone—No more thorns, thistles, bugs, or pesky insects. Things will be as they were in the garden before the fall of Adam but even more spectacular. They shall live in God's presence and finally see His face and live. His name will be in their foreheads as an eternal sign that He is their God, and they are His people. Will the church be in the New Jerusalem? I don't see why not. At this point in prophecy, all will be one body in Christ.

"And there shall be no night there; and they need no candle, neither light of the sun; for the Lord God giveth them light: and they shall reign for ever and ever." - Revelation 22:5 KJV

The Holy Spirit reiterates that there is no night in the New Jerusalem. There is no candle, no electricity, no power plants, no switches on the wall, and no sunlight as the Lord God gives His light for the entire city. The inhabitants of the New Jerusalem will reign with the Lord Jesus Christ forever and ever, ruling the nations. It is difficult to put this into words as we have nothing in our world to compare the splendor and grandeur that is to come. Words are simply insufficient.

The Closing

"And he said unto me, These sayings are faithful and true: and the Lord God of the holy prophets sent his angel to shew unto his servants the things which must shortly be done. Behold, I come quickly: blessed is he that keepeth the sayings of the prophecy of this book." - Revelation 22:6-7 KJV

The Revelation of Jesus Christ is over, and now we come to the closing statements of the book. John reiterates that the teaching of the Book of Revelation is "faithful and true." The Lord God has revealed this entire prophecy to His angels and His servant John. These prophecies will soon come to pass, meaning that they will happen quickly once they begin to unfold. All the prophecies about the second coming of Jesus Christ will happen in rapid succession once the 7-year Tribulation begins. A blessing is in store for each person that takes the prophecies of the Book of Revelation to heart.

"And I John saw these things, and heard them. And when I had heard and seen, I fell down to worship before the feet of the angel which shewed me these things. Then saith he unto me, See thou do it not: for I am thy

fellowservant, and of thy brethren the prophets, and of them which keep the sayings of this book: worship God." - Revelation 22:8-9 KJV

John is overcome by what he has seen and falls at the feet of the angel to worship him. The angel quickly instructs John not to do that as he is a fellow servant of the Lord, just like John. We are to worship God through our Lord and Savior Jesus Christ and him alone.

"And he saith unto me, Seal not the sayings of the prophecy of this book: for the time is at hand. He that is unjust, let him be unjust still: and he which is filthy, let him be filthy still: and he that is righteous, let him be righteous still: and he that is holy, let him be holy still." - Revelation 22:10-11 KJV

The angel instructs John not to seal up the book so it can be copied and distributed to the assemblies for the "time is at hand." That was written by John 1900 years ago, so how could the time be at hand? The time was at hand until Israel proclaimed their final rejection of their Messiah Jesus in Acts chapter 7. Stephen testified before the Jewish council, and they vehemently rejected him:

"Ye stiffnecked and uncircumcised in heart and ears, ye do always resist the Holy Ghost: as your fathers [did], so [do] ye. ... When they heard these things, they were cut to the heart, and they gnashed on him with [their] teeth. ... Then they cried out with a loud voice, and stopped their ears, and ran upon him with one accord, And cast [him] out of the city, and stoned [him]: and the witnesses laid down their clothes at a young man's feet, whose name was Saul. And they stoned Stephen, calling upon [God], and saying, Lord Jesus, receive my spirit." - Acts 7:51, 54, 57-59 KJV

With the rejection of Stephen's message, Israel's last chance to receive Jesus as their Messiah passed. God judged Israel and called

Saul of Tarsus, the apostle Paul, to take the gospel of grace to the Gentiles.

Israel's prophetic kingdom program was set aside so God could save Gentiles in the dispensation of grace. After the rapture, God will restart Israel's prophetic program with the 7-year Tribulation.

The Holy Spirit declares that the filthy or unjust will remain that way as they show no desire to follow the Lord. But let the righteous and holy continue to be righteous and holy still as they have the desire in their hearts to follow the Lord. We all know people that are spiritually filthy and unrighteous. Apart from a miracle of God, they will stay that way. So too, with the righteous and holy. They will stay that way because of the power of God flowing through them.

"And, behold, I come quickly; and my reward is with me, to give every man according as his work shall be. I am Alpha and Omega, the beginning and the end, the first and the last." - Revelation 22:12-13 KJV

The Lord is coming quickly, especially now as we approach the end of the church age. Soon the rapture will remove the church from the earth, and the Tribulation will begin. When the Lord returns at the end of the Tribulation, his rewards for Israel will be with him. Each rewarded according to their works. The saved have good works planned for them by the will of God. The lost have their sinful works of iniquity they must account for. The Lord Jesus Christ is Alpha and Omega, the beginning, and the end, the first and the last. He is the beginning of creation as he created all things. He is the ending of all creation as nothing was made apart from Him. Everything was and is designed for His divine purpose. He is all in all.

"Blessed are they that do his commandments, that they may have right to the tree of life, and may enter in through the gates into the city. For without are dogs, and sorcerers, and whoremongers, and murderers, and idolaters, and whosoever loveth and maketh a lie." - Revelation 22:14-15 KJV

There are two groups mentioned here. Those who keep the Lord's commandments have the right to enter the New Jerusalem and eat from the tree of life, Israel. They can come and go from the city at will. Remember, the kingdom of God is not just the New Jerusalem but the entire planet.

Outside the kingdom are the dogs, sorcerers, whoremongers, murders, idolaters, and anyone else that has no love for the truth. They are not outside the walls of the city but the kingdom. They are not on planet earth but in the lake of fire completely removed from the kingdom of God. The Lord is saying that no evil person will be anywhere near His kingdom or His city.

"I Jesus have sent mine angel to testify unto you these things in the churches. I am the root and the offspring of David, and the bright and morning star. And the Spirit and the bride say, Come. And let him that heareth say, Come. And let him that is athirst come. And whosoever will, let him take the water of life freely." - Revelation 22:16-17 KJV

This prophetic testimony is to be distributed among the churches, assemblies of Jews in the Middle East. The Revelation came directly from Jesus to His angels and then to the Apostle John. What greater chain of custody could exist? Jesus is the "root and the offspring of David," meaning that He is a warrior as He returns to "judge and make war."

Jesus is the "bright and morning star." The morning star, Venus, is a planet but referred to as the morning star. She is the brightest of all heavenly bodies except for the sun and moon. The morning star arises early and is a sign of hope for the new day. Before the GPS technology, the morning star was used for navigation and direction. Jesus' word is our guide and guidance in this world, and as the bright and morning star, He illuminates our path. Jesus is a unique person. Venus is a unique planet as it is the only planet that rotates clockwise and the hottest planet even though she is not the closest to the sun. Jesus, as the bright and morning star, will shine brightly for all eternity.

The invitation is given to "Come." All those that thirst after truth and righteousness come. Anyone who comes to the Lord may drink the water of life freely. Let whosoever wills, come.

"For I testify unto every man that heareth the words of the prophecy of this book, If any man shall add unto these things, God shall add unto him the plagues that are written in this book: And if any man shall take away from the words of the book of this prophecy, God shall take away his part out of the book of life, and out of the holy city, and from the things which are written in this book." - Revelation 22:18-19 KJV

Jesus gives a dire warning to all that would tamper with the word of God. Many false teachers and pastors manipulate the word of God for their purpose and greedy gain. Modern bibles have removed words and whole verses simply because those texts did not support their preconceived notions of what the Bible should say. How about Thomas Jefferson removing entire chapters from his Bible? These men and women are in grave danger of the fires of Hell. God will not tolerate these people, and their judgment will be most severe.

Also, do not use a so-called Bible that a man has manipulated. For example, the Message Bible, Living Bible, and the Amplified Bible were each created by a single person that wanted to rewrite the Bible according to their desires and way of thinking. That is an abomination unto God. These bibles are an abomination. So too with the modern versions like the NIV, TNIV, NAS, NASB, ASV, ESV, and the HCSB. Those bibles are all built upon flawed, corrupt Greek manuscripts compiled by Westcott and Hort, then Nestle and Aland or the United Bible Society. Get an accurate Bible, get a King James Bible!

*"He which testifieth these things saith, **Surely I come quickly. Amen. Even so, come, Lord Jesus**. The grace of our Lord Jesus Christ be with you all. Amen." - Revelation 22:20-21 KJV*

The Lord Jesus Christ says, "surely I come quickly." When the Rapture happens, all the prophetic events will come quickly with increased intensity and frequency.

Even so, "come Lord Jesus."

May the grace of God be with us all, Amen!

Briefing

Point of interest:

a) chapter 1 – vision of glorified Jesus Christ.

b) chapter 2-3 – issues with Jewish assemblies in the Tribulation.

c) chapters 4:2 – chapter 19:3 details the 7-year Tribulation.

d) chapter 19:11-21 the second coming of Jesus Christ.

e) chapters 20-22 the Millennium, the final rebellion, the great white throne judgment, the new heaven and new earth, the new Jerusalem, the perfect age.

Persons of interest:

a) Antichrist aka white horse rider, beast from the sea; cast alive into the lake of fire at Jesus second coming.

b) false prophet – religious leader working with antichrist also cast alive into the lake of fire at Jesus second coming.

c) 144,000 Jewish preachers; 2 witnesses, Moses and Elijah at the temple; tribulation saints enter the kingdom.

Outcome:

a) vast global destruction, mass deaths of unprecedented scale, strange phenomenon in the earth and the skies, false flag alien invasion exposed.

b) massive final BATTLE OF ARMAGEDDON as Jesus Christ returns.

c) THE ENEMIES OF GOD ARE GATHERED TO PREVENT THE SECOND COMING OF JESUS CHRIST.

d) ALL GODS ENEMIES ARE DESTROYED AND THE MILLENNIAL REIGN OF JESUS CHRIST COMMENCES.

e) Satan loosed at the end of the 1000 year reign of Jesus Christ to test those born during that time.

f) Final satanic rebellion crushed by fire from God. Satan cast into the lake of fire.

g) Great White Throne Judgment for all the lost souls.

h) New Heaven, New Earth and the New Jerusalem begin the perfect age.

i) Jesus Christ reigns for all eternity.

APPENDIX A - THE CHURCH

What is the Church Not?

The church, the body of Christ, is NOT a continuation of the Jewish dispensation (Old Testament believers) under a new name.

"The law and the prophets were until John: since that time the kingdom of God is preached, and every man presseth into it." - Luke 16:16 KJV

John the Baptist was the last Prophet under the Law.

"For the law was given by Moses, but grace and truth came by Jesus Christ. - John 1:17 KJV

Since God has separated these two dispensations (Law and Grace), let not man join them together (rightly divide the Word of Truth).

"Study to shew thyself approved unto God, a workman that needeth not to be ashamed, rightly dividing the word of truth." - 2 Timothy 2:15 KJV

Some believe the Christian Church is but another phase of the Jewish Church. They insist on observing the Feasts and Jewish holidays. They emulate the Jewish priesthood with garments and rituals. That is the error of the Hebrew Roots movement. Nothing wrong with understanding the Church's Jewish roots and the culture in which the Lord and the Apostles lived. But the Law has been fulfilled for us in Jesus Christ. If we are indeed "in Christ" and He is in us, then the Law has been fulfilled.

*"But now we are **delivered from the law**, that being dead wherein we were held; that we should serve in newness of spirit, and not in the oldness of the letter." - Rom 7:6 KJV*

*"But if ye be led of the Spirit, **ye are not under the law**." - Galatians 5:18 KJV*

*"But now hath he obtained a more excellent ministry, by how much also he is the mediator of a **better covenant**, which was established upon **better promises**." - Hebrews 8:6 KJV*

The Old Testament believers are not part of the Church. The Jewish believers will be resurrected at the second coming Jesus Christ, the first resurrection. Christians are resurrected at the rapture, 7-years before the second coming of Jesus Christ.

The Church is NOT the Kingdom. John the Baptist preached the gospel of the kingdom.

"In those days came John the Baptist, preaching in the wilderness of Judaea, And saying, Repent ye: for the kingdom of heaven is at hand." - Mat 3:1-2 KJV

Jesus initially preached the gospel of the kingdom also.

"And Jesus went about all Galilee, teaching in their synagogues, and preaching the gospel of the kingdom, and healing all manner of sickness and all manner of disease among the people. - Mat 4:23 KJV

Jesus sends the twelve out preaching the gospel of the kingdom.

"These twelve Jesus sent forth, and commanded them, saying, Go not into the way of the Gentiles, and into any city of the Samaritans enter ye not: But go rather to the lost sheep of the house of Israel. And as ye go, preach, saying, The kingdom of heaven is at hand." - Mat 10:5-7 KJV

However, the Jews rejected their King, and the Kingdom was postponed. There cannot be a Kingdom until the King returns as King of Kings and Lord of Lords at the end of the Tribulation. Study Luke 19 about the Nobleman receiving the kingdom.

Jesus receives the postponed kingdom in Revelation Chapter 11

*"And the seventh angel sounded; and there were great voices in heaven, saying, **The kingdoms of this world are become the kingdoms of our Lord, and of his Christ; and he shall reign for ever and ever**. And the four and twenty elders, which sat before God on their seats, fell upon their faces, and worshipped God, Saying, We give thee thanks, O Lord God Almighty, which art, and wast, and art to come; because **thou hast taken to thee thy great power, and hast reigned**.* - Rev 11:15-17 KJV

The earthly kingdom of Jesus Christ begins after His second coming, so the Church is NOT the Kingdom.

The error of Kingdom Theology is there is no Rapture and no second coming of Jesus Christ at the end of the 7- year Tribulation to set up His Kingdom. The Kingdom will be set up by the Church overcoming the world. Some names for this Kingdom Theology are Latter Rain Movement, Manifest Sons of God, Restorationism, Reconstructionism, New Apostolic Reformation, Kingdom Now, Dominionism, Word of Faith, Third Wave Movement, Joel's Army. They are all in error.

Summary:
The Church is NOT a continuation of Jewish OT believers. The Church is NOT the kingdom of Jesus Christ on earth. The Church is spoken of as a "House," a "Temple," a "Body," but NEVER a Kingdom. Jesus Christ is the "Head" of the body of believers, the Church. Jesus is never spoken of as King concerning the Church. The Kingdom of Messiah was well known in the OT. But the Church was a mystery revealed by the Apostle Paul.

What is the Church?

The Church is a "Mystery."

*"Of which **salvation the prophets have enquired and searched diligently**, who **prophesied of the grace** that should come unto you: Searching what, or what manner of time the Spirit of Christ which was in them did signify, when it testified beforehand the **sufferings of Christ**, and the **glory that should follow**. Unto whom it was revealed, that not unto themselves, but unto us they did minister the things, which are **now reported unto you** by them that have preached the gospel unto you with the Holy Ghost sent down from heaven; which things the **angels desire to look into.**"* - 1Peter 1:10-12 KJV

The OT prophets prophesied about Grace and searched diligently as to the timing of its revealing. They did not realize that between the sufferings of Christ (the Cross) and His glory (the Millennial Kingdom) there would be a period of grace (Dispensation of Grace) wherein believers in Jesus Christ would make up His Body, the Church. The time of Grace was hidden from the OT prophets but has been revealed by the Holy Spirit to the apostles and those that preach the gospel of grace. What was a "mystery" to the prophets and even the angels has been revealed; the dispensation of Grace wherein Jesus Christ will build His Body, the Church.

The revealing of the "Mystery of the Church" was given to the Apostle Paul.

*"For this cause I Paul, the prisoner of Jesus Christ for you Gentiles, If ye have heard of the **dispensation of the grace of God** which is given me to you-ward: How that by revelation he made known unto me the **mystery,** (as I wrote afore in few words, Whereby, when ye read, ye may understand my knowledge in the mystery of Christ) Which **in other ages was not made known** unto the sons of men, as it is now revealed unto his holy apostles and prophets by the Spirit; **That the Gentiles should be fellow heirs, and of the same body, and partakers of his promise in Christ by the gospel."** - Ephesians 3:1-6 KJV*

*""Whereof **I was made a minister,** according to the gift of the grace of God given unto me by the effectual working of his power. Unto me, who am less than the least of all saints, is this grace given, that **I should preach among the Gentiles** the unsearchable riches of Christ; And to make all men see what is the **fellowship of the mystery,** which from the beginning of the world hath been **hid in God,** who created all things by Jesus Christ: To the intent that now unto the principalities and powers in heavenly places **might be known by the church the manifold wisdom of God, According to the eternal purpose which he purposed in Christ Jesus our Lord.** - Ephesians 3:7-11 KJV*

From these Scriptures, we see that the Church was unknown to the OT patriarchs and prophets. The salvation of the Gentiles was known, but the mechanism was not. The "Mystery" was that God was going to do a complete "NEW THING," composed of both Jew and Gentile called "THE CHURCH."

The Church is a "Called Out" Body.

The word for Church is "ecclesia" meaning an assembly or congregation of like-minded people. The term "ecclesia" was also used for the assembly of Jews called out of Egypt.

*"This is he, that was in the **church in the wilderness** with the angel which spake to him in the mount Sinai, and with our fathers: who received the lively oracles to give unto us:" - Acts 7:38 KJV*

That was a national calling, not a personal calling.

"Simeon hath declared how God at the first did visit the Gentiles, to take out of them a people for his name. And to this agree the words of the prophets; as it is written," - Acts 15:14-15 KJV

Peter was first to take the gospel to the Gentiles at the house of Cornelius. The bulk of Paul's ministry was to the Gentiles. God is now calling individuals from "every kindred, people, tribe and nation" among the Gentiles into His Church. The "ecclesia" of Israel was national. The "ecclesia" of the Church is individual and personal.

The "elect": the elect of Israel are those chosen in Abraham through Isaac. The elect of the Church were chosen "before the foundation of the world."

*"According as he hath chosen us in him **before the foundation of the world**, that we should be holy and without blame before him in love: Having predestinated us unto the adoption of children by Jesus Christ to himself, according to the good pleasure of his will" - Ephesians 1:4-5 KJV*

National Israel was chosen through Abraham. The Church was chosen in Jesus Christ before the foundation of the world. Therefore, they are distinct and separate entities.

It is the "Body of Christ."

*"And hath put all things under His feet, and gave Him to be the **Head** over all things to the church, **Which is his body**, the fulness of Him that filleth all in all. - Ephesians 1:22-23 KJV*

Jesus being the HEAD of the Church was not possible until after His resurrection and ascension to the right hand of the Father. Also, the mystery of the church and the dispensation of grace was revealed to the apostle Paul after his Damascus Road conversion in Acts chapter 9. Consequently, the Church was conceived after Acts chapter 9. Believers were first called Christians in Acts chapter 11:26 at Antioch. Therefore, it is a unique entity in God's plan for humanity, precisely His plan to save Gentiles. So, there is one body, the Church, and one head, Jesus Christ.

*"For as the body is **one**, and hath many members, and all the members of that **one body**, being many, are **one body**: so also is Christ. For by one Spirit are we all baptized into **one body**, whether we be Jews or Gentiles, whether we be bond or free; and have been all made to drink into **one Spirit**." - 1Corinthians 12:12-13 KJV*

Believers are incorporated into this "one body" by the "one Spirit," the Holy Spirit.

*"There is **one body**, and **one Spirit**, even as ye are called in **one hope** of your calling; **One Lord, one faith, one baptism, One God** and Father of all, who is above all, and through all, and in you all." - Ephesians 4:4-6 KJV*

The fact that the Church is a body made up of living members shows that it is not an organization but an Organism. Since the Church is the body of Christ, we manifest Jesus Christ to the world. If we are "in Christ" and Jesus Christ is "in us," then He has chosen us to show Himself to a lost and dying world. We are to be Jesus' disciples, His ambassadors, His witnesses showing Christ in our daily lives. We are to be the "perfect body" for the "perfect Head," Jesus Christ.

"And he gave some, apostles; and some, prophets; and some, evangelists; and some, pastors and teachers; For the perfecting of the saints, for the work of the ministry, for the edifying of the body of Christ: Till we all come in the unity of the faith, and of the knowledge of the Son of God, unto a perfect man, unto the measure of the stature of the fulness of Christ:" - Ephesians 4:11-13 KJV

"For we are labourers together with God: ye are God's husbandry, ye are God's building. According to the grace of God which is given unto me, as a wise master builder, I have laid the foundation, and another buildeth thereon. But let every man take heed how he buildeth thereupon. For other foundation can no man lay than that is laid, which is Jesus Christ. Now if any man build upon this foundation gold, silver, precious stones, wood, hay, stubble; Every man's work shall be made manifest: for the day shall declare it, because it shall be revealed by fire; and the fire shall try every man's work of what sort it is." - 1Corinthians 3:9-13 KJV

We are the Temple

*"If any man's work abide which he hath built thereupon, he shall receive a reward. If any man's work shall be burned, he shall suffer loss: but he himself shall be saved; yet so as by fire. Know ye not that **ye are the temple of God**, and that the Spirit of God dwelleth in you? If any man defile the temple of God, him shall God destroy; for the temple of God is holy, which temple ye are." - 1Co 3:14-17 KJV*

Previously God's Glory was manifest through the Tabernacle after the exodus from Egypt, then Solomon's Temple followed by

Zerubbabel's Temple. But now, in this dispensation of grace, while national Israel is out of fellowship with God, we, the Church, are God's ambassadors on earth through which He manifests Himself by the Holy Spirit.

*"Now therefore ye are no more strangers and foreigners, but fellowcitizens with the saints, and of the **household of God**; And are built upon the foundation of the apostles and prophets, Jesus Christ himself being the chief corner stone; In whom all the building fitly framed together groweth unto **an holy temple in the Lord**: In whom ye also are builded together for an habitation of God through the Spirit."* - Ephesians 2:19-22 KJV

Previously God's presence was manifest in the Tabernacle in the Shekinah Glory. In this dispensation, we, the Church, are the visible "habitation of God" on earth.

The true Church is God's witness on the earth. Once the Rapture of the Church happens, God will allow the Jewish Temple to be rebuilt in Jerusalem, call out His 144,000 Jewish men, and His two witnesses in Jerusalem.

The Mission of the Church

As we have seen, the Church is not an organization but an Organism. Therefore, it is not a Social Club organized and supported solely for the benefit of its members. It is not a place of amusement or entertainment to pander to the carnal nature of members. It is not a House of Merchandise for the sale of commodities, whereby the money of others can be secured to alleviate saints from a little self-sacrifice.

The Church is not a Reform or Improvement Group. Social service in all its forms is commendable, but that is not the Mission of the Church. All the evils we see today existed in Jesus' day. But He never told anyone to organize a relief society or protest Rome. He knew man's problem is Sin. Jesus came to regenerate the human heart, saving individual people's souls forming a "new creation".

The Mission of the Church is to carry the Gospel to the World; everything else is secondary. The Gospel is not a Code of Ethics or Morals. It is a Proclamation of Salvation.

"For I am not ashamed of the gospel of Christ: for it is the Power of God unto Salvation to every one that believeth; to the Jew first, and also to the Greek." - Romans 1:16 KJV

The purpose of the Gospel is not to save Society from its ills but to save individual from the condemnation of their sin. Then they can become "living stones" building up a Spiritual Temple, the Church.

A great mistake of the Church has been to appropriate the promises of an earthly kingdom and glory that belong exclusively to Israel. When the Church enters an alliance with Governments, Agencies, or NGOs consisting of ungodly men and women, she loses her spiritual power and becomes helpless as a redeeming force. Preach the Gospel first and foremost. That is the Mission of the Church!

APPENDIX B – HOW TO STUDY YOUR BIBLE

Expository Bible Study

We are going to examine two issues. One, how to do expository, exegetical Bible study. Two, which Bible is the true Word of God. That can be a very detailed study in and of itself. Many books have been written on this very subject. However, I will keep it to a minimum and recommend some additional resources at the end of this chapter for further study. How you read and interpret the Bible is called hermeneutics. I interpret the Bible literally.

I believe the Holy Spirit means what He says and says what He means. The context of the passage determines symbolic language usage. Some passages must be taken as symbolic as the literal interpretation would be absurd. For example, Jesus said in John Chapter 6:53, "*Verily, verily, I say unto you, Except ye eat the flesh of the Son of man, and drink his blood, ye have no life in you.*" That is symbolic as Jesus was not promoting cannibalism. "Eating" His flesh is to consume His Word, the Bible, as He is the living Word of God. To "drink" His blood is to be cleansed by His blood continually for the forgiveness of our sin.

The most important rule of Bible study is "stay in context." The context of the surrounding verses, the chapter, and the entire Bible. Staying in context is something that we all understand, but so many violate as they are not taught how to do it. We are so accustomed to sermons where the pastor preaches on a single verse. We are indirectly taught that the Bible is a collection of independent scriptures and stories but, in reality, is one integrated off-planet message from the Most High God. It was given to us by the Holy Spirit working through men.

Exegetical Bible study is letting the scriptures say what they want to say without any presuppositions. Eisegesis is the contrary when we force our preconceived ideas and meanings upon the text. Sadly, many Christians do exactly that and drift into error.

So, precisely what is Expository Bible study. There are three steps to expository study.
1. Observation – what does the text say? What is the plain, straightforward literal reading of the passage?
2. Interpretation – what does the passage mean? It means what it says. Here we need to be sure to stay in the context of the preceding verses and try to understand the background, if possible. Here is where many have difficulty as they bring a preconceived assumption to the text that is not there.
3. Application – how does the passage apply to Christians? The application must be based on the meaning of the passage. Many Christians miss-apply scripture due to an incorrect understanding out of context. That is a source of much error in the Church today. We must identify the speaker and the intended audience of the passage. That will guide us to its proper application.

Steps 2 and 3 are where we must be careful as a faulty or erroneous interpretation will yield an improper application. That will always lead to error and false doctrine.

Let's look at an example of how exegetical bible study works. In Luke 13:3, Jesus says, "I tell you, Nay: but, except ye repent, ye shall all likewise perish." Let's examine this verse using the three parts of expository Bible study.

1. Observation – what does the text say? It says that without repentance, all will perish.

2. Interpretation – what does it mean? Here we must look at the context. Jesus states, "I tell you, Nay:" which must refer to the context of previous verses; otherwise, the "Nay" would have no meaning and be superfluous. Verse 1 and 2 of Luke Chapter 13 speak of Galileans that Pilate executed. Some supposed that they were the worst sinners in Galilee because they suffered and died at the hands of Romans. Hence they would perish in hell for their sins. But Jesus said, "Nay," not so, even you that hear me will die like them if you do not repent.

3. Application – how do we apply this interpretation to ourselves? Many Christians look at others who are suffering and ask what sin they committed to deserve such suffering? They elevate their self-image at the expense of others. Jesus is saying that mentality is wrong. Whether you suffer or not, live or die, all will perish in hell unless they repent. No matter what our lot in life, we must repent of our sin to be saved and escape perishing in the fires of hell. Repentance is the first step to Salvation. Everyone starts there. No repentance, no salvation!

The exegetical Bible study method will significantly help us arrive at what the Holy Spirit would have us to learn from His Word. God gave us His Word so we could learn His Truth. The Bible is the living, powerful holy Word of God. It is not another piece of historical literature. We do not have the right to formulate our own opinions about God's Word. We do have the privilege to study and learn His Truth.

"It is the spirit that quickeneth; the flesh profiteth nothing: the words that I speak unto you, they are spirit, and they are life." - John 6:63 KJV

Which Bible

Sadly, there are many English Bible translations on the market today. Too many Christians are not aware of what lies behind the English Bibles, so they pick one that seems easy to read. But is "ease of reading" a qualifying characteristic of God's Word? Not hardly! Let's look at two popular English Bibles, the King James Bible (KJB) and the New International Version (NIV) by Zondervan a subsidary of Harper Collins Publishers. We will consider the source documents for their New Testament only.

Let's look at the NIV first. Bear with me on this as it is vital. The source manuscript for the NIV New Testament is the Nestle Aland Greek New Testament (Novum Testamentum Graece). Currently, the editors of Nestle are on edition 28 (NA28). The basis for the NA28 and all previous editions is the Westcott-Hort Greek New Testament of 1881. The two primary manuscripts used by Westcott-Hort are the Codex Vaticanus and Codex Sinaiticus, two ancient manuscripts of the Alexandrian text-type dating to the 4th century A.D. The Alexandrian text line is also called the Minority text as there are very few documents in this class. Their origination in Alexandria, Egypt, is a crucial factor, as we will see.

The King James Bible uses the Textus Receptus, the Received Text, as its underlying manuscript. The KJB is also called the Authorized Version (AV). Erasmus completed the Textus Receptus in 1522. The source documents and manuscripts behind the Textus Receptus are the Majority text or the Byzantine text because they are the most numerous, over 15,000 documents and counting. This text line is called the Antioch text line as the manuscripts can be traced back to the hub of the New Testament early church centered in Antioch, Syria. Many of the Apostles worked out of Antioch. Paul's missionary journeys started in Antioch. There is no record of any Apostle visiting Alexandria, Egypt.

Now that you have some basic information on the NIV (Alexandrian text-type) documents and the KJB (Antioch text type), what does the Bible say about these two cities? Can we determine if God has chosen one over the other? Let's look at the Scriptures.

Alexandrian Text Line

The rule of First Mention in scriptures is interesting as we see how God initially treats the subject. The first mention of Egypt is:

*"And there was a famine in the land: and Abram went down into **Egypt** to sojourn there; for the famine was grievous in the land." - Genesis 12:10 KJV*

You are probably familiar with this story. God has called Abram from Ur of the Chaldees down to the land of Canaan. Abram arrives only to be greeted by a harsh famine. Abram decides to travel to Egypt. Upon arriving in Egypt, Abram tells Pharaoh that Sarai is his sister, not his wife. He knows the Egyptians are pagan barbarians and will quickly kill him for his beautiful wife. The first mention of Egypt is negative.

A few centuries later, another Pharaoh tried to kill all the young children, but Moses escaped, placed in a basket and set afloat on the Nile River.

During the Exodus, Moses states:

*"And Moses said unto the people, Remember this day, in which ye came out from Egypt, out of the **house of bondage**, for by strength of hand the LORD brought you out from this place:"* - Exodus 13:3 KJV. *Another negative for Egypt, the house of bondage.*

*"But the LORD hath taken you, and brought you forth out of the **iron furnace**, even out of Egypt, to be unto him a people of inheritance, as ye are this day."* - Deuteronomy 4:20 KJV.

Egypt is an iron furnace of slavery.

"But he shall not multiply horses to himself, nor cause the people to return to Egypt, to the end that he should multiply horses: forasmuch as the LORD hath said unto you, Ye shall henceforth return no more that way." - Deuteronomy 17:16 KJV

The Lord tells Israel not to buy horses from Egypt and never to go that way again. Did you get that? Never go that way again!

After the exodus, Pharaoh sought to kill all the children of Israel. But God wiped out Pharaoh's armies.

*"**Woe to them that go down to Egypt for help**, and stay on horses, and trust in chariots, because they are many; and in horsemen, because they are very strong; but they look not unto the Holy One of Israel, neither seek the LORD!"* - Isa 31:1 KJV

It seems like the creators of the NIV have done precisely that, "gone down to Egypt for help" with their bible manuscripts. In scripture,

Egypt is a type of a pagan, corrupt world. So, why would you want a Bible from Egypt?

What about Alexandria? Founded by Alexander the Great in 331 B.C. to promote Greek philosophy and pagan Greek mythology throughout the region, it quickly grew to be one of the greatest cities of the Hellenistic world — second only to Rome in size and wealth. They were conquered by Arabs in 641 A.D., falling into a long period of decline. It is now a leading port and industrial center for petroleum, textiles, and paper products.

Did God ever say anything about Alexandria? Yes, He did. He mentioned Alexandria four times in scripture. Scholars from Alexandria, Egypt disputed with and killed the first Christian martyr, Stephen (Act 6:9) (First mention - negative).

*"Then there arose certain of the synagogue, which is called the synagogue of the Libertines, and Cyrenians, and **Alexandrians**, and of them of Cilicia and of Asia, disputing with Stephen." - Acts 6:9 KJV*

Those from Alexandria help stone Stephen! It is a place where erroneous bible teaching originated. Apollos, from Alexandria, was learned in the scriptures but was unsaved (knowing only the baptism of John). Aquila and Priscilla explained the gospel - that Jesus was the Christ - and Apollos corrected his theology and was saved. (Acts 18:24) A mixture of bad theology blended with Greek philosophy permeates Alexandria, Egypt.

It is a place that leads people to bondage and death. The Apostle Paul was taken to be executed in Rome by a ship from Alexandria. (Acts 27:6) They almost died at sea.

After surviving the shipwreck and a nasty snake bite, Paul was taken to Rome for execution by another ship from Alexandria. (Acts 28:11) The vessel bore the flag of Castor and Pollux. Castor and Pollux are twins of the Greek gods. Each twin had a different father. Only the Greeks, right. Nothing good originates from Egypt or Alexandria! Not even ancient manuscripts.

Antiochian Text Line

What about Antioch? Does God say anything about Antioch?

Antioch is the only hometown city mentioned from which a man of honest report, full of the Holy Ghost and wisdom came, and was appointed over church business (Acts 6:3-5) (First mention – positive).

The first appearance of Antioch and Alexandria occurs in the same book of the bible and the same chapter, Acts 6 as if God is highlighting the two options we have from which to choose. (coincidence? Not likely.) "Choose wisely."

Antioch is where the first great awakening of the Gentiles occurred. The persecution following Stephen's death scattered the believers, who preached wherever they went. They preached to the Grecians, and many believed and turned unto the Lord (Acts 11:19-21).

Antioch is a place where many people were added unto the Lord. It is also where the people were glad, rejoicing in their heart to cleave unto the Lord. Barnabus was sent to Antioch, and these things resulted. (Acts 11:22-24)

God established the headquarters of his New Testament church in Antioch. Barnabus sought Saul and shepherded him back to Antioch (not to Jerusalem and certainly not to Alexandria), and assembled with the new church (Acts 11:25,26)

Believers were first called "Christians" at Antioch (Acts 11:26) It is the place to which God moved his prophets, signifying his blessing on Antioch, while the world was plagued with scarcity. (Acts 11:27,28)

God blessed those at Antioch for keeping his word. The disciples were told to preach the gospel to all the world, but some didn't and remained at Jerusalem. Then, relief for Jerusalem was needed from Antioch, where they had been faithful - which they sent at the hands of Barnabus and Saul. (Acts 11:29,30)

 It is the place from which God sends missionaries (not from Jerusalem, and certainly not from Alexandria). Paul and Barnabus went on the first great missionary journey from Antioch (Acts 13:1-3)

It is the place to which two envoys traveled from Jerusalem; Their decisions had consequences. One (Judas) returned to Jerusalem and into oblivion; the other (Silas) stayed in Antioch and became a tremendous missionary partner of Paul. (Acts 15:23-27)

The second great missionary journey began at Antioch (not Jerusalem and certainly not Alexandria), with Paul and Silas as the missionaries (Acts 15:40,41).

So, what about the horses? In I Kings 3:1, Solomon, the wisest man who ever lived, ignored God's commandment to avoid Egypt and NOT buy horses from Egypt. But he bought the horses and married the Pharaoh's daughter anyway. The result was that his heart was turned away from God (I Kings 11:3,4), he began worshipping other gods (I Kings 11:5-9). God pronounced judgment on him (I Kings 11:9-43), all because he ignored God's command and went down to Egypt.

Conclusion

So, here's the pertinent question. If God holds these opinions of Alexandria and Egypt and commands his people not to buy horses from there, how likely is it that he would want us to get a BIBLE from there?   Conversely, would he recommend a BIBLE from Antioch, where "the word of the Lord was published throughout all the region?" (Acts 13:49) I think so since that is where the Bible originated.

Were there manuscripts published in Alexandria? Absolutely. But they were not the words of God. Those were manuscripts generated by Origen, founder of a school of philosophy in Alexandria, Egypt, and others of like mind. Their job was to blend Greek philosophy with Christian theology to diminish the deity of Jesus Christ and elevate pagan humanity. Both Clement of Alexandria and Origen denied the deity of Jesus Christ, the virgin birth, and Jesus' bodily resurrection. Do you want to visit their house for Bible study? That is what you are doing when you use one of their bibles.

Vaticanus, Sinaiticus, and Alexandrinus (the three primary manuscripts underlying modern Bible versions) are believed to be copies of Origen's original works. Vaticanus was found and remains secluded in the Vatican archive. Sinaiticus was found in a garbage can at St. Catherine's monastery in the Sinai Peninsula (Egypt).

These works are filled with errors, strike-outs, contradictions, and deletions. Yet, they form the basis for what was compiled by Westcott and Hort in their 1881 Greek New Testament (GNT) manuscript that underlies the Nestle Aland GNT and all modern Bible versions. The Nestle Aland GNT continues to be edited and is presently on version 29 as of this writing.

Can anyone honestly believe that: Bad manuscripts = Good Bible??

In summary, the Word of God was published in the regions around Antioch and was accepted as scripture by the early Church when they received it (hence "Received Text" underlying the KJB). Many fragments of these writings constitute the "Majority Text," which Erasmus and the King James translators used to compile God's Word.

 In opposition to this move of God, Origen, Eusebius, Augustine, the Catholic church, Westcott and Hort, Nestle, Aland, and many others generated and continue to propagate many conflicting accounts of what God's Word says. These deceivers bring into question scripture passages by giving alternate, watered-down, inferior meanings from pagan Greek. They add or omit many words and phrases, creating confusion with many contrary versions. (... God is not the author of confusion. (I Cor 14:33).

The choice is clear! Get a King James Bible.

APPENDIX C – THE PARABLE OF THE TEN VIRGINS

Do the ten virgins represent the church, the body of Christ, or Israel?

What is the significance of the oil?

Why were the five foolish virgins excluded from the marriage feast just because they were late?

The parable of the ten virgins found in Matthew chapter 25:1-13 is much misunderstood. Many so-called prophecy experts interpret the parable as a stand-alone passage without asking basic questions that should be asked and answered with every passage of scripture.

1. Who is speaking?
2. Who is the intended audience?
3. What is the timeframe or setting?

Only by correctly answering these questions can one make a proper application of the passage. Let's read the passage; then I will answer the three questions.

*"Then shall the kingdom of heaven be likened unto **ten virgins**, which took their lamps, and **went forth to meet the bridegroom**. And **five of them were wise, and five were foolish**. They that were foolish took their lamps, and took no oil with them: But the wise took oil in their vessels with their lamps. While the bridegroom tarried, they all slumbered and slept. And at midnight there was a cry made, Behold, the bridegroom cometh; go ye out to meet him. Then all those virgins arose, and trimmed their lamps. And the*

foolish said unto the wise, **Give us of your oil; for our lamps are gone out**. But the wise answered, saying, **Not so; lest there be not enough for us and you**. but **go ye rather to them that sell, and buy for yourselves**. And while they went to buy, the bridegroom came; and they that were ready went in with him to the marriage: and the door was shut. Afterward came also the other virgins, saying, **Lord, Lord, open to us**. But he answered and said, **Verily I say unto you, I know you not**. Watch therefore, for ye know neither the day nor the hour wherein the Son of man cometh." - Mat 25:1–13 KJV

Question 1, who is speaking? Jesus is speaking.

Question 2, who is the intended audience? From Matthew chapter 24, we know the audience is the 12 disciples. Jesus is giving them a private briefing on the coming last days.

Question 3, what is the timeframe or setting? To properly answer that question, we must begin in Matthew chapter 23:

"O Jerusalem, Jerusalem, thou that killest the prophets, and stonest them which are sent unto thee, how often would I have gathered thy children together, even as a hen gathereth her chickens under her wings, and ye would not! Behold, **your house is left unto you desolate**. For I say unto you, **Ye shall not see me henceforth, till ye shall say, Blessed [is] he that cometh in the name of the Lord**." - Mat 23:37–39 KJV

Jesus is lamenting the continual rebellion of Israel against God. They killed the prophets God sent to them and rejected Jesus as their Messiah. Jesus longed to gather them to Him as a hen gathers her chicks, but they denied Him as the Son of God. Their judgment was clear; your house, your nation, will soon be desolate. They would never see their Messiah again until they cried out in brokenness and humility; Blessed is he that cometh in the name of the Lord.

The setting in this passage is Jerusalem, the focal point of the coming desolation.

Let's continue to define the setting with a passage from Matthew chapter 24.

"And Jesus went out, and departed from the temple: and his disciples came to [him] for to shew him the buildings of the temple. And Jesus said unto them, See ye not all these things? verily I say unto you, **There shall not be left here one stone upon another, that shall not be thrown down.** *And as he sat upon the mount of Olives, the disciples came unto him privately, saying,* **Tell us, when shall these things be? and what [shall be] the sign of thy coming, and of the end of the world?**" - Mat 24:1–3 KJV

Jesus and His disciples are in the vicinity of the Temple, admiring the magnificent renovation. Herod sponsored a complete makeover of the second Temple, Zerubbabel's Temple, which had stood for over 400 years. Jesus' response to the disciple's admiration of the Temple must have come as a surprise. He foretold of its destruction; "There shall not be left here one stone upon another, that shall not be thrown down."

When they reached the top of the Mount of Olives, the disciples asked Jesus 3 questions.

1. When shall these things be? In other words, when will the Temple be destroyed?
2. What shall be the sign of thy coming? What sign shall precede the second coming of Jesus back to the earth?

3. What sign will bring the end of the world? Or the end of the age?

The setting for the ten virgins parable is Jesus giving a private briefing to the 12 disciples about the coming destruction of the Temple, His second coming, and the end of the world. The context of the setting is Jerusalem, the Temple, and the Mount of Olives. Remember, the 12 disciples are disciples of Israel, not the church, the body of Christ. In Matthew 19, we read:

"And Jesus said unto them, Verily I say unto you, That ye which have followed me, in the regeneration when the Son of man shall sit in the throne of his glory, ye also shall sit upon twelve thrones, judging the twelve tribes of Israel." - Mat 19:28 KJV

The "regeneration when the Son of man shall sit in the throne of his glory" is the second coming when Jesus inaugurates His Millennial Kingdom. The 12 disciples will sit on 12 thrones, judging the 12 tribes of Israel. Therefore, they must be apostles to the 12 tribes of Israel, not Gentiles.

Are you starting to get the picture here? The setting is entirely Jewish. Jerusalem, the Temple, the Mount of Olives, the Jewish Messiah speaking to 12 Jewish disciples about His second coming to restore the kingdom to Israel.

Now, let's deconstruct the passage of the ten virgins.

Verse 1.
   "Then shall the kingdom of heaven be likened unto ten virgins, which took their lamps, and went forth to meet the bridegroom." - Mat 25:1 KJV

"kingdom of heaven" – The kingdom of heaven is an earthly kingdom where God's will is "done on earth as it is in heaven." John the Baptist, Jesus, and the disciples preached the gospel of the kingdom; "repent for the kingdom of heaven is at hand." At hand means close or near, on the earth. In Acts chapter 1, Peter asks Jesus, "Lord, wilt thou at this time restore again the kingdom to Israel?"

The original land grant given by God to the descendants of Abraham, Isaac, and Jacob runs from the Nile River in Egypt to the Euphrates River in Mesopotamia (Iraq, Syria, and Turkey). Also, the phrase "kingdom of heaven" only appears in the gospel of Matthew, which is fitting as Matthew presents Jesus as the King of Israel.

So, the context of the ten virgins parable is the coming earthly kingdom promised to Israel.

There are ten virgins, obviously representing the nation of Israel. They took their lamps and went out to meet the bridegroom. Who is the bridegroom?

Let's read a few verses.

*"Then came to him the disciples of John, saying, Why do we and the Pharisees fast oft, but thy disciples fast not? And Jesus said unto them, Can the children of the bridechamber mourn, as long as **the bridegroom is with them**? but the days will come, when **the bridegroom shall be taken from them**, and then shall they fast." - Mat 9:14–15 KJV*

Jesus is referring to himself as the bridegroom. His disciples do not fast because the bridegroom of Israel is with them. They will fast when "the bridegroom shall be taken away from them."

*"He that **hath the bride is the bridegroom** but the friend of the bridegroom, which standeth and heareth him, rejoiceth greatly because of **the bridegroom's voice this my joy therefore is fulfilled**" - John 3:29 KJV*

John the Baptist, the "friend of the bridegroom," stands and rejoices upon hearing the voice of the bridegroom, Jesus. Jesus, the bridegroom, has the bride, Israel.

Most Christians are told that they are the bride of Christ. That's why they try to force the church into the interpretation of the parable of the ten virgins. But is that true?

The term "bride of Christ" is nowhere found in the King James Bible.

But we do find two passages about the Lamb's wife.

"Let us be glad and rejoice, and give honour to him: for the marriage of the Lamb is come, and his wife hath made herself ready." - Rev 19:7 KJV

"And there came unto me one of the seven angels which had the seven vials full of the seven last plagues, and talked with me, saying, Come hither, I will shew thee the bride, the Lamb's wife." - Rev 21:9 KJV

The woman in this marriage is referred to as the "wife," not the "bride" as one would expect. Could this be a remarriage to a previously divorced wife?

We read in Jeremiah:
*"And I saw, when for all the causes whereby backsliding Israel committed adultery I had put her away, and **given her a bill of divorce** yet her*

treacherous sister Judah feared not, but went and played the harlot also." -
Jer 3:8 KJV

Here the Lord gives Israel and her sister Judah a "bill of divorce" for adultery, spiritual fornication with idols, and false gods. As long as Israel lives, God cannot marry another as that would be adultery. So the Lord must remarry Israel, and that is exactly what He does at the second coming.

In the parable of the ten virgins, the bridegroom is Jesus, and the five wise virgins represent the remnant of Israel redeemed by Jesus at His second coming. That has nothing to do with us, the church. We might be spectators at the marriage supper but not participants.

*"And the woman fled into the wilderness, where she hath a place prepared of God, that they should feed her there a thousand two hundred [and] threescore days. ... And to the woman were given two wings of a great eagle, that she might **fly into the wilderness, into her place, where she is nourished for a time, and times, and half a time, from the face of the serpent**." - Rev 12:6, 14 KJV*

The woman in these verses is the believing remnant of Israel protected by God during the last half of the 7-year Tribulation. Many other Jews will compromise with the Antichrist system and be lost. The 5 foolish virgins symbolize them.

Verses 2-4
"And five of them were wise, and five [were] foolish. They that [were] foolish took their lamps, and took no oil with them: But the wise took oil in their vessels with their lamps." - Mat 25:2-4 KJV

Five virgins were wise and took extra oil for their lamps. Five were foolish and took no extra oil for their lamps. I have always been amazed by preachers and teachers that equate the oil with the Holy Spirit. They conclude that five are saved because they have oil and five are lost because they have no oil. How ridiculous, they all came together with oil in their lamps. You can't run out of the Holy Spirit. That is yet another feeble attempt at injecting the church into passages meant for Israel.

Verse 5.
"While the bridegroom tarried, they all slumbered and slept." - Mat 25:5 KJV

The bridegroom has indeed tarried. He's been gone from Israel for almost 2000 years. There's an interesting passage in Hosea that possibly touches on this point.

"Come, and let us return unto the LORD: for he hath torn, and he will heal us; he hath smitten, and he will bind us up. After two days will he revive us: in the third day he will raise us up, and we shall live in his sight." - Hos 6:1– 2 KJV

The apostle Peter states that a day with the Lord is as a thousand years. Then Israel being torn and smitten for two days could mean 2000 years. The Lord will heal, bind and raise Israel on the third day, the beginning of the third millennia. We are on the cusp of the third millennia right now.

The modern nation of Israel is still looking for its Messiah. Rabbis frequently declare His coming close. They are looking for his first coming. They will at first get a false Messiah, the Antichrist. Seven years later, Jesus returns as King of Kings and Lord of Lords. The third day begins the Millennial Reign of Christ, the Messiah of Israel.

Verses 6-8

"And at midnight there was a cry made, Behold, the bridegroom cometh; go ye out to meet him. Then all those virgins arose, and trimmed their lamps. And the foolish said unto the wise, Give us of your oil; for our lamps are gone out." - Mat 25:6–8 KJV

At midnight the coming of the bridegroom is announced. Everyone rises and trims their lamps as it is night. But the foolish virgins have run out of oil for their lamps. The bridegrooms coming is the second coming of the Lord Jesus Christ at the end of the 7-year Tribulation. The setting is just before Jesus' second coming.

Verse 9

"But the wise answered, saying, [Not so]; lest there be not enough for us and you: but go ye rather to them that sell, and buy for yourselves." - Mat 25:9 KJV

The wise virgins refuse to share their oil. (Can you imagine the outrage on social media?) They tell the foolish virgins to go to town and buy oil from those that sell. Head on over to the local hardware store and buy some lamp oil.

That is the critical verse that almost everyone misses. Remember, the setting is the imminent return of the Lord at the end of the 7-year Tribulation. What is required to buy and sell during the last half of the Tribulation? That's right, the mark of the Beast.

"And he causeth all, both small and great, rich and poor, free and bond, to receive a mark in their right hand, or in their foreheads: And that no man might buy or sell, save he that had the mark, or the name of the beast, or the number of his name." - Rev 13:16–17 KJV

The five foolish virgins had to take the mark of the beast to buy oil from those that sell. Taking the mark of the beast sealed their doom as everyone that takes the mark will be cast into the lake of fire.

Verses 10-13

"And while they went to buy, the bridegroom came; and they that were ready went in with him to the marriage: and the door was shut. Afterward came also the other virgins, saying, Lord, Lord, open to us. But he answered and said, Verily I say unto you, I know you not. Watch therefore, for ye know neither the day nor the hour wherein the Son of man cometh." – Mat 25:10–13 KJV

When the Lord returned, the five wise virgins entered into the marriage, and the door was shut. Later the foolish virgins return and implored the Lord to open the door. Jesus treated them like strangers saying, truly, I know you not. The Lord rejected the five foolish virgins because they had taken the mark of the beast. They were not allowed into the marriage nor the kingdom.

Jesus closes the parable with a command to "Watch." The foolish virgins should have stayed with the others and watched for the bridegroom instead of heading off to town to buy the oil they did not need. Five working lamps would give enough light for ten people. They should have stayed and watched whatever the cost. Had they done that, they would have entered the marriage and the kingdom.

Let me summarize what we have covered.
1.   The timeframe is just before the second coming of Jesus at the end of the 7-year Tribulation.
2.   The setting is Jerusalem, Israel.
3.   The ten virgins represent Israel, not the Church
4.   Five foolish virgins run out of oil for their lamps.

5.   They go to town to buy oil from those that sell.

6.   To do that, they must take the mark of the beast.

7.   Taking the mark enables them to buy oil but condemns them to the lake of fire.

8.   When the bridegroom, Jesus, returns for the marriage feast, the five wise virgins enter; they are the remnant of Israel.

9.   Later, the five foolish virgins return and ask to enter the marriage.

10. The Lord rejects the foolish virgins as they took the mark of the beast

11. The foolish virgins should have stayed with the wise instead of taking the mark to by oil; they should have watched and waited.

Now let's answer the three beginning questions.

1. Do the ten virgins represent the church, the body of Christ, or Israel? They represent Israel. The five wise virgins represent the believing remnant, and the five foolish the ungodly.

2. What is the significance of the oil? Nothing really, indeed not the Holy Spirit. Just the vehicle to test the five foolish virgins as to whether they would take the mark of the beast to buy oil.

3. Were the five foolish virgins excluded from the marriage feast just because they were late? No, they were excluded for taking the mark of the beast.

God Bless!

Paul Felter

www.ingramcontent.com/pod-product-compliance
Lightning Source LLC
Chambersburg PA
CBHW060244100426
42742CB00011B/1639